The
Kit Car
Manual

The complete guide to choosing, buying
and building British and American kit cars

The **Kit** Car Manual

Iain Ayre

The complete guide to choosing, buying and building British and American kit cars

Second Edition

Designed by Jelena Ayre

First published 2003
Reprinted 2004
Second edition published 2008

A catalogue record for this book is available from the British Library.

ISBN 978 1 84425 521 4

Library of Congress catalog card no. 2002117289

Published by Haynes Publishing,
Sparkford, Yeovil, Somerset BA22 7JJ
Tel: 01963 442030 Fax: 01963 440001
Int. tel: +44 1963 442030 Int. fax: +44 1963 440001
E-mail: sales@haynes.co.uk
Web site: www.haynes.co.uk

Haynes North America Inc.,
861 Lawrence Drive, Newbury Park,
California 91320, USA

Illustrations courtesy of the author except where credited.

WARNING

**Jurisdictions which have strict emission control laws may
consider any modifications to a vehicle to be an infringement of
those laws. You are advised to check with the appropriate body
or authority whether your proposed modification complies fully
with the law. The publishers accept no liability in this regard.**

**While every effort is taken to ensure the accuracy of the
information given in this book, no liability can be accepted by
the author or publishers for any loss, damage or injury caused
by errors in, or omissions from the information given.**

Printed and bound in Great Britain by J. H. Haynes & Co. Ltd, Sparkford

Contents

Introduction

Individualist cars started in about 1927 with a chap called John Bolster, who was dissatisfied with dull, modern production cars and experimented with games such as wooden chassis and jamming four JAP bike engines into a car. So twin-bike-engined Tigers are actually quite retro. The kit scene gathered momentum in the 1950s with early GRP bodies fitted to the separate chassis of old family Austins and Fords, to produce cars such as the Hamblin Cadet.

Kits became more sophisticated as time went on, and the Falcon Caribbean is a body design that can hold its own against almost any period production sports car. Lotuses and TVRs with quite good chassis could be bought in kit form without paying purchase tax at one time, but that tax loophole was soon closed. Many kits then regressed into some pretty dire vehicles that involved scrap Beetles and Fords, with slabs of wattle-and-daub fibreglass. The Cobra explosion and the spread of the Lotus Seven replica revitalised the kit world, and the recent re-introduction of bike engines has brought it to a wider audience. The industry has matured, and there are now fewer but better cars about.

Author and journalist Iain Ayre has been writing about kit and performance cars for ten years, after a career in advertising that finished up at JWT in Berkeley Square. He has published books on TVR, Maserati, Ferrari, Porsche and replica Cobras, and launch-edited *Classic Ford* magazine. He currently writes for *Classic & Sportscar*, *MiniWorld*, *Kit-Car*,

The Ayrspeed Six project has had its ups and downs, but has provided Iain with a fast and gorgeous car and the readers of Kit-Car magazine with plenty of stories and a few laughs.

Below: The Swallow was an appealing little trike, but its chassis was too heavy.

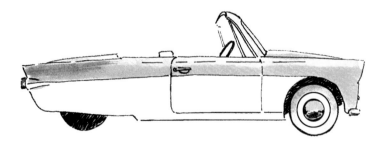

6

Ultra VW, Jaguar World, MG Enthusiast and *Triumph World* in the UK; *The Mini Experience* in Australia, and *Corvette Fever* and *Kit Car Builder* in the USA since emigrating to Canada.

His kit CV starts with the first six-cylinder Midge, a wooden-bodied pre-war MG lookali'. Next up was a Cobra look with a Chevy small-block .id Jaguar running gear. Re grettably this had to be sold to pay the bills incurred in building it.

The next scheme was his own design – a Mini-based four-seater trike with '60s British/Italian styling at the front and fins at the back, immortalised in Chris Rees's book on three-wheelers. Too heavy to qualify as a motor tricycle, its production numbers remained at one.

The Ayrspeed Six followed – a fairly close replica of the gorgeous Jaguar XK120. Three of these were made, but economics and 4.2 Jaguar engines caused too many problems. Iain's Ayrspeed Six is now an Ayrspeed Eight, as its third and last Jaguar engine has been replaced by the rebuilt Rover V8 featured in this very book.

His latest design project is the Ayrspeed Police Cobra, which recycles American V8 cop cars

and BMW V8s into Cobra replicas, and the budget EcoCobra, using the 40mpg Mazda MX-5 as a single donor. There are also talks with Marcos Heritage about future Ayrspeed-Marcoses or Marcos-Ayrspeeds.

Right: The Ayrspeed Police Cobra takes shape. Will I never learn? Why don't I just buy a nice Jensen CV8 and keep out of trouble? US model uses modern cop-car V8, British version uses BMW V8 and Mazda DOHC four. Updates on its progress appear on website www.ayrspeed.com.

Above: The Cobretti with a Chevy V8 engine and Jaguar running gear was a wicked car, but went way over budget and had to be sold.

Chapter 1

What is a kit car?

The range of objects that can be called kit cars is almost as wide as those that can be called cars. A Trabant is a car, and so is a De Tomaso Pantera. The reasons why you might want to buy or build a kit are also numerous, but whatever you want out of the world of kit cars, you will find it if you look for it.

Budgets go from £50 for a second-hand Dutton to £50,000 for a top Ultima kit, and anywhere in between. Top speeds range from 70mph (2CV trike) to 210mph (Ultima) while power can go from 39bhp (Triumph Herald-based Midge) to 1,000bhp (blown, nitrous-injected Cobra). Build times can be just a few weekends (Caterham Classic) to 23 years (Gentry MG TD replica).

The basic idea of a kit car has evolved rapidly over the last couple of decades. The general public's view of kit cars is probably still based on some admittedly ugly plastic sheds built from dead shopping cars, but that's well out of date.

What you get from modern kit cars is serious performance, a massively strong chassis and a light but tough GRP shell. The steel used for kit chassis is many times thicker than any production car, and will probably last for 50 years or more. The GRP body will last indefinitely, although red gelcoat colours tend to fade over the years.

The improved performance is based on getting rid of a very heavy, four-seat, fully glazed, four-door monocoque production shell and replacing it with a steel chassis and plastic body weighing less than half that of the original donor car.

Let's take a budget kit based on Ford Sierra mechanicals, with a 2-litre Pinto engine of 95bhp. Cutting the weight by 50 per cent gets exactly the same performance result as doubling the power – therefore the cheapest of kit cars has the same power-to-weight ratio as a Sierra Cosworth Turbo.

So any old bottom-grade kit goes like a Cossie, even when it's powered by a bog-standard

Caterham's Seven is as much fun on the track as off it. This track version is fitted with a rare Ford BDA engine, and is soon to be registered for the road.

Westfield are the second major manufacturer of Seven-style cars – they also have a big club and a dedicated racing series.

Pinto, and that's before you start fiddling with the engine. Take more weight off, put more power in and you're looking at a lot of kit cars with 0–60mph times of five and six seconds. When kit people watch TV features on production 'sports' cars, you can hear them sniggering at what the presenter and sports car people think is fast.

There's also a general opinion that kit cars are flimsy, dangerous things, when in fact the opposite is true. My first Cobra replica was a Chevrolet/Jaguar Cobretti, which had a massive steel chassis with a solid GRP body bolted, riveted and bonded to it. In a 70mph head-on crash with a Land Rover, a similar Cobretti sustained body, wheel and suspension damage, a cracked windscreen and a bent upper wishbone mounting bar. The Land Rover was a mess, with its front spring shackles almost touching each other, and the driver's door had to be forced open to get the driver out and into an ambulance. The kit car driver was uninjured, other than seatbelt bruising across his chest. The Cobretti chassis was undamaged apart from one end of one front suspension beam. That's partly why I bought a Cobretti. Occasionally you see newspaper pictures of a coned-off accident scene with a lump of unidentifiable wreckage and a damaged kit car under a tragedy/miracle escape headline. The production car involved is usually unrecognisably mangled, and the kit car always seems to lose a single wheel. The police are always 'astonished' that the kit car driver walked away uninjured. Kit car owners are not astonished by this.

The key is that even a basic kit car ladder frame is very strong, and when triangulated into a spaceframe it becomes even stronger and also lighter. It's very hard to bend a spaceframe. A production monocoque has to survive a specific impact to pass standard tests, but there are financial limits to the strength of a production car. It's made for profit,

not for ultimate strength. If you want to be safe in a production car, buy the biggest and heaviest you can afford.

The only down side to having an immensely strong chassis is that there are limited soft structures to absorb a big impact. If you hit a production car, no problem – you can use its crumple zone to soften the impact. If you hit something very solid like a tree or a house in a kit car, the deceleration is more violent, although the car will generally retain its shape and you won't be trapped in it. If you plan to drive hard when you've finished a kit car, fit good full harness belts and keep them very tight.

The UK's Single Vehicle Approval test (SVA), or whatever it's called now, which all new kit cars have to pass, is tough and getting tougher. I wouldn't expect a production car to pass it. Anything that can get through an SVA test is a pretty damn good car, and very safe indeed.

The choice of kit cars is immense, and the first criterion

has to be whether you're more interested in building one than in driving it. If the construction process is the attraction, then you have the benefit of being able to build with virtually no cost at all. Something like Ron Champion's Locost has to be a good idea, although the supposed budget of £250 for a complete car does rather rely on finding a set of matched coilover shocks for a tenner at a boot sale. A genuine no-budget car is the Midge, still available in plan form from the Midge Club. You can build one of these from a Triumph Herald/Spitfire chassis, which means you can get an MoT-failed (and tax-exempt) donor car almost free. The bodywork is cut from sheets of 3/4in plywood, and then skinned with thin aluminium. The steel mudguards are from trailers, and the whole thing is hand-made from bits and pieces. If built well, the end result is a charming little car that looks remarkably like a pre-war sports car, and which gets more attention than a Ferrari Testarossa.

Further upmarket, there are

America's Superformance is actually imported from South Africa, and is a well-sorted car running Mazda Miata running gear.

This low-budget MK Locost uses a Honda FireBlade bike engine, and is hard to drive smoothly, but very quick when you let it loose.

many complex kits, which require serious commitment and a long time to build. Any Lamborghini Countach replica is going to require big money and a big commitment, as it can take weeks just to make the doors open and shut properly. If it's the building of the car that interests you, any supercar replica with a roof is going to keep you quiet for a good while.

If you're more interested in using the car than building it, the picture changes, and the car's function becomes much more important. The majority of kits are for short-range weekend fun, and are fast, hard and lively. They usually only have two seats, with comfort coming after performance and handling.

One aspect of kit cars that I tend to forget is the impression they make on the general public. I'm used to driving cars that get a lot of attention, and take it for granted. If you enjoy making a big impression, ten grand's worth of kit will draw a lot more attention than £60,000 worth of BMW, Porsche, Ferrari or whatever. It's also positive rather than negative attention – people are fascinated by genuinely unusual cars,

whereas the usual 'aspirational' sports cars are . . . well, usual, and in the case of BMW and Porsche are becoming increasingly boring. The fun-per-quid ratio with kits is obviously very high, but for attention-per-quid, kit cars leave everything else standing – just as they do at the traffic lights.

LOTUS SEVEN STYLED CARS

Caterham's Seven is still the Lotus Seven in all but name: Caterham

Cars used to be a Lotus dealer, and when Lotus went upmarket and stopped making the Seven, Caterham changed the badges and carried right on producing the car. They still do. The pure Seven remains available, but on the balance of practicality versus performance, practicality doesn't get a look in. It is possible for a standard-sized human to squeeze into a Caterham with the roof on, but you have to be pretty flexible. Even leaving the roof off, which most people do nearly all the time, you have to wiggle your legs past the little steering wheel and down the tunnel, then squeeze your bum into the space between the outside of the car and the spaceframe transmission tunnel. Then you have to find the straps, connect them all up and tighten them until you can't move. That's tight enough to be safe. The steering's heavy at parking speeds and operating the gear stub is hard work. The clutch is sharp, and the chassis records every bump.

However... once you come to a bit of clear, bendy road you can immediately see the point, and you can also see the reason why so many people buy these for weekend racing. Their cornering abilities are immense, and the lack of any significant weight allows an ordinary Rover K-series engine

Carroll Shelby is selling self-assembly GRP-bodied Shelby Cobras with continuation CSX chassis numbers. This has to be the top kit car ever. (Pic courtesy of Shelby American)

At the budget end of the Cobra replica spectrum is the UK's Pilgrim. With a very good gelcoat finish and the option of a Rover V8 it offers excellent value for money.

to sing. You wouldn't believe how hard you can push one of these along an A-road – they just grip and go. Make a mistake, go into a corner too hard, and you get some tyre shrieking, but no drama. Just hang on and keep your foot down and you'll get round.

The Caterham is at the top of

LA's Superformance car is another import from South Africa, but this one runs a Ford Windsor V8 rather than a little Mazda four.

the Seven tree, and although you pay handsomely for the privilege, the kit contains every last nut, bolt and washer, and fits together like an Airfix kit, although the bits are too big to get lost in the carpet. The resale value of a Caterham remains pretty high too, and the number of writs the company has issued

against other companies copying the Seven suggests that it was well worth copying in the first place.

There are dozens of Seven-style cars available, and some are very good. Westfield, Tiger and Sylva all do very well in kit racing, and Caterham, Westfield and Locost all have their own series. I've always rather liked Tigers, which currently show how it should be done with a 0–60mph time of 2.8 seconds with a twin-bike-engined car.

There are some remarkably cheap Seven-styled cars at the bottom of the market that offer remarkable fun-per-quid, although the less you pay the more work you have to put in yourself.

Ron Champion's Locost introduced the idea of very low-budget road-racers made from plans – you just buy a MIG welder and some steel, a GRP nose cone and some mudguards, and then make the whole car yourself. Even if you buy lots of parts from the many small-scale manufacturers

The Coddington/Image 427C/I is the excellent old Contemporary Cobra re-jigged by a chap who spent 20 years building kits for customers. Think hot big-block Ford, and reflect that these Palm Desert cars don't need windscreen wipers. Grrr.

Southern Roadcraft's SRV8 always had a good reputation, and has recently reappeared under new ownership: welcome back.

This glorious Auburn Speedster replica runs on big-block Ford wagon engine, chassis and running gear. Exterior is detail perfect, with butter-smooth chrome.

If you fancy a Testarossa but can't handle the purchase price or the garage bills, RV's Nemesis with V12 Jaguar power should definitely blow your frock up.

Healey replicas are more popular Stateside than in the UK. Some have evolved into Cobra-style monsters, others remain period replicas. The Nissan straight-six is remarkably similar to the Healey straight-six, but with a different head.

who sell Locost bits and pieces, this is still very affordable fun, and again, there are race series for these cars.

The advent of using motorbike engines for these cars has also changed the face of the Seven scene. Modern Japanese bike engines produce 150bhp, weigh as much as a bowl of sushi and rev to 12,000rpm through a six-speed sequential gearbox. For a pure adrenalin speed rush, bike-powered cars are hard to beat. The power-to-weight ratios

are absurd, and they just keep screaming to the red line in every gear until the scenery blurs. You wouldn't want to tour in one, but for clearing a week's worth of mental cobwebs out on the track they're the business.

If your reason for wanting a kit car is to go budget racing, Locost has to be one of the best ways to go. Cheaply and very cheerfully, you can learn about racing and developing cars without making expensive mistakes, and then you can either just enjoy the fun

at weekends or progress to more expensive formulas.

This whole scene with Seven-inspired cars seems to be European only: at the last Los Angeles kit car show there was only one Seven-style car. Ayrspeed.com is investigating transatlantic import and export to open up more options for both Brits and Americans. Luego's Viento offers room for both V8s and American-sized humans, which is a bonus.

REPLICA COBRAS

The replica Cobra is a big part of the kit car world on both sides of the Atlantic, and recent good news is that you can still buy a Shelby Cobra from Carroll Shelby, with a CSX chassis number: you can buy it in component form, and you can buy it with a GRP bodyshell.

Also very close to the real thing are Hawk's ally or GRP-bodied replicas, one of which is not just a Cobra replica but a reproduction of a specific racing Cobra, 39 PH. In the USA there are longer and wider Cobra replicas as well as dozens of more accurate versions, while in the UK there is a family of cars including Cobretti that have bubble front arches and an extra foot of track to run standard

Porsche Speedsters are a worldwide favourite. Still based on Beetle pans and warmed-over flat-fours, they're very authentic in spirit as well as in style.

The UK's Pimlico is more of a replacement shell than a replica, but its GRP monocoque will last for ever.

Mad-looking Malone Skunk is actually a beautifully engineered ultra-light bike-powered rocket, and is capable of terrifying speeds, with the handling to deal with them.

Jaguar XJ6 suspension all round. Not very original-looking, but the handling reflects the extra track. They stick to the road better than a disgraced politician hangs on to his job.

It's possible to build a replica Cobra on a weeny budget with a teeny four-cylinder engine, although it's as uncool as wearing supermarket jeans that your mum bought you. On the bright side, there's always the possibility of putting a proper engine in later. The budget of a Pilgrim Cobra replica can be kept very reasonable by sticking to a single donor, and by using their very good gelcoat finish rather than paint, vinyl seats, a stripped-out race-style ally-and-rivet interior and steel wheels, some of which look quite acceptable.

With the vast number of Cobra replica kits on the market worldwide, there is something to suit everyone, but please use a V8. It doesn't have to be a big-block – a Rover will do fine.

There's more than a chapter to be written about Cobra replicas: there's a whole book, so that's what I might write next. (If my writing hasn't already irritated you enough to make you eat your own arms, keep an eye open for it.)

OTHER REPLICAS

You don't have to stick to Cobra and Seven replicas. As far as

Blackjack Avion is the latest success story based on the Citroën 2CV. Very tidy design work, a sort of retro-futuristic Dan Dare job. Top quality, too.

replicas go, you may have always seriously fancied a Ferrari, a Porsche Speedster, a D-type Jag or whatever, and resigned yourself to the fact that you'll never own one. You can get pretty damn close with some kits, though. Take the Speedster. The original is basically a Beetle floorpan with a Beetle-based engine, although Porsche fiddled with many of the Beetle components. The replicas are also on Beetle pans, but the kit bodies are lighter, stiffer and much stronger, and won't ever rust. The engine will be a modern, big-bore Beetle engine, stronger than the original Porsche. The Speedster replica might not be a genuine Porsche, but it's a better car.

Personally, I really wanted a new XK120, but that hasn't been available new for 50 years, so I designed and built a replica. This actually cost more than a real XK, but it has huge, four-pot vented brakes, the wiring is new, the three dodgy early 4.2-litre Jaguar engines have been abandoned in favour of a lightweight V8 (which I couldn't in all conscience have done to a real XK) and the car is a massive improvement on the original, but looks just as gorgeous.

Want a Testarossa? You can't have one without selling your house. The price is mad, and the running costs hysterical. You can have a very competent 5.2-litre V12 replica though, for about £30,000.

Want a D-type? Forget about it – even if you could afford it, there are none for sale. You can't even buy a drive in one. However, a good Jag-based replica with a tuned 3.8-litre XK engine is going to get you pretty damn close to what it felt like to drive the real thing – and you can take your British Racing Green GRP period hommage out for a genuine, original thrash any time the spirit moves you.

Some people drive kit cars for eminently sensible reasons, not just because they find production

The Tomcat off-roader starts with a shortened Range Rover chassis and adds a massively strong rollcage for psycho competition use. The GRP skin resembles a Land Rover.

The Ultima is the first 200mph-plus kit car; 1,000bhp engines are no bother, handling is awesome, and the only problem is parking with the polo-mint steering wheel.

The Beauford is another very familiar design, and has evolved into a successful wedding limo. Sierra power and service costs, Packard looks. It makes a nice tourer as well.

The first Marlins are now old enough to be classics themselves. The latest Marlins are among the first to use increasingly cheap and available BMWs as donors.

cars dull. A thick steel chassis and plastic bodywork are not just strong and pretty, but will last indefinitely. If you have to buy your own production car rather than being required to pay indirectly for a company car, you may find it annoying to lose big money every time you buy a new vehicle. In Britain, new car buyers are also charged extra by car manufacturers. It's not clear why the British pay this, but pay they do. They also lose a third of the new car's value as soon as it's registered, so buying a brand-new, cheapish family car means losing a lot of money instantly. That lost dosh would go a long way towards buying a practical kit car instead: let's say a Beauford, which is a Packard-inspired convertible tourer/limo. This seats five or six, will destroy a Golf in an accident, will take 50 years for the chassis to rust, and runs on dirt-cheap mechanicals and Nissan (or any other suitable) engines. It's fine for long trips or touring, it gets more positive attention than Kylie Minogue, and you will never have to buy another car as long as you live. It seems mad not to, doesn't it?

TRIKES

Many people derive a lot of fun from missing one wheel. Having played with (or rather, conducted sober professional evaluations of) several different three-wheelers, I can confirm they are definitely and officially a hoot. They can also be frighteningly quick. The Malone Skunk is based around a big bike engine, and all unnecessary weight has been trimmed – including the rear axle and one wheel. Weather protection is a helmet and jacket. The custom suspension and brakes look spindly and inadequate, but are designed precisely to deal with the stresses they face. The fat back Yokohama tyre is from a car, because that's the only way to achieve enough grip to get the

You can't write a book about kit cars without mentioning beach buggies, which are currently enjoying a resurgence in popularity as a new generation discovers what fun they are.

power down. The front tyres are from a bike: they squash out and grip when you load them up by piling into a corner at what feels like 40mph too fast.

Even the more conventional (!) three-wheelers, based on higher-torque Vee-twin bike engines and car front axles, provide a fair amount of speed, and what they provide as well is a unique blend of a bike and a sports car. There's something visceral about riding a bike that you lose in a car, but too many bikers are maimed and killed by dim punters (frequently in Volvos) not paying attention: 'Sorry mate, didn't see you.'

Trike controls are feather-light and very sensitive and responsive, and trikes with single rear wheels are remarkably stable. There's no tail to swing out and lurch out of shape: you can't get de-stabilising rear-end weight transfer if there's

no weight to transfer. So you can drift the rear end out under real control and slide round sharp corners steering on the throttle. Do that in a four-wheeled car and most of us will simply crash.

At the other end of the tricycular spectrum, Citroën's mad but clever flat-twin 2CV chassis still powers many well-loved trikes on trips to the Arctic Circle, Africa and all points in between. The running costs are pennies and the fun factor huge. Front-wheel-drive means that if you go mad and lift a wheel, you lose power and it comes back down again. True, you get laughed at by Toyota drivers, but who cares what people in beige cardigans think anyway?

OFF–ROADERS

The off-road kit scene has been growing of late, with lots of off-

road toys available. The jump from competition off-roaders to kit cars is not a big one, and the Tomcat exactly straddles the fence. It's basically a rollcage welded to a Range Rover or Land Rover chassis, and has some GRP panels that make it look enough like a Land Rover to qualify for formal competition. Although extremely competitive in serious sport, it's also a usable fun car a nd strong enough to take more abuse than you dare put it through.

The Tomcat's chassis-testing procedure involved accidentally going off a cliff and rolling to the bottom: stitches were required for the driver, but the Tomcat was simply pushed back on to its wheels and driven home. Tomcats are pretty serious bits of kit, with redesigned suspension and steering for off-road racing,

17

but there are also plenty of other kits at the bottom of the off-road budget range. There are little off-road fun cars based on Skodas, Minis and two-cylinder Fiats, which can be put together very quickly and for very little money. You don't need to bother about paint jobs and matching carpets if you're just going to play in a puddle, do you?

ORIGINAL DESIGNS

Some of the industry stalwarts have been around for years – Marlin, NG and JBA for example. There are new British and American kit car designs appearing every few months – some horrible, some delightful, but beauty is very much in the eye of the beholder. Go to the kit shows, take out a subscription to a kit car magazine and make sure you've seen all the people at the wilder end of the spectrum, which are normally small and obscure outfits. Even if you finish up with a Cobra in the end, you'll meet some fascinating eccentrics and drink lots of glassfibre-flavoured tea. I guarantee you won't be bored.

A fascinating exercise is to wander round the kit shows looking for the angle at which the original designs look good. That's usually side-on, and is usually the way the designer saw it in his head and first sketched it. Getting the rest of the 360° looking good as well is the tricky bit.

Whatever you fancy, there's almost certainly something to suit you from the world of kit cars – all you have to do is find it in the Appendix.

Left: Funbuggies make this on- or off-roader, with a Mini engine at the back. It can probably go further off the road than many 4x4s, and is certainly tougher than most 4x4s.

Below: This exquisite 250GTO replica was built from a Datsun-based kit by two girls from Chicago, who lengthened the monocoque, designed a custom fuel injection system and fitted a BMW V12 engine, all to get as close as they could to their dream car.

Right: Sherpleys are often beautifully executed tributes to 1930s Le Mans Bentleys, but are based on the very humble but surprisingly period-authentic beam-axled Sherpa van chassis. Hence the name Sherpley. Berpa would have sounded silly, of course ...

Right: JZR make proportionately very accurate replica '20s Morgan trikes with either Honda or Moto Guzzi V-twin bike engines. As a member of the Morgan club, John Z would have been beaten up if the Morganatics hadn't liked the JZR. I like them too: they're pretty, fast, fun, very involving and handle better than four-wheelers.

Below: There's nothing stopping you having a completely mad idea and just pursuing it doggedly until you make it work. As long as you can get it past the SVA test, you're in business. They can't fail your vehicle just because it's mad.

Chapter 2

Donors kebabbed

What car should you choose as a donor? Don't, basically. Choose the kit you want, then see what donor options come with it. Don't make the familiar mistake of buying a kit to suit the scrap car in your drive. A remarkable number of people spend £10,000 building a kit car chosen purely on the basis that they own a scabby old Ford that has failed its annual test and is now worth £30. Even if your sad old Sierra is a good choice for a donor, you'll almost certainly be able to buy a far better and lower-mileage one for a small amount of extra money. Of course, if you really want to reincarnate your favourite manky old shopper, by all means get on with it – after all,

you're a kit car builder, so you can officially do whatever the hell you want.

Ford have given us thousands of excellent kit car donors, and still do in the States, with the current Mustangs sporting a V8 at the front end and drive at the rear end. In Europe the situation is changing with the Sierra being the last of the rear-drive Fords. Modern Zetec engines are good, but require a rear-wheel-drive conversion and a gearbox, which no longer come with the donor and have to be paid for separately.

This chapter may give you some ideas about what to use or avoid if you get the chance, but it has to be better to figure out first what sort of kit car you want, and

then deal with what component choices you have, if any. Some excellent kits are based on a specific car and can't practicably be re-engineered for a different sort of engine. A front-wheel-drive (FWD) Fiesta-based kit car is stuck with FWD Ford gear.

However, some kits are appearing that take the whole Fiesta (and other) front-wheel-drive packages, transfer them to the back end and re-use them as a rear-engine, rear-drive system with the trackrods bushed to fixed mounts on the chassis and used as tracking adjusters.

If you plan to potter about in your kit car just for fun, it really doesn't matter what basic donor type you use. A FWD Fiesta

The Chevy 350 has to be a top donor engine if you can afford the fuel. Tough, tunable and very cheap to build for reliability and power.

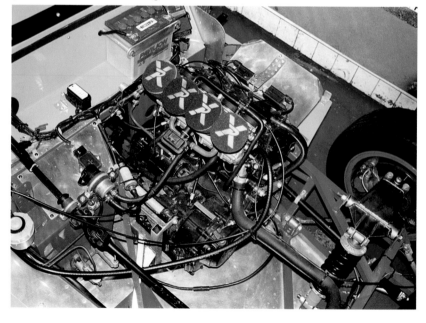

A neat bike-engine installation in a Sylva. Its light weight means the engine position is flexible. Correct air filtration is critical for top performance with bike engines.

Above: Ford's Zetec is increasingly affordable and available. Strong, lots of power, and it looks good decorated with a tidy four-branch manifold.

Fortunately for Porsche replica enthusiasts, the Beetle flat-four is pretty close to the original 356 engine.

The Mini's complete engine and drivetrain assembly is still a very useful package for those inventing their own cars, with endless cheap spares and tuning gear.

package is okay for a light fun car, and its steering characteristics tend towards safety if you overcook it. Even a Beetle package for a Porsche Speedster replica is okay, as the wheezing flat four doesn't really have enough power to get the back end swinging out far enough for the engine that's hanging off the back to pull you off the road. However, if you're planning any serious driving, you will probably be heading for a lightweight, rear-wheel-drive, mid front-engined open roadster resembling a Lotus Seven.

There is a big range of engine options with Seven-styled cars, although it's far easier to change kit brands than to fit the 'wrong' engine to the particular car you fancy. If you want a V8-powered Seven-style car, then use either a Westfield Seight kit or a Luego Viento; don't try to jam a V8 into a Caterham Classic. Having said that, this is the world of kit cars, and if you want to badly enough, you can do whatever you can think of. One kit manufacturer once built a Seven-styled stainless steel monocoque car with a Jaguar V12 crammed into it. It made no commercial sense, and nobody ever bought one – he just felt like doing it. Top man.

The Jaguar V12 is a good engine, but you really need a GT40, Testarossa or Lambo replica to make sense of it – there's huge power and torque, but the V12 is so heavy it needs to be mid or rear-mounted to feel good. Pop one into a Nemesis kit, and feel good it does – turbine-smooth and very strong, with a unique exhaust song.

Back to the real world, and as the Sierra dies out, the only mass-market front-engine, rear-wheel-drive donor will be BMW, whose cars are now where Ford Capris were ten years ago. Kit car enthusiasts still seem to believe that BMWs are too expensive for donors, and certainly the prices of spare parts can be silly. Any exclusivity BMW once had is fading fast as every London street

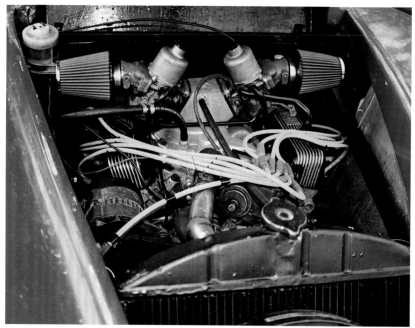

The Buick/Rover all-aluminium V8 provides plenty of grunt and the crucial offbeat throb, but weighs no more than a Pinto: top engine.

Alfa Romeo's 1960s twin-cam still offers good power and a standard five-speed gearbox, and it looks good too.

contains half a dozen new ones and a couple of dumped old ones. As BMWs become mass-market cars to rival Ford and Nissan, non-branded spares will become available more easily and cheaply. German and Swedish Car Spares in London are leading the way in bringing BMW parts prices down to sub-Ford levels. Using a 3-series BMW will soon become as natural a donor path as a 2-litre Pinto Sierra used to be. Marlin have led the way with BMW

Scrap MGBs on both sides of the Atlantic are still providing comprehensive donors for period sports replicas: torquey, reliable, long-stroke, and traditional.

donors, and more will follow.

When it comes to stripping a donor, there are two crucial issues. First, do it quickly and get the carcass 'Hi-Abbed' away ASAP, or the neighbours will start bitching. Secondly, do it methodically. Label the wiring loom, and put nuts, bolts and washers back where they came from on the components, rather than in a collection of grubby pickle jars. Each Jaguar front axle has 4,000 parts, and having blended them with the 4,000 parts from the back axle, you could spend a year or two sorting them out again when it's build-up time.

When taking springs off, bear in mind that each one normally supports a quarter of a ton of car, so use proper clamps and treat springs with fear and respect. They make a real mess if they get loose, and hands look so much nicer with the same number of fingers on each of them.

The same applies to jacking and axle stands – never put any bits of yourself that you value under a casually supported car if you want to use those bits again. Remember also that if you're scrapping the donor because it's rotten, you're going to have to find some solid parts of the shell to rest the car on as you fillet it.

DONOR OPTIONS

Donor car	BMC A-series	BMC B-series	Rover K-Series
	Mini, Metro, Sprite, Midget, Morris Minor 850cc, 1,000cc, 1,100cc, 1,275cc	**MGB 1800, Marina TC 1,500cc, 1,600cc, 1,800cc, (2,000cc)**	**Metro, MG, 200, 25, 400. 1,400cc, 1,600cc, 1,800cc, 1,800cc VVC**
Good/bad points:	Convenient complete engine/box/subframe package. Cheap, available, universal cheap parts, reliable, but – heavy, slow, noisy timing chains and gears. Morris Minor RWD gearbox delicate.	Strong, cheap, torquey, simple, nice exhaust note, vintage-style lever arm shocks and live rear axle on cart springs, independent suspension kit available, but – tall, heavy, lazy, archaic suspension, updated independent suspension kit expensive.	Engines light, powerful, and have an unusually competent and reliable ECU. Older K-series donors very cheap, but – engine has a tendency to blow head gaskets, needs good cooling system.
Power:	50–120bhp.	84–180bhp.	103–160bhp.
Unleaded fuel?	No.	No.	Yes.
Gearbox options:	Integral four-speed, or Midget four-speed/Type 9 Ford five-speed conversion for RWD.	Four-speed, four-speed O/D, T5 conversions.	MGF (AP1) gearbox for rear engine/rear drive, conversion to Type 9 Ford box for conventional RWD.

Donor car	Rover V8	Triumph	Ford Kent
	Rover P5, P6 and SD1 saloons, Range Rover, Land Rover. 3,500cc, 3,900cc, 4,200cc, 5,000cc	**Spitfire, Herald/Vitesse, TR6. 950cc, 1,100cc, 1,300cc, (1,500cc shared with Midget), 1,600cc, 2,000cc and 2,500cc sixes**	**Anglia, some Cortinas, Corsair, some Escorts, some Capris, KA. Crossflow and pre-crossflow. 1,000cc, 1,200cc, 1,340cc, 1,500cc, 1,600cc, (bored 1,700cc).**
Good/bad points:	Range Rover chassis excellent for kit conversion. Top low-budget light alloy engine, big torque, strong, reliable, tunable, but – old engines leak, airlocks common, cams wear, late 3.9 cylinder liner overheats and leaks due to over-lean standard chip fuelling.	Entire chassis/drivetrain usable for some vintage-styled kits. Cheap, simple, reliable, vintage-looking engines, sixes smooth, good spares support, but – chassis rot, dodgy handling from transverse rear leaf spring, suspect top end oil feed and crank thrust washers on sixes.	A late 1950s engine design, but good enough for revival in the Ka. Light, strong, balances well, tunable, Escort rear axle is light and strong with many ratios available, but – some spares tricky, blocks becoming rare, front MacPherson struts no use for kits.
Power:	160–450bhp (on carbs).	39–100bhp.	39–150bhp.
Unleaded fuel?	Yes – all post-1976 engines.	No.	No.
Gearbox options:	Rover four-speed and five-speed, BW 35 auto, T5 for stronger Rover engines.	Usually four-speed, some overdrive (O/D). Vitesse boxes weak.	Usually four-speed, Type 9 five-speed conversion, Ka FWD transverse five-speed.

Donor car	Ford Pinto	Ford Zetec	Ford Cosworth
	Sierra/Pinto, Transit (low comp), Granada. 1,600cc, 1,800cc, 2,000cc, (USA) 2,300cc	**Zetec Escort, Fiesta 1.6Si, Mondeo, 1,600cc, 1,800cc, 2,000cc, Focus**	**Sierra, Escort Cosworth, (Turbocharged Pinto). 2,000cc**
Good/bad points:	Cheap and tough, good cheap engine tuning parts available, all RWD with good gearboxes, Sierra independent rear end wide but strong, but – engine is crude, heavy, tall, no nice noises.	Very reliable, strong, cheap, economical, tunable engine, but – all FWD, engine is tall, high oil pressure fouls up hydraulic tappets, engine needs careful coolant bleeding, head gaskets can be unreliable, not the easiest amateur rebuild.	Beefed-up internals, good DOHC Cosworth head, lots of power, very tunable with chip/turbo upgrades, tractable compared with some other turbo engines, uprated Sierra running gear is good kit, but – anything Cosworth is expensive.
Power:	75–180bhp (on carbs).	100–210bhp (on carbs).	205–500+bhp.
Unleaded fuel?	Only on very late models.	Yes.	Yes.
Gearbox options:	Four-speed, five-speed.	Conversion to RWD boxes – Type 9 Ford, Euro type T5, Mustang T5.	Usually T5 five-speed; US T5 is stronger.

Donor car	**Ford V6** Granada, some Sierras, Capri, a few Cortinas. V6 Essex 3,000cc, Cologne 2,300cc/2,800cc/2,900cc	**Ford Small-Block V8** Mustang 289 and 5.0, sedans, vans, pick-ups. 5,000cc	**Chevrolet 350 V8** Small-block. Caprice and other sedans, pick-ups, light trucks, Camaro, Corvettes with small-block V8
Good/bad points:	Cheap, smooth and strong, nice noise, all RWD with north-south gearboxes. Live axles can be useful, but – Essex oil pump shaft rounds off, cam gears dodgy, all-iron engine weighs same as iron V8, not powerful or economical. Struts no use.	Mustang makes good donor. Ford V8 gives good muscle, parts and tuning cheap, reliability good, construction simple, but – heavy cast-iron block/heads, old/new 302 parts compatibility less good, less tuning options than Chevy; 289s getting rarer.	Commercial and high-power blocks have standard four-bolt mains. No nonsense about front-wheel drive. Millions of engines made, parts and tuning very cheap, big muscle, very reliable, simple, interchangeable old and new parts – but heavy cast-iron blocks and heads.
Power:	112–160bhp.	200–600bhp (on carbs).	200–600bhp (on carbs).
Unleaded fuel?	No.	All post-1976 US engines are lead-free.	All post-1976 US engines are lead free.
Gearbox options:	C4 auto, four-speed, four-speed O/D, five-speed. (Five-speed Capri gearbox weak).	Auto, or Ford T5 Mustang box, older four-speed top-loaders etc, uprated Toyota Supra Turbo five-speed.	Auto, or Saginaw/Muncie/Tremec four-speed and five-speed, Toyota Supra Turbo (with bigger bearings), T56 six-speed.

Donor car	**Big-Block V8** Ford, GM, Chrysler large sedans, trucks, vans. 7,000cc+	**Small Fiats** Panda/Uno are FWD. X1/9 is RWD, rear-engine. 900cc–1,400cc	**Fiat/Lancia** Twin-cam Mirafiori, 124, Spider, Beta. 1,400cc, 1,600cc, 1,750cc, 1,800cc, 2,000cc
Good/bad points:	Vast torque and power, Chevy parts availability and prices, authenticity for 427 Cobra replicas, but huge weight can spoil light cars; 427 side-oiler Ford now rare; fuel costs inevitably high.	Very cheap; light, long-lived, compact engines, but – FWD, dodgy FIRE distributors, gear bearings and head gaskets on late engines.	Indestructible, well-developed, pretty engine, Mirafiori RWD box useful and strong, but – no longer common; US examples often well worn.
Power:	200–750+bhp (on carbs).	45–114bhp (Uno Turbo).	106–200bhp.
Unleaded fuel?	All post-1976 US engines are lead-free.	Nearly all.	Doubtful – assume not.
Gearbox options:	Auto, and big four-speed and five-speed gearboxes.	Conversion to RWD Ford Type 9 box (MRH, 01634 290451).	Mirafiori four-speed.

Donor car	**BMW 3 and 5 series** 1,600cc, 1,800cc, 2,000cc, 2,500cc, 2,800cc, 3,000cc, 3,500cc	**Jaguar XK DOHC Straight Six** XJ6, MkII, S-type, E-type, 2,800cc, 3,400cc, 3,800cc, 4,200cc	**VW Beetle** Air-cooled flat-four. 1,000cc–2,200cc
Good/bad points:	Quite good if old-fashioned engineering, donors cheap, all RWD, M version engines can be amusing, bigger cars almost free, six-cylinders nice and smooth, but – parts prices silly, sixes can burn oil, front struts no use, 3 series rear suspension heavy, with suspect geometry. Sulphur in petrol has damaged some six-cylinder engines, so always check cylinder compressions.	Excellent rolling gear, big disc brakes. All RWD. Various axle ratios, some LSD. Engines strong and smooth, cheap UK availability, good power per £, some parts cheap, but – some parts prices silly, engines massively heavy, big and long. Earlier 4.2 unreliable, 2.8 burns pistons, ally/steel corrosion problems; manual gearboxes rare.	Floorpans rebuildable from strong central tunnel. Cheap to run/repair, seized barrel/pistons easily replaced, tuning parts cheap and available, no radiator, but – noisy, crude and not as reliable as VW enthusiasts insist. Floorpans usually need rebuild.
Power:	Four-cylinder 316 75bhp; six-cylinder M535 260bhp.	170–250+bhp (on carbs).	20–240bhp.
Unleaded fuel?	Yes.	Post-1968 engines can run on unleaded.	Late heads will run on unleaded.
Gearbox options:	Mostly Getrag and five-speed.	Moss four-speed O/D, XJ6 four-speed O/D, Getrag five-speed.	Standard VW four-speed box and diff is strong, compact and free.

Donor car	**BMW V8s** **Assorted 5, 7 and 8-series from 1992 to date** **3,000cc, 3,500cc, 4,000cc, 4,400cc, 4,800cc**	**Vauxhall DOHC 16V 2-litre** **Cavalier, Calibra, Astra, Carlton from 1989** **2,000cc**
Good/bad points:	Smooth and quite well-engineered, and getting cheaper all the time as BMWs become ever more common. Plenum chamber covers and cam covers are attractive, engine looks modern and sexy. Light for its size, all-alloy construction. But – silly parts prices, and computer-driven so there will be ECU issues. Also physically a big engine. Carbs/distributor not an option. Prior to 1997, M60 engines are made of porridge, and sulphur in cheap petrol dissolved the cylinders: but early engines that are still usable should remain usable. More than 15% cylinder leakdown means walk away. M60 3-litre engines with 1 745 871 engine numbers are OK, and M60 4-litres with 1 745 872 numbers are OK. Later, the Nikasil cylinder blocks are replaced by Alusil, and the engines are good. M62 V8s of 3.5, 4.4, 4.6 and 4.9 litres have Alusil blocks and 232-394bhp, and are OK.	150bhp in cooking spec. GTE spec with Webers gets 180bhp, and a cam takes it to 210bhp. XE is the desirable version, ECOTEC is the later watered-down vegetarian environmental version, but it's cheap, available and can still be encouraged to perform.
Power:	218–394bhp.	150–210bhp+.
Gearbox options:	Usually fitted with a good but electronically operated autobox: manual gearboxes are available but quite rare.	Conversion to Type 9 Ford 5-speed, or find a rarer Opel Manta box by Getrag, which only needs a spigot bush for RWD conversion.

Donor car	**Ford Duratec DOHC 16V** **Mondeo, Focus, Fiesta** **1,800cc, 2,000cc, 2,300cc**	**Toyota 4AGE twin-cam 16V** **MR2, Corolla** **1,600cc**
Good/bad points:	All Ford engines sold in Europe are now called Duratec, which is unhelpful. Variations are enormous, and engines are made in Spain, USA, Mexico and China. Post-2005 Duratecs are Mazda engines. The Duratec usually used in kits would be the 2-litre 4-cyl engine, which is a development of the Zetec. Focus RS version is supercharged to 215bhp. Westfield and Toniq sell a Cosworth version with 220–260bhp. Duratec V6 3-litre 24-valve engines give 200bhp and seem free of major problems. But – Duratecs need ECU management, can be tricky to start from cold unless the ECU program is good. Misfires may be plug leads – apparently it's worth using really good ones for longevity.	Tough, reliable screamer with a redline of 8,500rpm. (9,500rpm is apparently survivable.) Looks and sounds nice too, very popular with Seveneers. Physically small, thus convenient for smaller engine bays. Pre-1992 engines are exempt from catalytic converter requirement. MR2 offers a supercharged option. 12,000rpm can be achieved with a forged crank.
Power:	130–260bhp.	135–200bhp.
Gearbox options:	Ford Type 9.	Toyota K-50 and T-50 5-speeds, or Type 9 Ford 5-speed is a good conversion option.

Donor car	**Ford Modular OHC V8** **Mustang (quad-cam) Police Interceptor (twin-cam)** **4,600cc and 5,400cc**	**Mazda Rotary** **RX7 Wankel rotary, optionally turbocharged.** **1,300cc**	**Jaguar AJ6 straight six** **XJ40 and XJS** **3,600cc, 4,000cc**
Good/bad points:	Remarkably efficient engine, capable of 25–30mpg in a full-size car. Very strong, cheap to import as a crate engine. Can be lightly supercharged/turbocharged without compression drop. Stock blown Mustang version exceeds 500bhp. But – needs ECU management, is as big as a 7-litre big-block, and heavy. Backwards component compatibility is poor.	1,300cc doesn't mean much with a rotary. They offer a complete RWD drivetrain and axle set with remarkable power, strange but interesting noises and a 7,000rpm redline. Made from 1978 on, rusty donors are cheap. Rear axle is live with a Watts linkage. An interesting Sevenesque donor, rarely used. But – they tend to be very loud, emissions-dirty and not very fuel-efficient.	Old XJ6s and XJ40s are just about worthless now, so they're a good option if you want a big six. The AJ6 engine replaced the old XK engine and was a much better motor with no major design faults or problems. Cheap muscle with a nice straight-six soundtrack. But – engine wear tends to go past the ECU's parameters, resulting in rough idling and bad emissions, but the ECU can be adjusted to some extent.
Power:	230–600bhp++.	135–300bhp.	221–235bhp.
Gearbox options:	Good 4-speed autobox comes free, or use Mustang 5- or 6-speed manual.	In-line RWD 5-speed (and rear axle) comes with engine.	Getrag 5-speed manuals are available with a little hunting.

Donor car	**Honda B-series** **Prelude, Integra, Civic, CRX** **1,600cc, 1,700cc, 1,800cc**
Good/bad points:	Goes from mild 1600 to wild 1800 Type R with variable valve technology and 200bhp+. Some versions redline at nearly 9,000rpm. 1800 blocks and 1600 heads can be mixed and matched for even more power. Indestructible, light, cheap. The ECU seems to be easier to recycle than some. Later K-series VTEC engines offer 280bhp: Powertec tel. 01733 331919. The Ariel Atom uses a blown Honda and is almost as fast as an Enzo. But – many Honda engines spin the 'wrong' way, and there are no common RWD gearbox conversions. If the whole engine/gearbox package is used as FWD as in many current Mini conversions, or as a rear-engined, RWD fitting in the back end of a suitable kit car, that could work well.
Power:	126–215+bhp.
Gearbox options:	Comes with good 5-speed. No common RWD conversion has emerged.

Above: Ford's Cologne V6 is heavy and not that powerful, but is smooth and very cheap to buy.

Above: If you really want to use a particular engine, you can find a way. This Mini runs a rear-mounted turbocharged Lancia engine, simply because the owner refused to take no for an answer.

Below: The Honda FireBlade engine isn't usually seen in a Mini: this one uses a custom transfer box and retains the Mini's front wheel drive.

Above: The Toyota 4AGE engine is a stalwart kit car engine, in this case supercharged by Omex: it's pushed closer to its limits, but still well within them.

Below: Red top Vauxhall engine in this Raw Striker is still a very good choice for a kit car that will get regular use. Heavier than a bike engine, but more drivable.

BIKE ENGINES

Donor bike	Kawasaki Ninja	Honda Blackbird	Honda FireBlade	Suzuki 1300 Hayabusa
Good/bad points:	Small, light, cheap, tough, but – frantic 12,000rpm redline, no torque, mad parts prices. Later bigger engines up to 1350cc are expensive.	Reliable, a little more torque than smaller bike engines, injection works well, but – quite tall; dry sump is advised. Massive cost if ignition key is missing.	The first bike engine used in kits; small, light, powerful, tough, common, not too expensive, but – needs sump baffles, not much torque and a bit frantic. Avoid injected version.	Small, tough, powerful, some torque as well, but – costs £3,000+ second-hand; grabby clutch.
Power:	105–110bhp standard.	135–170bhp.	103–180bhp.	175–285bhp.
Gearbox options:	Integral six-speed sequential.	Integral six-speed sequential.	Integral six-speed sequential.	Integral six-speed sequential.

Donor bike	V-Twins for Trikes	Triumph	Yamaha R1
Good/bad points:	For Morgan replicas there are two main options in addition to the Citroën 2CV: Honda CX and Silver Wing engines of 500cc and 650cc, and Moto Guzzi engines of usually 500cc, 750cc or 1,000cc. The Honda engine with 50bhp at 9,500rpm feels faster, but the Moto Guzzi with 48bhp at 7600rpm is less frantic, more torquey, gets 50mpg plus in a bike and is a beautiful piece of Italian engineering sculpture sticking out of the front of your trike. Whereas the Honda engine, although indestructible even by dispatch riders, has all the visual panache of a garbage disposal pump. But could last 200,000 miles with timing chain changes every 50,000. Both have useful shaft drive.	British for a change. Odd, interesting engines: smaller ones usually transverse triples, bigger ones fours. Sizes 600cc, 1,000cc, 1,200cc, 2,300cc (a cool inline shaft-driven triple with 147lb ft torque. Surveys say Triumph have top reliability, happy customers: times have changed.	Short, compact 1000cc engine. Big power, starting at 150bhp. Built to be the fastest bike ever
Power:	48/50bhp for 500cc: 65bhp for Honda 650cc, 81bhp for Guzzi 1,000cc.	104–147bhp.	150–180bhp.
Gearbox options:	Usually 5-speed sequential on older bikes.	Integral six-speed sequential. (Rocket has 5-speed).	Integral six-speed sequential.

Right: Citroen's 600cc flat twin also powers many kit trikes. It has a small carb and a roller bearing crank, so it's extremely tough and still worth thinking about.

Below: Honda's 500cc and 650cc V-twin bike engines are excellent fun in a trike, but not the prettiest.

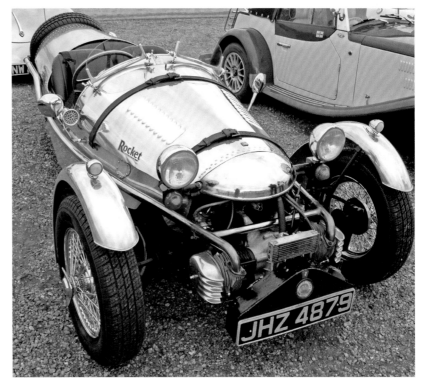

Chapter 3

Estimation and motivation

Think of a number and double it. That applies to both time and money, and the formula works with many kit car builds. Going over budget by 100 per cent on both time and money is not unusual. However, let's get it into perspective. You can't possibly waste as much in percentage terms as any single government project of any kind, because you're not sufficiently dim or negligent.

If you buy a new car in Britain you'll pay £5,000 over the odds compared with other Europeans, and you'll lose another £5,000 in depreciation as soon as the registration document has your name on it as well. So don't buy one. You've just saved ten grand to spend on a kit. You could also have taken up yachting, in which everything costs even larger amounts of money, so by avoiding that you've saved another £10,000 per annum. You're already up £20,000 – and that's just this financial year. With your new kit-builder's financial world-view firmly in mind, read on.

The first problem is creeping 'that-would-be-nice'. Your original budget calls for cheap steel wheels and recycling the original dash and instruments . . . but a set of split rims would be really nice. The Halibrand replicas are a one-off investment, your wife may take pity on you at birthday time and suddenly you've just copped for another £1,200. Likewise the instruments. A matching set of Autometer dials would look so sexy, and they're more accurate than the old standard stuff . . . but with the full set, the senders, the sensors and VAT, suddenly the credit card takes a battering. The dash looks the business, though, doesn't it?

It is possible to keep on top of your financial budget and avoid too much in the way of wallet

This is the image to keep in mind in freezing February when your spanner slips off a nut and you bash your knuckles on the chassis. Stick a photocopy of it on the garage wall.

On a high-class Cobra such as a Jag/Chevy Cobretti, you need to spend big bucks on leather seats, a decent wheel, a tinted screen . . . fortunately the Audi-sourced handbrake lever only cost a fiver.

injuries by spreading the buying of expensive parts of the car over a few years. If you pick a kit that can be supplied in a gelcoat finish good enough to be polished up and used, you save at least £1,000. Many kit car manufacturers' body finish is excellent, and you genuinely don't need to paint their

cars. You can also buy relatively cheap steel wheels that really don't look too bad at all, and will do fine until there is enough spare money for the serious wheels you need to get the car properly finished.

The second and less easily malleable problem is time. It has to be said that a lot of

manufacturers' build-time estimates are complete drivel. Just to confuse matters, some of them stubbornly tell the truth. The problem is that once one person has said that their Cobra replica was built in 150 hours, everybody else feels they have to claim a similar number, even if it's total nonsense.

Some of the figures are based on genuine build times. If you were a manufacturer and habitually built complete cars, it might well take you just 200 hours to finish one of your own cars to a high standard, assuming all the bits were to hand. A hobbyist enjoying the build can probably double that.

For a start, the number of productive hours in a weekend day is not very high. You don't get into the garage at 8am with your tools ready and your next task fully planned and under way a minute later. You take out a cup of coffee after a leisurely breakfast and potter about for a bit, deciding which bit you feel like doing, and avoiding painful or boring tasks. And so you should – this is supposed to be fun, not work.

If you spend your working life in an office, your neck muscles will not be strong enough to hold your head up at a 90° angle for an hour, so you're going to take a lot longer to organise a handbrake fitting under your car than a pro kit builder would.

If you want to speed things up, you can buy other people's time and also avoid the bits of the build you don't fancy. It takes a full week to prepare a car body to be anywhere near ready for painting, and it's hard graft. Skip it if you don't fancy it, and knock a couple of months off the build time. In the same way, if the thought of delving into the guts of an engine is daunting, either use a known good one, or buy a new one.

Wiring terrifies most people, although fitting a new loom to a new kit car is about as easy as auto electrics gets. If you think there are too many evil spirits

A full set of matching Smiths clocks is actually good value compared with replacing the electronic instrument pod on a newish production car, but it's still not cheap.

Michaela makes the Stardust Jaguar D-type replica look good. On the other hand, the car makes Michaela look pretty good too . . . just as it would make your other half look good.

lurking in a wiring loom, skip it and find somebody else to do it.

If cash is your shortage rather than time, consider saving serious money by buying and taking over somebody else's abandoned project. The sad truth is that a 90 per cent-finished kit car is worth only a small percentage of the money and work that has been poured into it, so there are always some bargains out there. However, these part-finished cars may have been built by half-wits, or even professional mechanics, which can be worse. You should budget for taking the whole thing to pieces and rebuilding it properly, but even so, you're still saving literally thousands of pounds.

There are other ways of saving money, too: the back pages of

Street Machine, *Custom Car* and *Classic Ford* are crammed with nearly new goodies at very reasonable prices, and you have the advantage of time on your side. Your car isn't going to be finished for a while, so you can wait until a set of the right wheels comes along at the right price. Use your imagination, and try some completely different ideas according to what bargains turn up – three-spoke wheels and a supercharged V6? Why not?

You can also save money by buying the right parts in the right places. If you want an American engine and gearbox, buy it in the States. The number of 350 Chevy engines built is in the millions, and the prices on tuning and rebuild parts are a revelation to Europeans. A brand-new Chevy

piston the size of a dinner plate still costs half as much as crispy Peking duck and egg fried rice. Conversely, Americans buying new Jaguar parts in the USA are likely to get hammered on prices – so use the UK's second-hand and budget Jaguar companies. Even with shipping charges and customs duty, there are big savings to be made on both sides of the Atlantic.

To get some idea of a genuine basic budget, you need to add in all the trivia that sends the final figure high enough to need hiding from your other half. This partial list may help.

Basic kit; all the other bits from the maker that are crucial to finishing the car; VAT or local purchase taxes; collection or delivery; a Haynes

Of course, if the whole kit car thing starts to look too daunting, you could always buy a production 'sports saloon' instead.

manual; overhaul, shot-basting, powder coating or painting of components; chassis treatments; disposal of donor wreck; brake pads, discs, cylinders, piping, fluid; bushes; shocks and springs; wheels and tyres; radiator, hoses, connections; oils; new hand tools and power tools; engine hoist and other plant hire or purchase; paint; trimming materials, glues, carpets, etc; seats; instruments; detailing chrome, mirrors, bumpers, badges, etc; steering wheel and boss; nuts and bolts, rivets, fasteners, sealers; windscreen wipers (and a windscreen to wipe); fuel cap; weather gear; a heater; wiring, lights and connectors. Oh, and an engine and gearbox plus rebuild costs, unless you simply paint, service and re-clutch the donor lump and bung it back in. And finally, a new kitchen and/or sofa to preserve domestic bliss.

Are you married? Are you really going to get away with a year and a half of disappearing into your garage most weekends and evenings, without a divorce? Would your other half join in? Would your friends or children join in?

I make a lot of jokes in *Kit-Car* magazine about the marital aspects of kit cars, and talk about the domestic currency of new sofas and kitchens, which tend to be traded for permission to buy and build a kit. There's a reality behind the jokes, though.

The kind of people who would consider building a car are usually adept at DIY, and it may not go down well if the household handyman completely ignores domestic maintenance for a couple of years. Unless you're single or unusually lucky, you will need to do as much preparatory work on your domestic situation as you will on your garage before you start.

Recently I answered the following agony letter in *Kit-Car*:

'This is not exactly a mechanical problem, but I hope you can help anyway. I understand that you have a Midge, an XK replica, a Range Rover and one or two other projects, and that you are also married. How do you manage this? I am about to get an inheritance of about £20,000 and my wife wants us to buy a proper new sports car, while I see this as my one and only opportunity to worship at the altar of the great Carroll Shelby. How would you persuade her towards the right course of action?'

My reply was as follows:

'Anonymous? Forget anonymous – if she reads this, you're dead. As far as my own domestic situation goes, I got the kit cars before the wife chose me. In any case, I'm dead lucky – my wife is a graphic artist, and also clever. As well as gorgeous. The Midge is pretty, the XK is a fabulous shape – she couldn't resist either of them. The Range Rover, bought mainly for health insurance while driving in London, was her choice anyway – as soon as she sat in it and heard the V8

A very cheap way into the kit car world without £10k and a two-year build is to start off by doing up a tatty old second-hand kit car like my Jeep. If you find that you enjoy the experience, gear up to starting a new build for real.

Any budget can get blown out of the water by bad luck. I tried three 4.2 XJ6 engines, one expensively rebuilt, before giving up and fitting a V8. A design fault in the early 4.2 means ovalised main bearing housings, and evil crankshaft vibration at 2,000rpm.

she said: "It's fab, we should buy this". She did get badly bored – as did I – with the Jag engines vibrating and breaking down, but with the V8 on the way the XK replica should rehabilitate itself. She's now making and selling limited edition screen prints of Facel Vegas, Cadillac fins and art deco Bugattis, so she's becoming a petrolhead too, which is a bonus. However, that was just good luck.

As to handling your own beloved, there are some straight facts she should know. For a start, £20k does not buy a new sports car. First, you have to knock off the £5,000 sucker tax for buying a new car in Britain, leaving you enough for an expensive shopping car or a cheap repping car. Secondly, as soon as the ink's dried on the registration document another £5,000 has just been flushed down the toilet. It's now a second-hand shopping car.

It will also increasingly be a cash cow for its manufacturer – future emissions failures will mean regular new cats at £1,000 a pop, and if any of its computers do what computers do outside warranty, budget for another £1,000 every time. If your wife wants a new production car, she'd

better start saving now to keep it on the road, or to pay for the next new car in a year or two – once you've joined the new-car game, you have to change them before you do many miles and before the warranty runs out. According to the AA, new cars now break down just as often as they did twenty years ago, but now they have to be recovered to main dealers rather than repaired free.

You can definitely have a brand-new Cobra replica for £20,000 though, and with that budget you don't even have to build it yourself. A Pilgrim would be a good bet, as your wife will be reassured to know that it passed the same German TUV structural tests as a Mercedes-Benz had to. The (GRP) body and (galvanised) chassis are obviously a lot newer than a 'new' production car that's been sitting on an abandoned airfield for a year due to overproduction. And of course you can still buy a brand-new Rover V8 engine and box. Add a new wiring loom and a new fuel system and all the regular breakdown problems are covered. Rebuilt Sierra running gear will do nicely for the rest, with new brakes and bearings. So she gets her brand-new sports car, but no

sucker tax, no depreciation, and no rust. Ever.

Your wife may also like to know that the bulging hips of a Cobra replica's rear end will make her bum look even slimmer than it already is by comparison, and that most people will think she is in a car that cost £150,000. So she'll look both rich and thin.

What paint and leather trim colours would she like? Would she like her new car to match the new sofa and kitchen she'll be getting from the savings from not buying a new production car?

Kit cars don't need dealer servicing to get the all-important stamps in the service book, which will save yet more. Would she perhaps like a little trip to Venice on the servicing savings? She could be chauffeured around the streets of Monaco in summer sunshine and enjoy the waves of pure envy coming from every other woman in the place who is not in a Cobra.

On the other hand . . . she can go to Asda in a dull new shopper. On her own. Anonymous. Unenvied. For stuff to cook on the old cooker.

Hope that helps.'

Okay, that wasn't entirely serious, but the idea that the first major task of the car in question will be to drive her ladyship along a sun-kissed promenade in the south of France will go down well. All this is a bit sexist, but let's face facts: something like 98 per cent of *Kit-Car's* readers are male, despite my own constant encouragement in the magazine for women to grab some spanners and join in.

So you're confident that you can handle the domestic aspect of the build, without having to sell the car to fund a divorce. How confident are you that you will get past the next hurdle – the dangerous 90 per cent-finished point? A depressing number of nearly finished kits are sold for very little money. Their owners have spent thousands of pounds and hundreds of hours getting the

Your head weighs about ten times more when you're trying to lift it off the deck as you fit propshafts, fuel and brake lines, gearboxes and so on from underneath. Expect some physical as well as financial pain if you start building cars.

Okay, I'm exceptionally lucky as my wife has a well-developed sense of humour, but if your other half isn't on side you could be looking at some real problems.

hard bits done, but they just can't motivate themselves to drag out a little more energy to finish the job and enjoy the car. If you think you might fall into that group, you have two choices – either sort out enough of a budget to get somebody else to finish it off if you get sick of working on it, or start off by buying some unfortunate person's abandoned 90 per cent completed project and finishing it yourself.

A good idea is to separate the process of building from the long-awaited enjoyment of the final car. Read Robert Pirsig's *Zen and the Art of Motorcycle Maintenance*, a sort of hippy biker philosophy classic from California. No point in rushing, you just slow down to the right speed to do the job well, and concentrate on the piece you're working on. The purpose of the kit during the time when it is being built is not primarily to

The Kit-Car *Le Mans long weekend can be made genuinely good fun for wives as well as kit-car mad husbands, and involves some seriously good restaurant food and a very civilised campsite half-an-hour south of the circuit.*

As Le Mans is already halfway down France, the natural thing to do is to thank your other half for his/her patience by driving the new kit car on to Venice for a few days. No cars there, just gondolas.

be a car, but to be your hobby. If your approach to it is calm, quiet and methodical, building it will be absorbing and therapeutic, and will provide relief from the stress of other aspects of your life.

If you get bored and annoyed with the whole thing, walk away for a while – building kit cars is supposed to be fun, and if it stops being fun, back off until you want to go back to it. If, like me, you just want to get the damn thing on the road so you can play with it, you should probably budget for getting some help towards the end, or like me you'll finish up always driving around in half-finished cars.

Do you have the skills and knowledge to build a car? Yes, you do. You certainly have enough to get started, and by the time you've got anywhere with the project your skills will be developing nicely. You may be absolutely clueless right now as to how an engine works, but by the time you've dismantled and inspected one with the help of the relevant Haynes manual, your eyes and hands will have made a lot of sense of what all the bits do. It can be physically difficult to tackle a car on a weekend basis, because your muscles and joints are not necessarily in the habit of being physically abused. This makes it hard work and makes you clumsier. Okay, you have to accept that your arms will get tired as you wind a ratchet back and forth at full stretch, your palms will blister as you grind in valves, and your neck muscles will hurt as you lie under a chassis holding a very heavy head up at 90° from its usual angle.

You don't have to do the whole thing yourself, though. If you join a kit club, you will get help, and you will give help later. It's considered polite to provide beer and tea, and once your problems are cheerfully solved by people who have already been there, you can plod along until you get stuck again.

If that all sounds too easy and comfy, you may prefer to drive an open trike over the Alps to Morocco and back, getting alternately frozen and burnt on the way. Endurance trips are increasingly popular, but not with me.

There are also professional kit car builders out there, some of whom are very good, although even at a reasonable hourly rate the bills do mount up. Bear in mind that it takes ten times longer to make new cars than to repair existing ones using bolt-on replacement parts.

You are completely free to pick and choose which bits you fancy doing yourself, or which bits you have enough confidence in your abilities to achieve, and you can simply pass on to somebody else those aspects of the build you don't fancy. Nobody's saying you have to do the whole thing on your own.

If you don't fancy rebuilding an engine, either buy a good second-hand one or have a new one built. If you don't fancy weeks of rubbing down, get somebody else to do the paint. If electrics sound scary – just overcome your nervousness and get stuck in. Fitting a new loom to a new chassis is dead easy, can be done in a weekend and gives a lot of satisfaction as everything hoots, flashes and pumps. If it all turns into a spaghetti nightmare, call an auto electrician.

Dealing with GRP bodywork is something similar – even if you do foul it up, you can always repair any damage you've done, and it gets easier the more you do it. I myself am fairly cack-handed and impatient, and easily unnerved by unfamiliar cam timing assemblies, but wiring and GRP are really no bother.

There will be cuts, bruises, strains, permanently black fingernails, cold, damp winter evenings, sulks from ignored families, pauses to redecorate rooms and visit relatives, and you may collect some permanent scars – one of my fingers is a slightly different shape after being hit with enthusiasm and a large hammer as I bashed out Jaguar hub bearings. One of my shoulders is also a bit suspect after a spectacular crash when my donor Jag overtook me, still on its trailer. However, although definitely a wordsmith rather than a blacksmith, I'm still playing about with kits after decades and still enjoying them. Computers have changed things substantially in the last ten years, both for the better and for the worse. On the plus side, you can get more power, reliability and economy out of donor engines than ever before. On the minus side, figuring out how to make an ECU work without its donor car still attached can be a bitch.

The internet gives you tremendous access to a huge amount of information, but on the minus side some of it is garbage uploaded by imbeciles. It is also cutting magazine circulation by 7% a year, as more and more people would rather have free, but often inaccurate, information than pay four quid to read material written by people who know what they're talking about. If you're reading this you're on the intelligent side of the fence.

If the above has really sunk in and has not put you off, you probably have what it takes, and we'll expect to see your freshly finished car at the kit shows in a year or two.

Chapter 4

Industrial secrets

Your kit car manufacturer is your tailor, so it's important to choose the right one. The kit car industry ranges from one guy in a shed to some quite impressive factories, and there are things to be said for both.

Cobretti in London represent the small end of the spectrum with their Viper Cobra replicas. Proprietor Bob Busbridge has seen the big money come and go, and his cars have changed hands at £30,000. The company used to occupy a big factory in the '80s, but has now contracted into a four-car garage at the bottom of Bob's garden. The Viper range still goes from budget four-cylinder Ford-based cars up to supercharged Chevrolet V8 powered Predator cars on Jaguar rolling gear, but Bob will not be expanding the business into a big factory again. He's happy with just a few customers and no pressure.

At *Kit-Car* magazine we have seen a good few people come into the market with big plans, big premises and big wage and rent bills, and sadly some of them have not survived the ups and downs that are inevitable in what is after all a luxury trade. Boat-builders face the same problems, with the same consequences. I've personally felt for a long time that when I go to review a car and company and find kit car makers working in a shed in a farmyard, it's a good sign – it means their costs and therefore their prices are lower, and they'll probably still be in business after the next recession.

If you deal with a one-man business, you're talking directly to the organ grinder, and if you want any changes in your kit they can usually be arranged. You will have a personal relationship with the car's designer and maker, and that

Here's a factory that's geared up to serious mass production – pile 'em high and sell 'em cheap. The computerised tube bender is certainly paying its way these days.

Right: A CNC machine being used to cut out body panels. For mass production, some manufacturers have more or less abandoned glassfibre, as it's expensive and supplies are unreliable compared with steel.

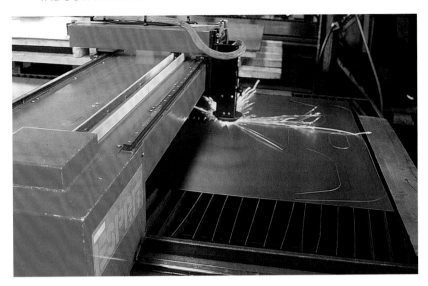

brings obvious benefits – as one of a small number of customers you're important and you'll usually become friends. After all, you've chosen his car from many options and made a significant personal investment in it, and that's quite a compliment you've paid him.

With the smallest companies you can get some hassles with details such as parts supply, and an attack of the flu means the whole company is stuck in bed drinking whisky and lemon and throwing the telly remote at Oprah, rather than welding your chassis together. So you need to be patient sometimes. Smaller companies also lack any clout when ordering bits and pieces. Take steering wheels. If you buy 500 wheels at a time from Mountney, so it's going to be 'Hello, sir, and how are you today?' When it comes to Cobretti it'll inevitably be 'Bob who?' because Bob buys five at a time. So you can budget for some parts delays with small companies.

If you go to the bigger and more efficient companies, you get a completely different product. Some manufacturers make and sell a lot of low-budget cars, on a rather impersonal basis. However, if what you want is pile 'em high, sell 'em cheap B&Q-style bargain prices and a whole kit car for a grand during special offer periods, this approach is what you're looking for.

If you want and are prepared to pay for service, attention and a thoroughly well developed, slick product, talk to somebody like

Right: This is the result of all that effort – the Intermeccanica car is a beauty. Sadly, bureaucrats prevent its sale as a turnkey car in Canada, so most of their cars go to the USA.

Above: Intermeccanica's Vancouver operation is geared to producing cars in the dozens rather than in the hundreds. They're not the cheapest, partly because the bodies are left in the moulds for two weeks to cure, which means having several costly moulds rather than just one.

At the other end of the scale is Jim Clarke, working on his own in a shed on a farm. He's a seriously talented bodywork sculptor, but commercial success has eluded him so far.

Caterham. They will receive you with a receptionist, sell to you with a salesman and support you with an engineer. The kit will plop together with the nuts, bolts and washers supplied, and is very unlikely

Jim's Manx was 2CV-based and not a big seller, but the point is that he produced this car with a superb gelcoat finish in a grubby shed on a farm – so you don't need to look for a big kit car operation to find excellent kits.

to cause you any unexpected problems. The Caterham option is expensive, but if time is more important than money, that's the right sort of kit for you.

Some of the bigger British and American Cobra replica companies have invested pretty serious money into development, and although you will have to pay fairly serious money for their product, they offer you a bargain when you compare their cars to anything else for sheer performance. If you're lucky, £30,000 worth of production sports car is going to get you to 60mph in eight seconds. Put the same budget into any good Cobra replica and you're looking at nearer four seconds than eight. You can also skip depreciation, deterioration and specialist service bills – all the serious Cobras do the business with cheap, simple V8 muscle.

I'm familiar with the economics of small kit car companies from personal experience, having made a few XK120 replicas. Using every trick in the book to save money, it still cost £25,000 to achieve the first prototype ... and that's the cheap bit. Selling them is the seriously expensive problem. Replicas are frequently bought by people who lusted after their dream car in their youth, and try to achieve one in middle age. Unfortunately the young men who lusted after XK120s in 1948 are now in warden-supervised accommodation in seaside towns, and well past their

car-building years. Had I been able to sell forty Ayrspeed Sixes a year I would have done very nicely, thank you, but if I sold four I would make a continuing fat loss. Four was obviously enormously more likely than forty, so I kept the production prototype and more or less packed the project in, although I still have the moulds and the occasional body is sold – the last going off to rebody a real XK, oddly enough. Many small kit car manufacturers have even less commercial sense than I do, and somehow manage to keep making cars – but it's in spite of the money and not because of it.

Glassfibre costs are continuously rising, although steel is cheap. It still costs around £300–400 for enough steel to make a chassis, before any labour is added. Nowadays it probably costs about £700 for enough GRP to mould a body, before any of the other chemicals and before labour. If one man welds up the chassis and lays the matting and resin for the body himself, he will spend something like two or three full-time weeks on it. He also had to pay £40,000 up front for moulds and jigs, and he needs to pay for rent, VAT, food, local council domestic and business rates, a mortgage, petrol tax, tools, electricity, national insurance/income tax, trousers, tea and bikkies. If he charges you £2,500 for the body and chassis kit, he's almost certainly giving it to you at a loss in the hope that he can make a bit later as you buy the rest of the bits and pieces from him. He's unlikely to have faced the fact that he's losing 50p an hour and would undoubtedly earn more money driving a bus. He's probably too busy to answer the phone, but when you turn up for a visit the first thing he'll do is put the fibreglass-encrusted kettle on.

The smaller the company, the more important you are as a customer, but the harder it is for the company to keep you happy and make a living. Kit makers are enthusiasts first and businessmen

Above: This is the buck for the author's Swallow design. The whole thing was created out of sheet steel and bits of Riley, Mini, Volvo and Renault, and was taken to a good enough finish to be painted. Months of work, but fascinating to see my design emerge in 3D.

The Swallow's perimeter chassis was massively strong, and the car was fast, comfy and very stable. Sadly, most trike enthusiasts only have motorbike driving licences, and the car was too heavy for them to drive it legally.

second, so pick one you like and trust, and be prepared to give them a break and be flexible – you'll get what you want in the end.

Don't, however, buy a kit without trying an example first. A surprising number of manufacturers don't have a demonstrator. This is not necessarily because they can't afford one, although they almost certainly earn less than you do. The problem is that they can't resist a good offer on their demo cars. A VAT bill turns up, a new MIG welder is needed, some money is urgently required to develop a new model or to replace an aging mould ... so when somebody waves a £20,000 wad, they usually get to drive away in the (ex-) demonstrator. If manufacturers don't have their own demonstrator, no worries as long as they can find you a customer's car. Most owners are delighted to show their cars off, and will also let slip more information than you might have got from the manufacturer. You don't even have to drive the car yourself – as a kit car writer, I find that I get a much better idea of a kit car's capabilities when driven as a passenger by someone who really knows the car and how to drive it.

Don't buy a kit without getting a ride, though. No two kit cars ever feel quite the same, as they are all much more different from each other than Ferraris or whatever, but you must have a ride in an example of a kit to find out whether you're fundamentally going to enjoy the car or not.

Two examples: first, 1970s Marcoses are fab. I nearly bought one once, but the shape of the seat hurt my back. The seat is the bodywork, so I can't have one without major structural changes, and I'm not that good at blind orthopaedic surgery. Second, the Raffo. It's a fascinating and radical shape, it's fast and it handles like a racing car, but the vibration from the uncompromisingly solid-mounted rear-mid engine spoils the experience at tickover and at low speeds. Both are excellent cars, but not for me, and the only way I could have found that out was by going for that crucial ride. Imagine spending two years and £10,000 on a car to find out in the end that you really didn't like it.

Being taken for a financial ride is actually an extreme rarity in the kit car world, particularly in the UK. There have been telephone deposit scams in the USA, but I'd say that over 99 per cent of kit manufacturers are if anything too honest for their own good. However, very occasionally a bank will pull the rug out from under their feet in the charming way that banks do. A sensible-sized deposit followed by cash on delivery for the big bits is a very satisfactory and safe way of doing business, and keeps your money out of the reach of bankers and lawyers.

I should have more sense, but I'm getting involved in making cars again, this time a Cobra that can be built either as a budget car or as a premium one, or can be built cheaply and improved later. All the other Cobra replicas seem to have evolved to become expensive these days – even the American version of the Pilgrim, the Factory Five, finishes

The prototype and the production prototype for the Ayrspeed Six, of which there are three examples in existence. Oh well, at least that's three times as many as the Swallow. More large amounts of effort and money down the pan, but at least this time the author finished up with what turned out to be a superb car.

up costing serious money, and like the Pilgrim the basic kit is inevitably built down to a price. That's not to say it's not a good design – it definitely is a good design apart from the location of the Mustang fuel tank right at the back, and the authentic but outdated drainpipe ladderframe. The chassis and body production methods are up to date, and the chassis uses design rather than a lot of metal to achieve its strength.

The body is likewise thin and lightweight, and uses the latest pre-impregnated glassfibre cloth and a very cool robot trimmer to get all the edges perfect. They have been bought by 6,000 people, and megabucks have been invested in production. Light weight and V8 power mean serious performance – people race them and get a lot of fun out of them. Earlier Factory Five cars were originally based on single-donor scrap Mustangs and the old 302 V8, but have evolved into being sold as complete new cars in kit form, although still mostly with the old engines. Factory Five has significantly raised the profile of the US Cobra replica industry all on its own.

So why didn't I just buy one of those, then? Too easy, and I always have this idiot tendency to want to do things my own way. Also, it seemed a shame to waste all the experience gained with the Jag XK replica project, and it is tremendous fun seeing what people achieve with kits you've designed.

The inspiration for the Ayrspeed Police Cobra came indirectly from watching police chase videos which are top fun, particularly when drunken retards in stolen pickup trucks are pitted into ditches by cop cars. What kind of car handles well enough to bash a large pickup into a ditch and stay under control, then? The Ford Crown Victoria P71 Police Interceptor, is the answer.

A little more research revealed that the P71 has a separate chassis, independent adjustable double wishbone front suspension, a live rear axle with an expensive Watts linkage on later cars, and a very efficient and powerful V8. It can also be bought in slightly wrinkled form at American police auctions for very little money. The engines are worked hard, but get oil changes every 3,000 miles; at 50,000 miles they're perfectly conditioned for Cobra use, so why waste money on a new engine?

My first thought was that the actual Ford chassis could be used, with some modifications and strengthening and a Cobra body on top. Not good enough, sadly. The Ford chassis rusts, it's not accurately made and it doesn't quite fit. OK, a new chassis would have to be designed, but it would use the standard donor P71 geometry and suspension parts: we already know that setup is excellent and will present no unpleasant surprises.

I'm not a big fan of the Tojeiro Ace drainpipes: that sort of crude ladderframe was fine for a vintage 2-litre AC sports car in 1955, but even a 289 V8 used to twist it rather dramatically, which is where its reputation for evil handling came from. Real Cobras can be driven very fast, but smoothness is key to keeping the chassis straight and the suspension geometry stable. My view is that drainpipes have had their day, unless an authentic-looking replica chassis is important to you. Again, you're a kit builder, so do what you like.

My own chassis has major side intrusion/structural side beams and a bi-level triangulated backbone chassis in a Lotus/TVR style, with steel floors and bulkheads, and chassis beams reminiscent of Isambard Kingdom Brunel as well as Colin Chapman. Extra steel is a waste of profit, but it's my way of doing it, and in any case I like the smooth ride and massive torsional stiffness and strength an overkill chassis gives

you. The body follows the same theme – it's not a stressed body, but better to slap on more GRP and get it really solid anyway.

The Ayrspeed Police Cobra continues to evolve: it's leapfrogged Factory Five in skipping the 302 and going straight for the new-generation 4.6-litre Ford modular V8 engine, and ignoring the old Mustang mechanicals completely. This much newer engine technology generated a nightmare with computing and electronics, but the necessary transatlantic research trip yielded both an excellent solution and a useful chapter extension in this very book.

Finer engineering tolerances and major changes in engine control mean big changes in engine efficiency, and allow either remarkable fuel economy – around 25–30mpg – or stonking power. The engine is so strong that it can be supercharged or turbocharged to between 350bhp and 400bhp without reducing the compression. American cop cars are no use to me, you might reasonably argue, as police car auctions in the UK merely yield sad FWD cars with small engines, and not large cheap V8s with proper axles. However, the new Ayrspeed chassis design has already been conceptually adapted to take the V8 and the drivetrain from ageing upmarket BMWs, the values of which are dropping encouragingly quickly. BMW 5-series are expensive new, but dirt cheap when a few years old and lightly bashed. They also come with very useful tubular steel subframes and a RWD drivetrain, so the rebirth of the traditional kit car idea of a low-budget single-donor Cobra replica, but now with a BMW V8, is a reality. Keep an eye open on Ebay Motors for suitable panel-damaged salvage, and you'll find a spot-on BMW V8 complete donor car for less than the cost of a decent Japanese bike engine. Keep an eye on www.ayrspeed.com for the project's progress.

Life at the sharp end of low-volume kitcar manufacture: the Ayrspeed Police Cobra project comes together during 2007 and 2008

Right: I drove my old camper 1,200 miles to California and came back with a Cobra body strapped to the roof to rebuild into a moulding buck. Age does not necessarily beget wisdom, apparently.

This is the last Thunderbolt body ever made: the manufacturer put a Beetle engine in a Cobra body for fun and got death threats, so he refuses to have anything further to do with Cobras. Two big deep outer beams provide massive strength, and the additional Lotus-style central spaceframe backbone adds torsional rigidity. Belt and braces.

It's always a delicate judgement call between getting the engine as far back as possible for perfect weight distribution, and leaving enough room for feet and pedals. Wide, high transmission tunnel frames also add rigidity.

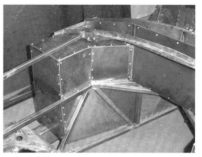

The bulkheads and footboxes are fireproof sheet steel rather than GRP. A little extra weight and cost, but that's the way I like it. Uhuh uhuh.

Below: The bonnet was a poor fit. In the end the only option was to blend the whole front end into a single sweeping curve, and then to re-cut the bonnet aperture.

There are no scrap V8 cop cars in Britain for $500, but 5-series V8 BMWs have a nice engine, and this excellent tubular steel suspension subframe will bolt right up to the chassis on the British version of the kit: a rolling chassis in a weekend, no bother.

Chapter 5

A factory in your garage

Turning a suburban garage into an engineering facility is easier said than done, but it is possible to build a car in a lock-up – my own Midge was built in one. Of course, it helped that the Midge is a tiny thing, and you would have trouble building a big car in a lock-up garage, but anything Sevenish is certainly feasible.

You do have to get the build in the right order: for instance, I used my rolling chassis as a convenient workbench and sawing horse to cut up the plywood to make the bodywork. If I'd built the body first I would have been in the poo.

Let's assume you've come to the kit scene as an automotive virgin, and have only fitted fuses and shelves before. You will need to invest in quite a lot of tools to build a car, but investing wisely will get you the best value, and the same tools will service your boring cars as well as your kit car, so the money is not wasted.

For some tools you need the best quality, but for others the best is a waste of money. It's worth spending out on a few really good screwdrivers, for example. If they're sharp, accurately manufactured and made of high quality, durable material, they will work and feel better. They will also avoid chewing up screw heads, and slipping off and gouging big scrapes right through a brand-new £5,000 paint job.

The same applies to your most-used spanners, which will be combination ring and open-ended 13 mm, 15mm and 17mm, and 3/8in, 1/2in and 9/16in AF (Across Flats) if you're still working

Your number one garage tool: a fire extinguisher. Keep one within arm's length wherever you are in the garage, particularly if you're welding or dealing with fuel and sparks.

Don't be tempted to borrow kitchen implements to use in car-building, as it causes big rages. For some reason, using her washing-up gloves to undo oil filters (very effective, incidentally) is worse than leaving the loo seat up. Safer to buy a chain wrench.

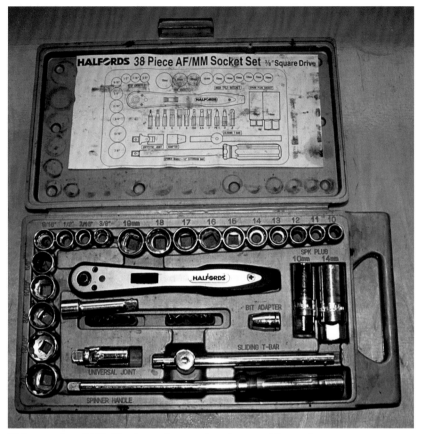

This manky old Halfords socket set has been with me for many years, and I've only lost one screwdriver bit. The set is not fancy or expensive, but it does the job.

A smaller socket set is needed for stripping carbs, alternators and so on: often securing nuts are in deep holes and you can't get to them without a small socket. I haven't lost any of this one yet.

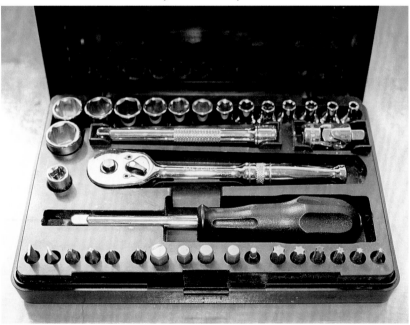

with older mechanicals. Just buy a few really good, tough, accurate spanners in those sizes. They will avoid chewing up bolt heads, and they will also save you losing an acreage of skin. When a cheap spanner rounds off a bolt and slips off, your knuckles will always hit something hard and sharp – it's a sub-clause of Sod's Law.

Don't buy cheap hammers, because they can chip at the edges and send flying shards of metal about. According to one kit manufacturer, the only thing worse than getting a flying sliver of steel in your eye is having it taken out again in Casualty after a five-hour wait.

For the rest of your tool kit, medium-priced socket sets and spanners will do fine. Avoid cheap chrome-plated tools, as chrome can flake off and lodge under your fingernails. You wouldn't believe how painful that is, and chromium is also poisonous.

If you're female or just not particularly strong, you can use brains instead of muscle. If you can't shift a rusted bolt with all your strength on a socket, soak it in WD40 overnight and then use an 'encouraging stick' over the socket handle – encouraging sticks are made from a couple of feet of tubular scaffold pole, available from your local scrap metal dealer for £1.

There are two main sizes of drive for socket sets. For big nuts you need a 1/2in-drive set, particularly for use with an encouraging stick. For general work you will find a 3/8in-drive socket set useful, and there are smaller sets still. These have sockets that go right down in size and are ideal for stripping carbs. An open-ended spanner may well round off a seized bolt head, but a socket exerts more even pressure all round and is a better idea. Ratchet spanners are nice, and are now a cheaply available luxury that saves time and effort.

Mega cheapo bargain bucket tool sets with 150 tools for £9.99 sound too good to be true, and

Left: Don't buy a cheap hammer, as bits of crystallised steel can chip off the edges and hit you in the eye. The difference between good and bad quality is only a few pounds. A soft hide or nylon hammer is also a necessary part of your tool kit.

Below: Halfords' Professional range of spanners seems to offer good value and high quality. You don't need to pay for seriously expensive brand names unless you use them every day to make a living.

Below: You will need a torque wrench, which is not expensive. Some suspension components and many engine components, particularly cylinder heads, need to be torqued down to a specific pressure.

that's because they are. Having said that, I do keep a £4.99 toolkit on board my car, which I regard as disposable – if it gets me out of trouble and then breaks, fine.

American Leatherman multi-tools have dozens of saws, scissors, knife blades, files and all sorts packed into them, and they're beautifully made, although expensive. Even when you're in a fully equipped workshop, you still find yourself reaching for your Leatherman first because it always seems to have the right widget in it somewhere.

A workbench is a very useful thing, and big DIY stores sell them surprisingly cheaply. You have to try to be disciplined about using one, or it'll just be another place to pile stuff while you carry on fixing things on the floor. However, the bench and its vice offer you the useful extra hand that is sadly not included in the human design. Autojumbles are a good source of large and ancient vices, which are quite useful as substitute extra hands. Get the biggest one you can find.

Shelving has two purposes – one is storage, the other is to bruise your head. Careful and high location of garage shelving promotes the former over the latter. I've tended to try to leave one garage wall clear and put shelves on the other side, which seems to work. DIY-store self-assembly shelving is pretty cheap, but you have to secure it to your

Left: For getting valves out of cylinder heads you need this sort of clamp to squeeze the valve springs and get the securing collets out. Care is needed, as collets are tiny and love to fly into corners and hide if they get loose.

Clarke make comprehensive MIG-welding kits for between £100 and £200, which include everything you need except gloves and overalls.

garage wall, or it goes squint and falls over if there's anything medium heavy on it.

Don't store reconditioned brake and clutch cylinders on garage shelves. There is more than enough damp in a suburban garage to rust them out in the time between rebuilding them and putting them on your car, unless you're pretty quick. Hide them in the house somewhere dry if you're not going to need them for a while. Engines are less vulnerable, but still need to have all their orifices plugged and their bores smothered in oil or grease if they're to be stored for any time.

If you stick to Caterham or to other very well established premium kits, you won't actually need that many tools, as top kits are largely a matter of assembly rather than building. This varies, though – ask owners' club members how hard their cars were to build and you'll get a variety of answers, sometimes expressed in quite colourful language.

If you buy a cheaper kit, you'll often find that you're expected to make your own arrangements for much of the detailed fitting-out. Let's take a bracket for a front brake hose. If it's on the kit, great. If not, you have to make one. You'll need a workbench, a vice, a drill, a hacksaw, a file, and if you want to do the job properly, a MIG welder. You can get by with nuts and bolts for securing a lot of things, but a welder is the best way to make sure something stays where it's been put. You will also find yourself thinking, just as with production cars, 'That's a stupid place to put a widget – I want it here instead.' It's a big deal for an amateur to redesign aspects of a production car, but with kit cars it's part of the point. There will be different ways you want to do things, and being able to weld gives you the freedom to fabricate your own ideas.

Getting really serious involves lathes and milling machines, which can sometimes be bought for a good price second-hand. This lathe belongs to someone who is making a car based around a Spitfire engine. (That's a 27-litre V12 Supermarine Spitfire aircraft, not a Triumph.)

It is possible to build a car in a suburban garage, but bear in mind that it can be tricky just driving a 427 Cobra into such a garage, never mind building one in it. However, once rolling it can always be pushed out for work and pushed back in afterwards.

Machine Mart in the UK are very well geared up to weekend engineers, and they make a big effort to have at least one guy on hand in each shop who really knows what he's talking about. Their 150TE kit is a 150-amp MIG welder that comes with some gas and welding wire and even a helmet. It's wise to invest in overalls that do up tight round your neck, and to wear boots rather than trainers, or little red-hot balls of steel spatter will get into places they're not welcome. Clever welding ideas are to use a 500w work lamp close to whatever you're welding, which will let you see enough through the very dark welding mask glass to position the tip before you press the trigger, and also to use CO_2 and argon mixed – it costs the same but works better. An important point is to make sure the steel you're welding is absolutely clean, or it will spit and weld badly. Yet another point to remember is to disconnect the car battery and alternator before wanging huge arc-welding amperages through the chassis and electrical system. MIG welders are very efficient at frying the electronic components of older alternators, and you can expect ECUs to suffer terminal internal injuries as well. If you look at a MIG welding spark with the naked eye, that part of your eye will be permanently blinded. If you're lucky and just get arc-eye, it feels like both eyes are full of sand for about three days until it begins to heal. Eighty quid now buys you an electronic instant-darkening welding helmet, making welding infinitely easier.

Which brings us to safety. Everything in the garage is just waiting to poison, burn, gouge, bruise, slash, crush and impale you: it's just like the Australian countryside. The combination of electricity and flammables that provides internal combustion in engines does the job just as well externally, and your garage and half-built car are a rich source of combustibles.

You absolutely must have a fire extinguisher literally within arm's length. Electrical systems and welding are excellent fire starters. However, grinder sparks and rags, or sparking electric drills and paint thinners do a top job too. It's worth keeping seriously flammable stuff such as cellulose paint and spare fuel outside the garage altogether, as long as it's not going to get stolen. Powder or CO_2 extinguishers are the favourites, as spraying water can just spread a liquid-based fire further and faster.

Tidiness with cables and tools is boring but worth taking a little

A random, lightning inspection of my own workbench is not too embarrassing, considering I'm writing a book rather than building a car at the moment: at least you can see the surface. This bench cost under £30 from B&Q, so it was cheaper than making one.

trouble over. In a confined space with a half-built car in it, tripping over a tool is guaranteed to land you on something sharp and nasty every time.

Some cuts and bruises are simply inevitable: using a big old socket to drive a bearing out of a Jaguar hub is a sensible approach, as long as you remember not to put your finger between the hammer and the socket. My nearside middle finger is never going to be quite the same again.

If you're grinding or sanding GRP, wear a mask as well as goggles. Some inhaled particles are large and get coughed up, some are small and get excreted through the bloodstream, but some are just the right size to stick in your lungs permanently.

Cellulose paint is reasonably poisonous, but it's nectar compared to two-pack paint, which will collect in your liver and kill you in about twelve weeks unless you're professionally masked up with a pressurised air feed.

Cars falling on you will do the same, but much more quickly. Unless you don't want to use it again, don't ever put any piece of yourself under a car that isn't solidly supported on axle stands. Hydraulic jacks are good for raising cars, but not for holding them up in the air.

When using tools, most of the personal injuries available are fairly obvious, but one unexpected mistake to guard against is holding a drill too lightly. If the drill bit sticks, the drill starts spinning instead: your wrist and anything else within range may not enjoy that.

Security is increasingly important. The same tools that intelligent people use for building cars are also used by assorted scum for stripping stolen cars, so a well-stocked garage will attract the attention of the local pond life.

Engraving every single tool you have with your name and your post code or zip code in large

This Midge was built in a single lock-up garage behind a flat in London, with power dragged out on an extension reel when it was being worked on. The smaller the car, the easier such a build becomes: Sevens are a good choice for the spatially challenged.

letters and then painting them all pink makes them less attractive in the first place, and may even get them back, but more to the point it gives the police a chance to prosecute.

In modern Britain you need to weld big bars over any garage windows you might have, and securing the garage door with four big padlocks will help to keep the risk down. For insurance purposes, keep an up-to-date list (with receipts, if possible) of all the tools you own, and after a burglary, don't leave the replacements in the garage at all for at least three months, because the same thieves will come back to collect your new tools. During this period, be as careless as you like about cluttering the floor with sharp objects, although actual booby traps are, of course, illegal.

The flood of cheap Chinese tools coming in through Wal-Mart at absurdly low prices allows useful savings, but you have to be more careful than ever to look at the value. A proper wheeled tool chest is expensive, but useful for keeping your tools and your approach tidy. A very cheap one,

even if it's relative garbage, will do a perfectly adequate job for a hobbyist so it's good value.

Don't buy anything dead cheap that will need spare parts, because there won't be any. A welder bought new for 75 quid is almost certain to be poor value, and the money could have gone towards buying one that works.

Welding helmets with screens that darken instantly used to be expensive, but now cost less than £100 and make welding infinitely easier. No more flipping the helmet down and moving the welder tip out of place. It's uncool to use one without custom-painting it first, though.

Chapter 6

Muscle

Part of the fun of kit cars is that you can use whatever power you like, within reason. You can even step outside the bounds of reason, if you feel like it. Say you go for a Westfield – you can fit a nice little 60bhp, 1,300cc Ford Kent crossflow engine for an amusing sports car, or you can use a 5-litre, 450bhp full-race Rover unit instead for a terrifying psycho beast.

Something to bear firmly in mind is power-to-weight ratios. A 90bhp Pinto engine does not shift a ton of rusting shopping-car about at impressive speeds. But – bin most of the deadweight and replace it with a spaceframe, four alloy wheels and some bits of plastic bodywork, and suddenly the Pinto is very lively indeed. Brake horse power tends to be pub horsepower – what you really want to know about is bhp per ton and torque figures, which give you a better guide to performance. A good example of applied torque is the venerable MGC, sporting a six-cylinder 3-litre Healey-derived engine weighing 600lb. This gets you 145bhp at 5,250rpm, which sounds pathetic from 3 litres. However, the 170lb ft of torque at 3,400rpm gives enough low-down grunt to allow it to climb big hills in overdrive top. It's a pleasant, relaxed long-distance cruiser with a respectable turn of speed when you need it. V8s and big sixes basically give you fat muscly torque, while little revvy bike engines provide lots of frantic bhp.

A seriously quick big-block Ford V8 nestling right back in the engine bay of a Bennett Cobra replica from San Francisco. Carroll Shelby was enthusiastic about Cobra replicas in 1993, because he signed the air cleaner on this one having seen it perform.

Starting at the sensible end of the spectrum, the older four-cylinder shopping Ford engines have a lot to be said for them. The old crossflow engine in 1,300cc, 1,600cc and (bored out to) 1,700cc sizes may be 40 years old, but it is still a good design – a short-stroke, fairly high-revving unit with decades of competition development behind it. If it was good enough for Ford to resurrect for the Ka in 1995, it can't be a bad engine, can it?

The transatlantic Pinto engine comes in 1,600cc, 1,800cc, 2,000cc and 2,300cc sizes, and was in some ways a retrograde step from the Kent. It's crude, smelly and cheaply made. However, its numbers are so vast that it's very cheap to tune, and is still readily available both in the UK

The good old Ford Pinto – cheap and available, and comes with a good rear-wheel-drive gearbox: still well worth considering for a budget kit.

Ford's cooking engines are very suitable for the novice home mechanic – they're simple and robust, and if you make a mistake, it won't cost a fortune.

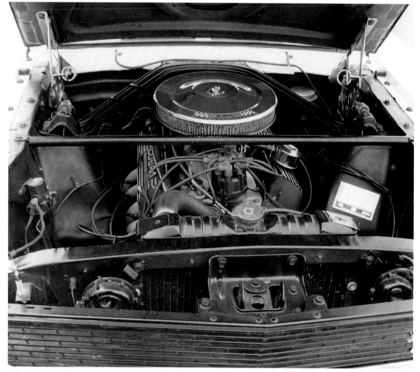

The Shelby GT350 Mustang has a lightly tuned 289 Ford engine. As this car sold for £46,000, it's unlikely that anybody will be using one as a donor.

Not one of my favourite sights – a 427 Cobra replica with a little Pinto engine. However, at least it gets somebody on the road, and the pose value is still there until they start it up.

and in the USA. The 205bhp Cosworth engine fitted to Cosworth Sierras is basically a Pinto, but quite a heavily modified version of the engine.

Of the later Ford engines, the CVH is not particularly attractive except in its turbocharged form from 1980s RS Turbo Escorts. The CVH uses oil, is not particularly powerful or strong, and because nobody tunes it up very much, performance parts are only made in small amounts and are therefore expensive.

The next-generation Zetec, on the other hand, is an excellent piece of kit. Good engineering tolerances, a heavy but well-balanced crank and a very tough bottom end mean you can expect 150,000 miles of enthusiastic driving before you wear one out. They're fitted to front-wheel-drive cars resulting in some drivetrain complications for kit car use, but nothing that can't be sorted out fairly easily. The RS Turbo boys in the UK have taken to changing the CVH bottom end for Zetec blocks, which is a good endorsement. A chipped and over-boosted turbo 'ZVH' in a Locost would be something of a weapon.

Mini engines were very important in the early days of kit cars, and the Mini is enjoying a resurgence with the availability of new Heritage shells and new performance options. The same doesn't apply to the 2CV Citroën air-cooled flat-twin – still an admirable design, but slow, noisy and an acquired taste.

The equally venerable MGB engine still has a lot going for it, though – particularly for classically styled roadsters. The 'B' engine has a long stroke and good torque, and will run for a long time once the cylinder head has been converted to hard valve seats (it will burn out the valve seats in 5,000 miles if it hasn't). It also makes a very nice growly noise. Parts are also readily available and very cheap wherever you live – the MGB was a huge success both

When you rebuild an engine, take the time to clean out the oilways and waterways. This crud came out of the water system on a Ford V6.

A very tidy installation of a small-block Chevy in an Ultima, bored out to 7 litres and attached to a Porsche gearbox.

at selling and rusting, so there are still hundreds of thousands of crumbly donors out there, and the owners' clubs keep spares available and down in price.

The same applies to Triumph Herald, Spitfire and GT6/Vitesse power units, although perhaps less so. There is still a healthy club scene, so in the same way as MGs, service and repair parts are at hobby prices rather than at modern, main dealer prices.

Vauxhall/Opel's recent 1,600cc and 2,000cc engines have a good reputation, and have been tuned successfully for racing. The double overhead cam, multivalve design means a lot of useful and expensive head work has already been done for you, so you can simply enjoy the power and reliability. Rover's engines of the last ten years have also developed quite a good reputation, and as the first MGFs rust out, the rear-

MkI and MkII Ford Cortinas are still scrapped because of rust, and can yield a good Kent 1,500cc engine and box, ideal for a low-budget Locost type of kit.

end power package will doubtless finish up in more interesting chassis and bodies. Watch the cooling, though – the MGF is getting a reputation for brewing up and doing head gaskets.

Duratec and later engines from the 1990s require a new approach. They tend to be more accurately engineered than the older engines, and more reliable. They also increasingly lack distributors and even the option to use carbs. Rather than stripping them for crank regrinds and rebores, you're more likely to be facing problems of making them fire up with an ECU that was not designed to operate just the fuelling and sparks. There's always a way, though.

Going right down in size, motorcycle engines have created a huge change in Lotus Seven-style sports cars in the last few years. So much so that the price of used superbike engines has risen quite a lot. The race replica engines are frequently genuinely developed from pure racing machines, but the engineering inside them is of such high quality that they last for incredible mileages as well as producing astonishing power. They never wear out in bikes, and they seem to last very well even when used to power a car that's several times the weight of a bike. Even the tiny clutches don't seem to cause problems, despite having to be slipped at 5,000 revs to get going. This level of longevity is rather wasted on bikes, which, on average, cover 10,000 miles in five years, unless they hit a Volvo first. The bikes that do hit Volvos provide engines for kit cars, and buying a complete but wrecked bike is a good move as you can sell other bits off it. Don't buy a bike engine without electrics and a key, though – the bill for a replacement Honda key can top £1,000.

The sort of power you get from a bike engine doesn't really suit a road car very well. Peak power is achieved when the engine is screaming at 10,000rpm or so, and there is very little torque at the bottom end of the rev range. For track use, great. Bike powered sports cars are exhilarating as they scream their nuts off through their (free) six-speed sequential gearboxes, but cruising at 7,000rpm is generally unpleasant.

For a more tractable bike package, check out what the motorcycle dispatch riders are using. They know what they're doing, and they look for torque and indestructibility.

At the other end of the spectrum we're into the big league, and Jaguar engines are an option, although immensely heavy. Although 3.4- and 3.8-litre XK Jaguar engines seem good, I gave up on trying to use the 4.2-

Bike-engined cars were being made fifty years before the current explosion. These delightful JAP-powered single-cylinder single-seaters are a lot faster than you would expect.

Citroën's air-cooled twin, fitted to an Avion. With unburstable roller bearing cranks, these can truck on a bit if you're prepared to ignore the noise and keep the revs up.

litre after three bad ones in a row. A veteran Jag restorer in Chiswick told me that the earlier 4.2 XK engines had been bored out too far, giving the crankcase the

Does anybody recognise this Ferrari engine? No? That's because it's actually a Pontiac Fiero engine. Naughty, but rather fun.

structural integrity of a wet paper bag, which resulted in oval main bearing housings. Whatever, I know I'd rather have hepatitis than another one.

The later XJ40/XJS straight-six engine, a newer design, is still very heavy, but gets you around 200bhp, lots of torque and 150,000 miles with regular servicing. The electronics will eventually fail, but until then you will get 30mpg in a light kit car so you'll have the time and money to source some spares.

Japanese car engines never seem to have caught on much in the kit car world, apart from in Beaufords and Healey replicas, which use the Datsun straight-six, which is a Healey engine with an overhead cam anyway.

The obvious exception to that is the Toyota 4AGE, which is nowadays used to great effect in all sorts of kit cars, and which will even tolerate moderate supercharging without a grumble.

BMW's engines are quite well engineered, although they have their problems. The sixes can burn a lot of oil, and the prices of spares can be comedic. Scrapping

another donor car is always an option, as old BMWs are very cheap now.

BMW's 1990s V8s are an interesting new option, and are becoming cheaper and more common every day. Early ones have serious bore wear problems connected to cheap petrol, but post-1997 they seem potentially good value.

The Rover V8 has become a favourite of mine, although I've been inside more of them than I would have liked. Once sorted, they give good power for a light road car, with 150–180bhp in fairly standard form. They have enough torque to haul a Range Rover about at a respectable speed, and overhauling them is not madly expensive if you avoid buying parts from Land Rover and use Real Steel and other specialists. The best feature of the Rover V8 is its weight. Its all-alloy block and heads give it the same weight as a four-cylinder Ford or MGB engine, so it keeps your car very light. Never mind the power, check the power-to-weight.

For serious muscle, we have to be looking at US-made Ford and Chevrolet small-blocks, of 5-litre and 5.7-litre capacities respectively. My favourite is the Chevy, which is one of the most successful and numerous engines ever made. It's incredibly cheap to uprate and rebuild, because the development costs of the tuning companies were recouped by 1965 and the engine has basically remained the same ever since. My own Cobra replica used a very low-budget 350 Chevy with a block from about 1976, heads from 1978 and a crank from 1992. With a £40 Taiwanese chrome dress-up kit to provide a sump and rocker covers, a rebore and new pistons at £10 each, I got 250bhp and around 300lb ft of torque for about £500. In a Cobra replica, that gave me a high power-to-weight ratio, even with the massively heavy iron block and heads. However, the sheer size of the engine and

The Mini engine/box/diff/shaft/steering/suspension/brakes assembly still offers a great package, but power is low, unless of course you use a mad engine, huge Webers, nitrous injection and straight-through stack exhausts.

The author's Ayrspeed XK replica, fitted with the first of its three 4.2-litre XJ6 engines. Apparently the 3.4- and 3.8-litre versions are more reliable.

its big torque meant that I didn't need a rampant camshaft and massive carburation, so the car was a pussycat until you put your foot down, at which point it would bellow and charge.

Sheer size gets you cheap and easy power, and not necessarily at a great cost in fuel – that Cobretti produced over 20mpg, and my XK replica with overdrive used to approach 30mpg when cruising, if one of its three 4.2-litre engines happened to be working well enough to be driven.

The Ford 302 is also not a bad engine by any means, although not quite as good value as the Chevy, and Ford's habit of changing things means you can run into problems with bits and pieces from different dates not fitting each other. There's also less cheap performance gear about for the Ford.

Big-block Ford, GM and Chrysler engines all benefit from the sheer number made, which

helps keep prices down. Some of them are physically very big, and in lightweight cars they make less sense than small-blocks.

If you want the correct engine for a 427 S/C Cobra replica, you need a big-block Ford V8. The genuine side-oiler big-block engine used to be found in Ford Galaxies as well as Cobras, but everybody knows that now, so there's been a very big price hike on any 427 engine that isn't actually scrap.

Ford 289s are also getting thinner on the ground, and the later 302 is a good engine, but is not the correct one for Cobra replicas which aim to be accurate.

A recent piece of very good news for those in the UK is that Germans are prohibited from driving their old cars unless they have aftermarket catalytic converters fitted – so these cats are now available for new kit cars going through ever stiffer pre-registration tests. Fisher Sportscars

have put a Sylva through the Single Vehicle Approval test with a Pinto and two 40 DCOE Weber carburettors, which is a dirty old engine by anybody's standards – but their aftermarket cat got it through. This is great news for those who want to tune up carbed engines – you don't need to use ECUs and injection unless you want to, provided your engine still has a distributor.

As a kit builder, indulge your freedom to choose whatever engine you like, and to play with it as much as you want to first – but please don't abuse that freedom by putting a four-cylinder shopping car engine in a 427 Cobra replica. That brings the entire kit car scene into disrepute, and is more uncool than Albanian pullovers.

DON'T BUY AN INVOICE

After messing about with cars for twenty years or so, I'm finally

beginning to take the advice I
keep handing out in *Kit-Car*
magazine.

First, if it's possible to buy your
main donor or engine donor as a
drivable car, do it. Newer engines
and V8s can remain healthy for
very high mileages, so if you
buy a good one, you can clean
it, paint it, transfer it straight into
your project and head for the hills
without getting your hands or
your credit card dirty.

If you buy an engine off
somebody's workshop floor, be
crystal clear that you're not buying
an engine, you're buying a base
unit for rebuild, and you should
only pay that price for it. The
engine may, as the owner says,
only have been driven delicately
for 10,000 miles by an old lady,
but even if he believes that, it still
may not be true. In any case, the
old lady could have been hanging
her handbag on the choke pull,
in which case the oil has been
washed off the bores and bearings
for 10,000 miles and the engine's
shot anyway.

Don't buy an engine that you
can't turn over, unless you are
taking it on as a collection of
spares. It could just be stuck, but
it's more likely to be rust-seized.
That guarantees a rebore – during
which you might find that it
can't be bored out far enough to
clear the rust pits off the bores.
You may hear the faint echo of
bitter personal experience here.
An engine that can be turned
over with a spanner should be
reusable, and may just need
new rings, if you're lucky: my last
Rover V8 didn't even need that.

If you prefer to rebuild an
engine before using it, fine.
Rebuilding engines should be
a calm, ordered process, and
therapeutic as long as you don't
have to rush. Even if you're a
novice, there's nothing you can't
manage if you want to. It all
looks a bit daunting the first time
you strip an engine, but as you
physically handle the components,
it all begins to make sense and

You can't get away from hard work with engines. The new hardened valve seats need to be ground in by hand. When the blisters on your hands reach 2in square, you're getting there.

you can see how it works and how
it should go back together.

For most older and simpler
engines, you don't need much
in the way of special tools or
experience – just the relevant

Haynes manual. At Haynes they
take cars apart and put them
back together again to write the
manual on them, so they started
in the same place as you are but
it can be annoying when they

The MG B-series engine goes right back to the MGA from the 1950s, in 1,600cc size. It's a good, strong unit and makes a nice grumbly noise, very suitable for a traditionally styled kit.

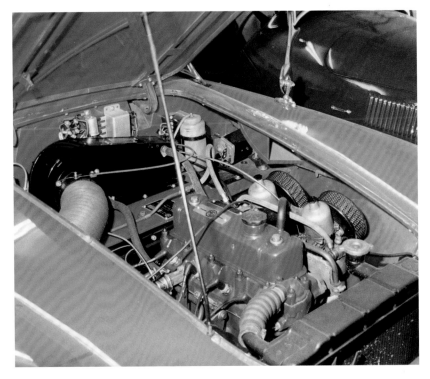

An American favourite, the Chevy 350 small-block. This one's confusingly painted Ford blue instead of Chevy orange, but on the Ford small-block the distributor is at the front.

Stripping the Rover engine revealed serious rust seizure, so it's off for reboring at the very least.

say 'now withdraw the widget from the whatsit' and you find it takes a day with slide hammers, sledgehammers, releasing fluid, blowtorches and swearing to get the widget out, but that's automotive life.

The single most important aspect of engine rebuilding is that every component must be squeaky clean. Engines will only tolerate oil, coolant and petrol going in. A few pieces of grit or steel swarf will wreck a rebuilt engine in about ten seconds.

The Rover V8 engine currently in my XK replica is a good example of what's involved in an engine rebuild: it's big and has eight cylinders, but is essentially simple, with a single camshaft in the block and pushrods operating the valves.

When bought, the engine was a non-runner, and unusually I obeyed my own rules. Was it seized? No, it turned over smoothly by hand, with enough resistance to suggest that the compressions were okay. The exterior nuts, bolts and washers were in good condition and all there, although they had been spannered. That meant the engine had been opened up before, but by somebody reasonably competent. If the exterior nuts are chewed and half the washers are missing, that suggests a bad mechanic has been at the engine, and is not a good sign.

With a V8, taking the fuel system and inlet manifold off can reveal some horrors – inches of carbon kak in the vee of the engine, left over from insufficient oil changes and two hundred thousand miles. In my case, this one was nice and clean. The cam lobes can be examined with the manifold and gasket removed, and on a Rover they wear quite quickly. In my engine, the camshaft was fairly new, but with a chewed mark on one lobe where a piece of metal or grit had been left in the engine. No problem, there was a new cam going in anyway.

Above: Before removing any big-end or main bearing caps, engrave their number and direction on them.

Use a nylon or rubber hammer for persuading seized engines to turn. Pieces of fuel hose pushed over the conrod bolts avoid damaging the bearing surfaces during removal.

If you can see grooves on the bearing surface or if the white metal has worn through to the brass beneath, you're probably looking at regrinding the crank.

If the timing chain and gears are a little worn, replacing them will keep the cam timing spot-on and the power up.

One of the big moments is when you pop the head or heads off, after undoing the head bolts in the right sequence to avoid warping the soft aluminium head castings. Examine the bore surfaces for obvious wear, and then feel with your fingernails for a lip around the top of the bore. There is a small area where the piston rings don't bear on the cylinder walls, and if you can feel a ridge there it means the bore walls have been worn away by the rings over the years. If there's a ridge, you'll need a rebore and eight pistons, but this is not necessarily a bad thing, as you'll then get another 100,000 miles out of the engine afterwards. If the pistons have nothing stamped into the tops, great – the engine is still a virgin and the pistons are the originals. If you see +10 marked on the pistons, that means it's already been rebored out by ten thousandths of an inch, but you can rebore it again. If you see +20 or +30, it's been bored out too far already – you probably need a new block or cylinder liners.

Tip the engine upside down, mark the bearing caps' numbers and direction and then pull off the caps on the mains and big ends. It's crucial that they're kept in the right order, as the main bearing holes were line-bored with the caps in their places during manufacture, and mixing them up will make the bearings either too tight or too loose when torqued down, with terminal results. If you mix up the caps, it is better to just throw the engine away and start again.

The bearing surfaces on the crankshaft should be visibly perfect, and they do need to be checked for size and ovality either with a micrometer or by an engineer. The bearing shells are also marked for size, so you can tell if the crank has been reground. If you're lucky, you can start rebuilding from about here and if you need a regrind, and in any case should you intend to give an engine any action higher up the rev range, it's worth thinking about balancing the crank and pistons. The engine will rev higher, increasing its power, and it will run longer and smoother.

It's worth having the mating surface of a head checked for flatness before reassembly, particularly with aluminium heads. Blocks don't generally warp, but heads do if they're overheated or have been torqued up incorrectly.

With older engines, timing chains and gears are quite cheap, and worth replacing if there's any sign of wear. Sloppy cam timing takes the edge off performance, and if a chain ever lets go, you've got a box of shiny mince where you used to have an engine. Later engines with cam belts rather than chains automatically need new belts, whether you're going to rebuild them or not. You have no idea when a cambelt was last changed, so assume it's overdue and replace it.

When your shiny new pistons, reground crank, fancy new cam and so on are all gleaming on the bench and ready to go back into your spotless engine block, which has had all the core plugs and gallery plugs removed and every cranny of the engine cleaned, you can start putting it back together.

Slop lots of oil everywhere as you go, and when it comes to refitting and torquing down the crank bearing caps, spin the crank every time you tighten one down. The whole thing should become slightly stiffer as you go, but if it jams solid at any point, you know where the problem is.

Of course, rebuilding your own engine is optional, and the whole kit car game is meant to be for fun. If you really don't fancy either the black-fingernail business, or if the thought of being unable to put it all back together without any bits left over is too intimidating, no worries – get somebody else to do it instead and just concentrate on the bits of the kit you know you will enjoy.

Above: This low-mileage engine had been stored with no spark plugs in, had rusted solid and needed a rebore and new pistons. I shouldn't have bought it.

Left: This oil pump is excellent, with no visible wear on the pump body or gears. It's relatively cheap to replace anyway.

Below: This was the worst seized cylinder, with quite deep rust pits in the walls. However, a 10-thou rebore and some honing got rid of the damage.

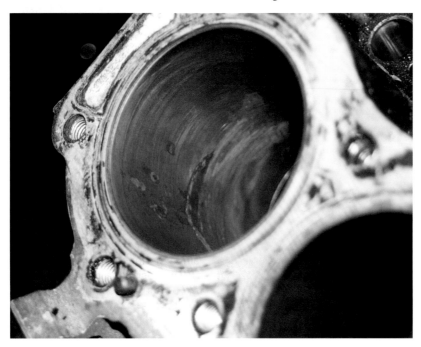

Above: The pushrods bear on the rockers and the cam followers, and must be kept in order even if new cam followers are fitted.

These 1972 oil gallery plugs have to come out to get the galleries clean. If heat and violence don't do the job, drill them out.

Change all the water gallery core plugs, as they can rust right through in just a few years, even if they look okay.

An internal micrometer is used to establish whether the conrod bearing surface is still circular or whether it's gone oval. Same for the crank.

TOO MUCH IS JUST RIGHT

When it comes to power, Carroll Shelby knew what he was talking about: too much is indeed just right. On the subject of tuning engines, there are as many opinions as there are motorheads. After ten years of writing agony columns for Ford and kit magazines, some general principles on tuning have become clear.

One very familiar theme concerns buying performance parts as a package. The best results come from buying all your goodies from an experienced performance shop that has used the same combinations successfully before. Many dyno shootout sessions for *Fast Ford* magazine revealed that someone had bought a camshaft at a car show, had saved up for a 'Stage III' head, had then bought some carbs from a friend and an exhaust from somewhere else again. They had spent bucket loads of money, only to discover in the cold light of the dyno reading that they'd lost 20bhp from the bog-standard engine spec. Incidentally, Stage I, II and III heads don't really mean anything as such. I would suggest that Stage I should mean smoothed port walls, Stage II is smoothed and opened-up ports matched to the manifolds and headers, and Stage III means all that plus big valves. Be clear about what a modified head has had done to it, and what can be expected of it.

Buy everything from a single knowledgeable speed shop if you can, and be crystal clear about what you're going to get for your money. Don't buy a head from anybody who doesn't have a flow bench to develop and test their head designs – doing it by instinct and experience went out in 1959.

The basic idea of improving the performance of an engine is to get more gas in and out of it. Getting it in is more important than getting it out. Start with a

Above: Cylinder heads and blocks are skimmed or decked on a machine like this. The block is held down rigidly while the spinning blade takes a few thou off.

Above: The cam and followers need special lubrication goo, which protects them during the crucial first start-up.

Above: The camshaft lobes are likely to be worn in a Rover. Replace the cam with something like a Piper 270 to get more power while you're at it.

The oil pump must be primed. The posh way is to spin it up with a drill and check the pressure.

On the other hand, packing the pump full of petroleum jelly and spinning the engine over usually does the job too.

You can get away with a lot where V8s are concerned, but one tool you can't manage without is a reasonable torque wrench.

performance filter, the bigger the better. A K&N filter claims an increase of 40 per cent in airflow over a standard airbox and filter – an excellent result for what is literally a bolt-on goody.

A common mistake is to leave a sharp edge on the intake of the carb. If you've spent loads of money on expensively smoothed ports in the head, there's no point in starting turbulence with a sharp edge on the carb intake before the air's even got into the engine. If you're going for serious performance, either smooth the edge or preferably fit a bell-mouth inside the filter. It's the collection of 1 per cent more power here and 2 per cent there that makes all the difference.

Having increased your airflow into the fuel system, you have leaned the fuel supply right out with too much air in the mix, so you need more fuel available to balance the extra air. In carbs, the needles or jets will have to be changed, and in modern engines, the fuelling will need to be altered.

The air/fuel mix is delivered to the cylinders next, via the inlet manifold and the inlet port. In an ideal world, each port will be a

For Top Dead Centre, mike up No. 1 piston, and use a timing wheel. ALWAYS spin the engine by hand before starting it.

If your finished bottom end looks as squeaky clean as this, your engine should have a long and happy life.

big, straight tube going directly from the air to the inlet valves via its own carb or injector, and in fact, an SBD-prepared Vauxhall engine does just that – the inlet bell-mouths are about a foot long and huge. They're also made of weightless carbon-fibre, have additional fuel injectors mounted on them, and cost £900 a set.

That's racing gear, though – a road engine has to be a collection of compromises. You can still achieve the ideal of a choke for each cylinder with two twin-choke Webers on a four-cylinder, and with two four-barrel carbs on top of a V8, but most of us will run something more economical.

Generally, head work involves enlarging and smoothing the ports, and is expensive because it means sophisticated and lengthy engineering work. However, you don't want chromium-smooth port walls, as fuel comes out of suspension and sticks to the sides, and neither do you necessarily always want huge ports. Ford's CVH engine already has big ports, and with the rest of the gasflow path being relatively restricted, enlarging the CVH ports

just drops the gas speed and the power.

Standard valve guides poke out into the ports, and have to be either changed for aerodynamic ones or shortened and shaped by hand. Beyond a certain stage, standard valves are too small and need to be replaced with bigger ones to keep the gasflow up. The shape of the edge of the valve and the seat itself are also important – three or more angles around the actual sealing ring of the seat mean smoother flow as the valve opens and closes.

A performance camshaft is really needed to obtain the best from a gas-flowed head, because it opens up the valves further and again lets some more gas in. To generate the most extra power from an engine for the least investment, the first moves are a better air filter and a performance cam.

Take my own Rover as an example. It's fitted with two K&N filters and a Piper 270(i) injection cam, and a pair of tubular headers. The official extra bhp you can expect from a Piper 270 profile fast road cam on a Rover is 24bhp. As it happens, the unofficial word from Piper is that lots of their

Above: With a balanced bottom end and a good cam, this engine should give 180bhp, 220lb ft of torque and 100,000 miles.

The better balanced an engine, the more power, revs and longevity. Pros use very accurate scales, but home balancing using digital kitchen scales still helps.

Above: This cam's high profile will push the valves way down in the combustion chamber, requiring engineering work on the heads.

Above: The pros balance both ends of a rod and piston assembly.

Crank balancing requires a machine like a lathe, and is not a DIY job.

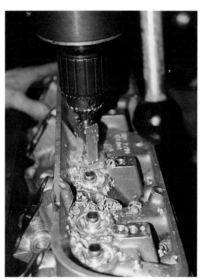

The valve springs will coil-bind and wreck the rockers unless depressions are cut in the head to allow them room to move.

This set of pistons has been balanced – their original weights are still written on them.

customers have been using the 270 injection cam on carbed Rover engines, because it gives 22bhp and a big slug of unspecified extra torque right down low – precisely what I want from the V8. I haven't radiused the carb intake edges, and I haven't in the end ported or polished the head. Getting 22bhp plus big torque from fitting a new cam – which needed replacing anyway – is well worth it. Extracting an extra 5bhp from about 30 hours of careful work with a drill is not worth it for my road engine. For racing, you have to go all the way, because an extra 2 per cent of power means you're four feet in front at the end of a long straight, which means you win rather than lose.

The exhaust side is less important, as you have to do quite a lot of development work on the inlet side before the exhaust becomes a restriction. Having said that, cast iron standard manifolds are often badly designed for gasflow, but very well designed for being cheap to cast, and therefore generating more profit. Profit is, after all, the original purpose of manufacturing a car engine. Bike engines can have problems with exhausts, as they're very highly tuned and sensitive to exhaust design.

In a kit car, you have the advantage (or disadvantage) of having to make a new exhaust system anyway, so you might as well design a decent exhaust manifold or pair of headers before you begin. A note here – second-hand performance manifolds are

Above: All the valve springs have to be shimmed to the correct height, to ensure even pressures on the valves.

Opening up and polishing ports is a DIY job, up to a point. This tool takes out port material, and is used on the end of a drill.

The split rod is easy to make, and is for polishing the port walls.

Emery paper is slipped into the split. You don't want the port walls chromium-smooth, as fuel comes out of suspension and sticks to them.

cheap: check out the classifieds at the back of performance car mags.

The old-fashioned term 'extractor manifold' means that when a pulse of gas has been pushed down the pipe, it leaves a vacuum behind it, which helps to suck the next exhaust charge through the cylinder.

If you do want to get serious about headers, get their shape as smooth as possible, avoid sharp corners, and match the primary pipes in length at 22in to 24in before they meet at a collector box. If you use a four-into-two-into-one design, you get a little more torque. If you go four-into-one, you will have a little more bhp.

The advent of electronics and turbocharging has changed things in the last few years, but not always for the better. If computers always worked, they would be a bonus. As it is, they're increasingly unavoidable, whether they work or not.

Newer engines can still benefit from traditional tuning techniques, but the results are less dramatic than with old engines, as a lot of natural development has taken place. A Zetec gasflow path is much better than a Pinto, although it can still be improved.

With turbocharged engines, you'll get the most extra bang from upping the boost and from chip changes in their ECUs or computers. The manufacturers' chips are designed to avoid warranty claims, and there is usually a lot of potential performance in new engines that has been managed out by the control electronics.

There is a lot of potential power in a turbocharger, and if you open the floodgates and let it in, you can jam enough fuel/air into an engine to produce an extra 100bhp from it, no bother. The standard Cosworth Turbo version of the Pinto gives you 205bhp straight from the box, but that can be chipped up to 300bhp simply with a set of bigger

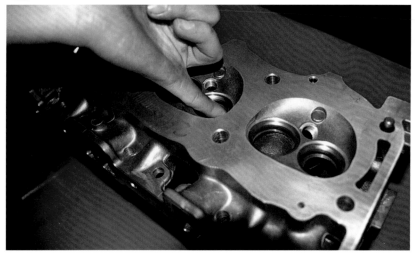

Above: If the port feels nice and smooth, you're getting there: more gas smoothly in and out equals more power.

The inside of an ITG performance filter has a bell-mouth to get a lot of air in smoothly.

Left and right: A standard four-barrel carb is a mass of sharp edges. If you want max power, soften every structure inside it until there are no edges left.

injectors to squirt a bit more fuel in. An extreme version of that engine can top 500bhp – but probably not for long. You also need to know what you're doing when driving with a powerful turbocharged and chipped engine, because the power tends to slam in all at once when the turbo gets up to speed, irrespective of whether you're halfway round a fast corner at the time. A wild cam will also do this to some extent: the Southern Roadcraft Cobra replica demonstrator of 1995 had a particularly evil cam in its small-block V8, as well as big carburation and some serious internal interfering. This caught me by surprise on a test drive: when the cam came on at 3,500rpm it felt like being hit from behind by a truck. The car stopped spinning fairly quickly, but it took a while for my head to stop spinning.

Turbocharging essentially involves using the exhaust gases to spin up a compressor that pressurises the fuel/air mixture to add power. It's now quite well developed technology and there is a lot of performance kit available today. The main disadvantage is turbo lag, which means you put your foot down, wait for the exhaust gas to spin the turbo up, then all the power comes in at once. Amusing, but risky. Turbos also spin at mad revs, and tend not to last that long.

Supercharging goes back 80 years, and also involves a compressor. The supercharger or blower is driven by a belt from the crankshaft, and the pressure is constant – so you get instant power, at the expense of some noise and a slight power loss at low revs. Both turbos and superchargers require lower compression ratio engines if they are to be used in earnest.

Nitrous oxide is a bottle of gas that increases the efficiency of the petrol burn by a considerable margin, and results in serious power gains. A good system can

Above: Left is a cast manifold off a Pinto. Cheap and profitable, but with very poor gas flow. Compare this with a performance header on the right – it's visibly better.

Basic head work – polishing and smoothing – is absorbing, but filthy. Most of the kak that comes off seems to go down your neck. This head has been partly skimmed as well.

Vernier cam wheels allow very accurate cam timing, as the camshaft position can be finely adjusted before being locked in place.

The cheap and cheerful way to big power. Nitrous oxide enables fuel to burn with big increases in efficiency and thus muscle, but make sure your mains and big ends are in good shape.

be a cheap and useful source of big power. You have to get the bottles refilled regularly, but then the same applies to the petrol tank.

Whatever you do to an engine it will be twice as effective in a kit car because it's half the weight. If you're new to kits, the smart move is probably to build your first car with a standard engine and learn

how to handle it, while building a spare engine into something evil for next year.

TURBOCHARGING AND SUPERCHARGING

It's worth a slightly deeper look at turbocharging and supercharging smaller engines, as fuel is not

going to get cheaper. As well as achieving more economy and efficiency, it will be increasingly wise to turn to small engines and forced aspiration as an alternative to big engines. 'Ain't no substitoot for cubes', certainly, but if we can't afford to feed big cubes we have to get more creative. Turbocharging and supercharging of smaller engines both yield relatively spectacular extra power without spoiling the inherent economy of them. The power increase can be 30–50% quite easily, and today's closer engineering tolerances and better engine materials mean that some useful blowing can take place within the stress limits of the engine and without the traditional need to change the pistons and

This Beetle nicely illustrates the principles of turbocharging. The exhaust gas goes up the lighter-coloured wrapped pipe (with the wastegate on it to keep the boost level under control) and spins the turbo, then goes back down to a silencer and out. The silver part of the turbocharger compresses the air coming through the air filter and pushes it through the blue hoses and through the intercooler to the other blue hoses, from where the cooled compressed air is forced through the carbs or throttle bodies and into the engine. More air and fuel in, more power out.

This straight-six Toyota Supra 3-litre engine started off with 240bhp and now produces around 1,000bhp. The turbo is enormous, internally polished and runs at a maximum of 34lb rather than the usual 7lb for a production turbo setup, the air piping is all very big bore and silky smooth internally, and the injectors are the size of fire hydrants. The car is brutal and nasty to drive, but more fun than a bag of monkeys.

lower the compression ratio, which used to be a prerequisite.

Turbocharging involves extreme heat, quite violent power increases, usually some lag before the impeller speeds up enough to produce the power, the need for intercoolers, lots of pipery, noisy blowoff valves and considerable expense. But it takes no engine power to drive itself as it uses waste exhaust gas to drive its pump, it's entertaining trying to retain control when the power comes in, the engine-bay bling can be impressive, and the alternating turbo screaming and blowoff valve chittering provides a new kind of soundtrack.

If you're planning a new kit or engine installation, it would be worthwhile buying a turbo engine as a package. Even if you upgrade it later, you start off with the turbo exhaust manifold, the turbo, wastegate, ECU programming, intake piping, suitable injectors, frequently an intercooler included in the engine radiator, and all sorts of other bits and pieces that cost a fortune when bought separately.

Most standard turbo installations run at somewhere between 5lb and 8lb of boost, which can generate a respectable extra slug of power. If you want more of a kick, the cheapest and most effective move is a stronger spring in the turbo's pressure relief system. The wastegate stops the engine overboosting and blowing up, by opening at a pre-set pressure to control the amount of turbo pressure. Putting a stronger spring in the wastegate, or controlling it with an electronic boost controller, raises the wastegate opening pressure to say 15lb, so the turbo puts twice as much pressure through the engine.

A problem with turbos is that when you close the throttle, the turbo basically stops spinning because you've just shut off the exit for all the air it was pressurising. That means big turbo lag before it speeds up and starts boosting again, and this happens every time you back off the throttle to change gear. A dump valve sits between the turbo and the plenum chamber, and opens up to atmosphere to let the turbo blow off pressure and keep spinning. A blow-off valve works in a similar way, but it equalises the pressure between the throttle body and the turbo, again allowing it to freewheel and keep up to speed. A problem with some turbo setups is that oil is shared between the engine and the turbo, so when the turbo lets go, all the resultant swarf and broken component particles are also shared with the engine.

A friend of mine runs a 1,000bhp Toyota Supra, and the key to its enormous power is mostly 34lb of turbo boost. Much of the rest of the engine work has been devoted to keeping it in one piece with that amount of boost going through it.

Superchargers are simpler, and involve lower stress, lower temperatures and a lower component cost. They also last longer than turbos, which rev at up to 100,000rpm and glow red hot. Superchargers cost a percentage of engine power all the time, as they are basically compressors driven by a belt from a crank pulley. There is also some heat inevitably generated by compressing air. But superchargers provide smoother and more controllable torque, and power that rises with engine revs. They're simple, they run cooler than a turbo and they also make a nice whine that tells the knowledgeable what you have under the bonnet.

If you're putting serious power and serious heat through your engine, it is best to know what's going on under the bonnet. This turbo Mini has a tacho, water temp, oil pressure, oil temperature, turbo boost and air/fuel mixture gauges so that the owner, the World's Fastest Clown, knows what's what.

Another approach to serious turbocharging is to use two smaller ones rather than one dustbin-sized one. This gives less turbo lag, as smaller turbos spin up faster. Using one smaller and one bigger turbo is also an option: the smaller one gets you going until the big one kicks in.

An interesting development going on right now is the intercooled, ECU-controlled supercharger system with a separate oil supply being developed by Omex specifically for the kit car market. One useful application for it is the popular Toyota 4AGE engine, which as it turns out can be supercharged from a stock 140bhp to 220bhp in a half-day installation without a compression-ratio drop – and it won't blow up as a result. There's another version that goes to 280bhp, but that probably will blow up unless you fit new pistons, rods and a head gasket.

When your car eventually becomes not fast enough, you have several options. Running a twin turbo system with a smaller turbo that spools up quickly and a bigger one that delivers the big power higher up the tacho can be quite effective, and so can running a supercharger as well as a turbo. You get the instant torque of the supercharger and then the turbo joins in as the revs rise.

All this power remains optional depending on how hard you put your foot in it: even a 280bhp 4AGE engine in a Raw Striker gets the fuel consumption of a lightened Toyota Corolla as long as you keep the revs down and take it easy.

Chapter 7

The drivetrain

Proper sports cars are rear-wheel drive. Cue chorus of outrage from makers of (very good) kits like Quantum and Midas, who make front-wheel-drive work as well as it can. However, there are no FWD racing cars, no FWD dragsters, and no high-performance FWD sports cars.

The reasons are simple. When a front-wheel-drive car accelerates, weight transfers to the back, the unloaded front wheels lose grip, lots of rubber smoke,

not much action. When a rear-wheel-drive car accelerates, the same weight transfers to the back, the driving wheels grip harder, the car accelerates: four seconds to 60mph.

With rear-wheel-drive the steering wheel is also neutral in your hands, not squirming horribly as FWD torque steer tries to put you in a ditch. Front wheels steer, back wheels drive – job done.

There has been some clever bodging and marketing to make

FWD seem less bad, but kit car people in general simply won't have it. FWD is fine for shoppers and reppers, but not for your real car. Stick with a front engine, rear-wheel drive donor combo if possible.

Ford used to supply endless cheap and rusty RWD donors, but nowadays they only provide engines. BMW donors are replacing Sierras: they are just as common, and dirt cheap when old, although genuine parts prices are silly. They offer

The heavy flywheel is bolted to the back of the crankshaft and its mass smooths out the engine's rotation. This one has been drilled and lightened for faster throttle response.

A clutch pressure plate and the clutch plate itself. There is no need to uprate unless your engine is seriously tuned, but it's always worth replacing the old clutch when the engine's out anyway.

It's still quite easy to find Rover V8 gearboxes which are shared with other cars and vans, but the SD1 aluminium bell housings are becoming harder to find.

reasonable engineering, five-speed gearboxes, lots of engines from 1,600cc upwards, and usable rear axles in different widths.

Smaller engines nowadays come with transverse transmission – i.e. no gearbox. Ford's very good Zetec engines and Vauxhall/Opel's good-quality smaller engines are examples – there are no standard RWD applications for these engines. Conversion to RWD is inevitable; it's always possible although it can be tricky, so conversion kits may be a better idea. Tiger have been converting Zetecs to face the right way for years. Most five-speed Sierra boxes have the right first motion shaft, and go straight on to four cylinder Ford engines. The four top bolts around the Sierra bell housing also bolt straight on, and the others can be bolted to drilled and tapped holes in the aluminium sump. A four-speed 2-litre Sierra box will also fit, although complications arose at one time with the starter and ring, but Tiger now supply a special starter motor,

Ford gearboxes are good value, and close-ratio gear sets are available. The best early Ford 'box is from the Corsair 2000E . . . but there aren't many of those left, sadly.

The Rover gearbox that went into my XK. Before fitting one, check that it has five gears – this one only had four, which only showed up on the first attempt to change into fifth.

Above: The guts of a Jaguar 'box, which is much meatier than the Ford. Chasing down a nasty vibration in my own car included stripping this box.

There was visible wear on the surface of this shaft, which had worn through the case-hardening but after a gearbox rebuild and replacement, the engine turned out to be the source of the vibration anyway.

Ford's popular Type 9 Sierra gearbox has a badly designed remote selector arrangement that sometimes results in a baulky and unpleasant action. A good remote quickshift usually sorts it out instantly.

When the Jaguar overdrive packed up, there were bits of broken internal clutch all over the inside. Given the option, always go for a simple five-speed gearbox and save yourself overdrive grief.

which apparently works even better than the correct one.

Several of the Zetec tricks could be useful for other cars. Tiger chop (and baffle) the Zetec's oil pipe and the aluminium sump down to $5\frac{1}{2}$in as there's plenty of clearance beneath the crankshaft. This can be very convenient to clear a crossmember, or to get an engine as low as possible without trashing it on a speed bump.

The five-speed Type 9 (Ford Sierra) box is also very useful for non-Ford engines, and has been used with V8 Rover, MGB, Zetec, Pinto, crossflow and smaller Vauxhall twin-cam engines. A beefed-up version is the T5, fitted to Cosworth Sierras. The ultimate version is the American spec T5, which is used for the 5.0-litre Ford Mustangs. It's rated at 330lb ft of torque, okay for the Ford V8 but pushing its luck with a 5.7-litre Chevy.

The Sierra Type 9 is still plentiful and cheap for the moment, but will not remain so for ever.

TYPE 9 FORD CONVERSION KITS

For Rover V8
Magnum Engineering
(01926 642122).

For Zetec
Tiger (01733 894328).

**For MGA and MGB
(and beefed-up boxes)**
HiGear (01332 514 503).

For Spridget
Frontline (01225 852777).

For Vauxhall
SBD (0208 391 0121).

There is a standard five-speed gearbox for the Rover V8, but it doesn't have a top reputation. It's also relatively rare, because most V8s are automatic. The box itself is okay, but there is major confusion about oil: 90-weight hypoid is apparently too thick, and

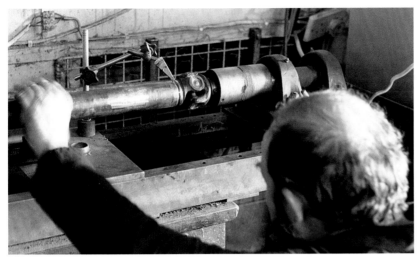

Getting propshafts cut, welded, fitted with new universal joints and dynamically balanced is usually a pro job, as everything has to be spot-on to avoid vibration. This is not usually too expensive, though.

automatic tranny fluid seems to cause premature wear. The newer LT80 version of the box is better, but expensive. Millers Oils, who make a lot of racing lubricants, suggest their TRX synthetic 75w–90w race gear oil, or 75w semi-synthetic.

American engines need strong gearboxes, and the old Ford top-loader is still a good option, although more recent American manual boxes are slicker and less agricultural. Tremec make aftermarket gearboxes for US V8s. Their standard five-speed will handle 400lb ft of torque, and their heavy-duty version with thicker shafts is the TKO. The top Tremec box is the T56 six-speed, rated at 450lb ft of torque, which is fitted as standard to some Corvettes.

A possible conversion for American engines is the Toyota Supra Turbo five-speeder. In standard form it's marginal with a V8, but with the two major bearings uprated, the box is supposedly up to the job. It's also slick and light to use.

For Lambo, GT40 and Ferrari lookalikes, the Renault 25 provides a good gearbox and transaxle. If the geometry is correct, you can run Rover V8s through these, and apparently even Jaguar and BMW V12s as well as Chevy and Ford

small-block V8s. However, if the first motion shaft geometry isn't spot on, you'll get 1,000 miles out of it if you're lucky. RV Dynamics (07802 813649) make conversion bell housings and kits, and have abused a Renault 25 box with V12 Jag power for 18,000 miles in their Nemesis without breaking it. Still, even if you trash one, replacing a standard R25 gearbox is not a big-budget problem. RV also sell a kit to convert the five-speed Getrag box from 3.6- and 4.0-litre Jags to the V12. Manual XJ12 donors are rarer than funny BBC sitcoms.

Automatic gearboxes are not automatically bad, particularly when used with big and torquey engines. With hi-stall torque convertors and trick valves, you can get faster launches than a manual box. The uprated torque convertor means the power slams in rather than squelching in, and the modified valves change up just after peak power revs are reached. A ratchet shifter prevents the selector going past second gear into third.

Click into 'Drive', boot it and red-line the engine, slap the shift up a gear, then again at the next red line. My first serious V8 Cobra replica was automatic, partly because the box came free with

the engine, and partly by genuine choice. If you have massive torque and a light car, it really doesn't matter if you lose some power through the autobox – you already have more power than you can use anyway.

PROPSHAFTS

Many kits come with a propshaft, but sorting one out from scratch is no big deal. At the front end you need a matching flange to bolt to the gearbox flange, or you can use the original slider fitting that comes out of the gearbox. At the other end you need another flange to mate to the one on the diff, and always somewhere along the shaft a flexible joint or slider is required to allow for movement. Short propshafts don't usually need a bearing or a mounting in the middle.

The measurement is taken from the end of the gearbox to the face of the diff flange, and your propshaft supplier will fit new universal joints and weld it all together into a shaft, then balance it. Bolt it on – job done.

Even if your diff is solidly mounted to the chassis, you still need a slider or flexi joint because of the movement of the engine (and therefore gearbox) on the mounting rubbers. If you have a live axle, the slider allows the axle to move freely.

Here's an advantage with FWD, finally – there's no propshaft at all; the driveshafts go straight from the diff to the wheels.

REAR AXLES

In the old live axle days, you had a self-contained casing with a differential and two internal shafts, suspended on cart springs. The 1967–80 Ford Escort axles are still used in many Caterhams and copies thereof. The real Lotus experience means a live axle, and they can perform very well if located properly.

The differential is the device

within the axle that allows the wheels to revolve at different speeds as the car goes round corners, and directs power from the propshaft to the wheels.

A limited slip diff (LSD) has clutches within it that allow quite smooth continuous drive if one wheel loses grip. A locking diff (the Detroit Locker, for example) is a more brutal mechanical version of this.

A normal diff loses drive if one wheel is slipping. Drive goes rather pointlessly to the slipping wheel unless there's a limited slip device to stop it. Most of the time an ordinary diff will do fine.

Independent suspension at the rear involves the diff being fixed centrally, with exposed driveshafts used to transfer drive from the diff to the wheels. This keeps the unsprung weight low by removing the single-piece encased axle/diff/shafts assembly. It also improves handling and ride. Jaguar and Sierra axles are good independent systems while BMW 3-series (and the old Triumph Herald/Spitfire) independent rear ends have dodgy geometry, but the BMW components are okay, and the

geometry will be improved by kit car manufacturers as time goes by.

On all driving axles, the diff ratio sets up the final drive and top speed of the car. The propshaft connects to a small pinion wheel inside the diff, which drives the big crown wheel that's connected to the wheels. If the pinion wheel spins 3.5 times for a single revolution of the crown wheel, the diff ratio is 3.5:1.

High and low ratio diffs are confusing, because they seem to work the wrong way round. A 4:1 low ratio diff means the engine will spin quite fast to achieve 30mph. A high ratio 2:1 diff means the engine will spin very slowly for the same 30mph.

Low ratio diffs mean engines reach peak revs and full power very quickly, so the car will take off like a dog-track bunny, but top speed will be quite low because the engine will run out of revs. This also means it'll be rather noisy and expensive on fuel. My Midge has low ratios and minimal weight, and even with a tired Vitesse engine it can still take a Porsche 911 at the lights. Only

for the first fifty feet, granted, but that's what counts.

High ratio diffs work best with big, lazy, high torque engines that have lots of grunt at low revs. Acceleration is slower, but cruising is more relaxed, and fuel economy is better. Current Corvettes run a six-speed box with a sky-high overdrive to get the fuel consumption over 30mpg with a 5.7-litre engine, which means it's barely ticking over at 60mph.

For serious performance and for circuit and drag racing, some people use Halibrand and other quick-change diffs to change the final drive ratio to suit a particular day's sport. That's over the top for a road car, but choosing the right diff is important. If you're lucky there is a little tag on the diff casing with the ratio marked on it. If not, open up the diff, count the teeth on the crown wheel and pinion, and divide one by the other – the result is your diff ratio.

The practical final drive ratio is also affected by the size of wheels and tyres, and many kit builders use big stuff. Big wheels and tyres do look sexy, so fair enough. For

The diff from IRS Jaguars is a hefty old lump, but it will take an enormous amount of power without breaking. There's a 427 replica in California that has been giving a Jag diff serious 700bhp abuse for ten years now, and no worries.

The diff from a Capri live axle. To find out what the final drive ratio is, count the teeth on the big crown wheel and divide it by the number of teeth on the pinion wheel at the front.

the SVA test, the speedo must not read even 1 per cent under the vehicle's actual speed, so unless your running gear is all standard and accurate you're going to have to get the speedo calibrated. The good news is that's not a big deal, as the calibration is calculated by pushing the car forward to rotate the wheels a few times while counting turns on the speedo cable. The numbers and speedo are then sent off for calibration.

If there's a big difference between the sizes of the original wheels and the new ones, you'll want to think about lowering the diff gearing. A Sierra-based Jeep with 15in wheels, big off-road tyres and standard Sierra gearing is going to have gear ratios that feel like 2nd, 3rd, 4th, 5th and 6th, but there won't be enough power to use the two top gears. A lower diff will sort this out to some extent.

In the time since the first edition of the *Kitcar Manual*, there have been some useful developments. BGH Geartech have developed a new Ford Type 9 (Sierra) gearbox with a long 1st gear. With kitcars being so much lighter than the hefty anchor of a full-fat Sierra, they don't need a very low first to get going, so the first gear ratios can be closer to the rest of the gears. Your first gearchange is thus delayed by a second or two, until you're across the traffic lights and in front.

The Freelander diff was previously too new to be easily available, but people are now crashing and breaking more of them, so their diffs are available to the kit fraternity. Why do we like it? The Freelander diff saves 14 kilos over a Sierra diff, that's why.

Quaife Engineering are now into kit cars in a bigger way than

My old Chevy's manual four-speed box, about to be upgraded to an overdrive autobox with a few performance tweaks – hardened steel pump components and uprated clutch bands.

Autometer's electronic speedos work off a sensor that plugs into the ex-cable drive on the gearbox, or works directly from the speed sensor. American components have been a bargain recently, with the US dollar not worth much.

ever, offering a new Type 9 Ford box with sequential six-speed guts, chain-driven diffs with cush drive and reverse gear for bike-powered Sevens, separate reversing boxes and a transaxle gearbox to replace the Renault 30 and Porsche 911 units in GT40s, Ultimas and so on. Their stuff is new and very expensive compared to second-hand production units, but you only have to buy it once.

I've personally discovered the General Motors 700R4 four-speed automatic. (The later electronic version is the 4L80E.) This comes free with many 1980s Chevy V8s, and is a personal favourite. One of my depressingly long list of projects is a 1958 Chevy Delray that used to be drag-raced, and had a very low-ratio rear axle and a four-speed manual gearbox. With a Z28 Camaro engine fitted, it was massive off the line but roaring its head off at 50mph. I changed the box for a 700R4, which got me a low 3.06:1 first gear, two intermediate gears and an electrically locking overdrive top gear that dropped my revs

by 35%, giving me better fuel consumption than the manual box as well as getting me a faster launch with the torque converter, rather than messing about with a clutch. Bear in mind that manual gearboxes strong enough to handle big V8s tend to be agricultural in construction, so fast gearchanges are not guaranteed.

Another drivetrain change that's now almost universal is the death of the speedo cable. Just a few years ago, electronic speedos were sexy high-tech widgets, and now they're just the way you do it. They're a distinct improvement over spinning cables and different-sized plastic speedo drive gears, and in any case, are more or less compulsory for enough accuracy to pass SVA. They operate by taking a pulsed signal from magnets secured to the propshaft, or from the Vehicle Speed Sensor, or wherever else they can get a signal from, and are designed to be calibrated by amateurs. Progress forwards rather than backwards.

Chapter 8

Putting a stop to it

There are two ideal approaches to kit car braking systems, both of which involve using complete designed systems. The builder of a single-donor kit is in the best position, as all he needs to do is to overhaul and transfer an entire braking system from the donor to the kit, making up new brake lines as he goes and re-siting the master cylinder and handbrake.

The second ideal approach is a complete new high-performance system, which consists of big front brake discs with multi-cylinder callipers, master cylinder(s) with an adjustable front-to-back bias, and smaller rear discs and callipers. All the components of such a system can be bought new, and should come from one source that has already sold similar systems to lots of other people.

I've always liked the idea of buying brakes from Merlin Racing, because they are actually on the racing circuit premises at Castle Combe, so their customers are race-testing their products just 100 yards away. If they sold people bad brake products, they'd be liable to get four-pot enemas from people who have just crashed.

For most of us, a standard donor brake system is twice as good as good enough, as our cars are half the weight of the donors. A standard system is powerful enough for most purposes, and by removing the donor's bulk you've just made the standard system twice as effective.

If the brakes worked well on the donor, they'll work even better on the kit. However, it has to be sensible to strip and check the components, to replace any cylinders that show signs of deterioration, and to replace all the rubber seals as a matter of course.

OVERHAULING

Don't split callipers. There are sealing rings that you can't buy, and the bolts that hold the callipers together are single-use only and won't torque back up correctly. If you have a really hard time prising the pistons out of the callipers to change the rubbers, you're probably better to buy new or reconditioned callipers anyway. There's also the reassurance that decently refurbished callipers will have been tested for cracks.

Brake fluid is hygroscopic, and once it's attracted water into the system, the steel cylinder bores and pistons will rust. On stripping them, any superficial crud that you can clean up with a cloth and brake cleaner is no problem, but visible rust pits in the bores will rip up the new rubbers and quickly start a leak.

Every scrap Jaguar provides very big four-pot brakes with vented discs, so even with a big V8 in a Cobra replica you have more brakes than you need, virtually free.

If you can't use Jag brakes, Wilwood offer very good systems with light alloy callipers at good prices.

Above: More and more standard donor-car brake systems are appearing with multi-pot callipers and discs all round, so aftermarket braking systems may not be necessary in lightweight kit cars. If you get the chance, build with standard brakes first and try them.

Master cylinders suffer the same problems and are approached in the same way, although there are enough additional complications caused by warning valves and dual brake system devices to make bleeding them something of a potential problem. The Haynes manual on the donor car will usually help you out with the procedures.

Brake servos either work or they don't, and they're not really repairable at home. Wait and see if you really need one: my Midge was originally fitted with a servo from its Triumph Vitesse donor, but it simply locked up

Above: Jaguar XJ6 and XJS have inboard rear discs that are very difficult to reach, so mechanics don't service them. Expect to carry out a full rebuild with new cylinders and discs.

Many rear brakes are still drums, which is fine as not much braking is done by the rears. You can expect to replace rear wheel cylinders, as they frequently weep fluid unless they've been replaced recently.

Above: If you don't change brake fluid regularly, it sucks up water. This rusted piston is from a scrap calliper – if you cleaned it up and put it back in, it would rip up the new seals within a week and start leaking again.

the front wheels as soon as you touched the brake pedal, so it was removed. Unless the brake pedal is unpleasantly heavy without assistance, leave the servo out. You get a better feel through the pedal, and you've eliminated a possible complication.

Clean and re-rubber brake parts, paint the callipers if you like, check that the connecting threads are in good condition, and then store them in your house. Don't leave overhauled cylinders in a damp garage – I did that with my Jag brakes and they went rusty again before I had the chance to use them.

Don't be tempted to mix and match bits and pieces of brake systems without understanding exactly what you're doing. There have been kits designed with big Jag rear brakes and small Cortina front brakes, and there have been big crashes caused by back brakes being more powerful than the front brakes. The bottom line is that front brakes should be roughly three times as powerful as the back brakes. If you're using a Jag four-pot big-vented-disc-braked front end and a Jag two-pot small-disc-braked rear end, perfect. Many of my Agony questions in *Fast Ford* and *Classic Ford* magazines were concerned with converting Escort RS Turbo rear brakes to discs, mostly for cosmetic reasons. It's easy enough to do, but then you have to virtually disable the new back brakes to achieve a safe back-to-front brake balance. Brake balance can be adjusted in the car with a brake bias valve, until a safe front-to-back balance is reached. This is essential for any custom brake system.

A serious set of high-performance brakes may be overkill for a light road car. For instance, the biggest and best UK brakes are made by AP Racing. Their kit is the dog's six-pot plums, but you should be sitting down when you check out the prices. You get what you pay for, and if you drive a 700bhp Ultima capable

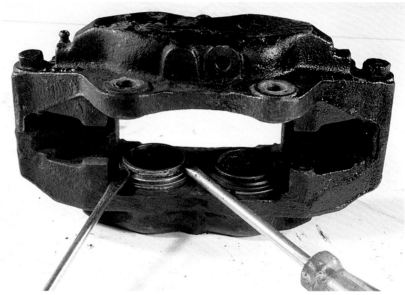

Above: When prising pistons out of brake cylinders, apply gentle and even leverage on both sides, or the pistons will jam. (If the system's still intact, you can also use hydraulic power via the brake pedal to help get them out.)

New brake master cylinders aren't too expensive, and are usually worth replacing – brakes are something you don't want to take any risks with.

If an old cylinder is in perfect condition with spotless bore and pistons, you have the option of just replacing the rubbers and seals and putting it back in, make sure the rubbers are fitted the right way round, though . . .

Making new brake lines in cupro-nickel is cheap and easy, but take care not to bend them too sharply, keep them neat and support them every few inches to stop them vibrating and chafing.

of 200mph plus, you'd better have some serious stoppers on board. Escort discs and pots will do nicely for a crossflow Seven, however.

A good compromise is provided by Wilwood, an American company who make rather old-fashioned but very cost-effective multi-pot aluminium callipers. These offer powerful braking for a reasonable price, and a Wilwood set-up will keep most people happy, even if they race at weekends as well as driving on the road during the week.

When it comes to hoses and piping, it's only cheapskate major car manufacturers who make steel brake pipes that rust out. Kits all use copper or copper/nickel lines, and you can buy cheap and effective flaring tools to plumb everything in. Brake lines must be run inside the chassis beams, so that none of them dangle down below the chassis or are run underneath it – otherwise the first speed bump will take out your braking system completely.

Most people now use flexible brake hoses with a braided stainless steel outer surface, which look nice and give you a firmer feel to the pedal as they don't expand like rubber hoses. However, do make sure that the hoses you buy are approved for road use, because the pure racing ones can wear out very quickly as the stainless steel braiding abrades the inner nylon core pipe.

Many people – including some MoT testers – believe that hydraulic handbrakes are illegal, but they're not. Provided that handbrake-operated cylinders have their own completely separate fluid, cylinders and piping, hydraulic handbrakes are fine. If you get MoT hassle, make them show you in the testing manual where it says handbrakes have to be operated mechanically.

Before there's any chance of having to use your brakes for real, take the car somewhere there's nothing to hit, get it up to speed and try a few genuine emergency stops. The SVA test goes through the theoretical static brake power and balance, but you need to know what's actually going to happen when you stamp on the anchors and all the car's weight transfers to the front tyres.

If you're going to fit ABS, fit a new system. Several Agony questions sent to *Fast Ford* concerned the one-sided failure of ABS on ageing brake systems, and if that happens when you really need the brakes, you'll have one side working and the other doing rather less, with predictable consequences. Better to learn cadence braking and keep things simple.

Lastly, if you're doing anything to the brakes of a car that's been painted, remember that brake fluid is a brilliant paint-stripper, almost as effective as coarse sandpaper.

Chapter 9

The rolling chassis

There is a fundamental difference between a kit car chassis and a production car chassis. The purpose of a production car chassis is to make money, and the purpose of a kit car chassis is to provide the foundation of the best car that the maker can create.

The less metal that a major car company can get away with the better – shaving down the steel cost by £2 a shell over 500,000 cars saves £1,000,000. A shell capable of passing the minimum safety tests can be created by spot-welding the minimum of stamped-out metal sheets into clever shapes, and a good job too. If most people weren't happy enough with that, we wouldn't have any donor cars. A kit chassis is a different animal entirely, however. Even the worst kit car chassis is immensely strong, largely due to the thickness of the

steel used. A basic ladder-frame kit car chassis will normally be box section with walls at least 3–4mm thick. That compares with production car steel of 0.5–0.7mm, and of course with a kit you also have a very strong GRP body firmly attached to the chassis as well.

A basic ladder frame will be found under most Cobra replicas, with assorted risers and hoops to provide door hinge, dash and screen supports, roll over bar mounts and so on. There's nothing wrong with a ladder frame – it's not sophisticated, but it does the job.

Spaceframes are usually found under Seven-style cars and other road/race types. Normally, there is no main backbone or big side rails, but a network of triangulated smaller bore square or round steel tubes. Spaceframes are immensely strong, as most of the stresses are translated into

compression or tension rather than bending.

So – whatever kit chassis is hauled off the truck and placed on axle stands in your garage, you really don't have to worry about its strength.

There are quite a few variations on the spaceframe theme. Gardner-Douglas use a backbone chassis, which is essentially a single narrow central spaceframe running front to back with wider structures at either end. TVR still used that method of construction for the final 200mph Sagarises.

Some multi-tube frames such as the Autotune chassis are a collection of triangulated frames attached to each other. These are also very strong for their weight.

There are even monocoques in the kit world, but unlike thin steel ones, these are massively strong and usually made of thick GRP. Midas use this method, and their shells have survived both laboratory crash testing and practical crash testing – *Kit-Car* magazine has had several letters thanking Midas for saving their owners' lives after big roll-over accidents.

Quite a few off-road-style kits don't exactly have a chassis, they *are* the chassis. A Tomcat, for example, is basically some of a Range Rover chassis topped by a hefty rollcage with some panels attached to it. So is a Dakar, and most of the fun off-roaders have been built this way as well – the Skoda-based RV Bugrat comes to mind.

If you have limited ambitions and time, it could be worth

This spaceframe comes from a Rotor rear-engined racing car made in Glasgow. Light and very stiff, with the cabin skinned in aluminium to save weight.

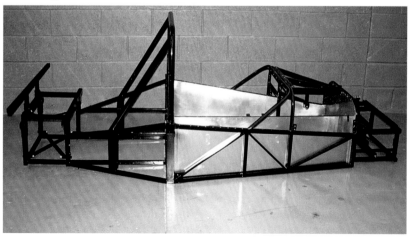

Above: A sophisticated American Cobra replica chassis. Steel panelling over a well-braced ladder-frame, with the door hinges and locks connected by what is effectively a side intrusion bar inside the door.

Even a simple ladder-frame will do the job very nicely as long as it's thick enough – and kit chassis nearly always err on the side of too much rather than too little strength.

A budget MK Locost spaceframe comes together. You can more or less pick it up and walk around with it, but these things are pretty stiff and can handle accidents at racing speeds.

considering a body conversion kit, which retains all but the outer skin of an existing production car. The Pontiac Fiero is a nice little American sports car that General Motors seems to have originally (and weirdly) built as an exact replica of a Ferrari – so it's a relatively easy matter to unbolt its exterior panels and turn it back into a Ferrari lookalike. There are a good few lookalike body jobs on Jap sports cars including a very cheeky BMW sports car fake on a Mazda Miata/MX5. These are hard to find because BMW launch a blitzkrieg of lawyers to bully anybody they find selling them. With these body conversion kits you get a finished car on the road with no chassis build, suspension or SVA problems, and you can complete them quite quickly.

SUSPENSION BASICS

There are several types of suspension on offer for kit car chassis. Cart springs or semi-elliptical rear leaf springs on their own are okay for shopping, but any serious driving gets the axle twisting and moving on the springs, which is not what you want happening during a fast corner. The axle has to be held in place so that it can only move up and down, not sideways. There are various ways of doing this, of which the simplest is a Panhard rod. This connects the axle to the chassis by a long rod going sideways across the axle, usually behind it. The ideal Panhard rod is as long as possible to make the arc of its up and down movement as flat as possible, and it runs from one end of the axle to the chassis at the other side of the car. Watts linkages, Mumford links and De Dion rear ends are all more advanced ways of achieving the same thing.

When cart springs are replaced by shock absorbers inside coil springs (coilovers), the axle needs even more location, and a good way to achieve this is by a four-bar link running forwards. Four parallel bars run from above and below the axle to mounts on the chassis, and the longer these bars are, the better. On Sylvas, you'll see the long bars outside the bodywork. The longer the bars, the flatter the arc of movement, the more the axle is restricted to just up and down movement, and the better the suspension.

Caterham Sevens still use live axles on some models, simply because they are still Lotus Sevens and that's just how they are. A well-located live axle remains a good solution, although more and more independent rear ends are available.

Kit car front ends are nearly all double wishbones. This is an effective and simple solution, and even when cars such as Sierras with MacPherson strut front ends are used as single donors, most manufacturers will adapt the front suspension to turn it into a double wishbone system. Coil springs with adjustable shocks or dampers inside them fit neatly into the gap between the wishbones; castor and camber angles are either adjustable or use standard settings; everybody's happy.

The author's Cobretti chassis. This took four people to lift comfortably, and the steel plates for the footwells, bulkheads and floors are about 1/8in thick. Still, it was comforting to know it would squash a Land Rover.

Inboard shocks use an extra lever to place the dampers and springs inside the chassis – this helps keep unsprung weight low, maintains the weight closer to the centre of the car, and looks sexy.

ASSEMBLY

So you've decided on a kit, tried out the demonstrator, joined the club, asked every question you can think of, squared off your other half and handed over your hard-earned. All the bits are on the floor and your chassis is perched solidly on four substantial axle stands – time to get on with building the car, and the first step is to paint the chassis. You don't really have to paint it at all – steel that thick will take literally decades to rust. However, it does look a bit manky all rusty, so the first job on a kit build is usually painting the chassis and running gear. Household exterior gloss paint is not a bad idea. It's apparently more flexible than some of the

This Ferrari replica is actually a Fiero. Fieros have a pretty good chassis for a production car, with reasonable crash protection. The original panels are swapped for Ferrari lookalikes, and the Fiero structure remains basically untouched.

Above: This is what you drag out from under a rotten Jaguar XJ6. Note the piece of floor still hanging on to the trailing arm: bits of the floor quite often come off with the suspension.

And this is what a Jag half-shaft looks like when it's been cleaned, shortened and TIG-welded, prior to being fitted with new universal joints.

Most of a Jag rear end has been fitted to this Coddington/Image chassis, which uses its own hubs and upper links. The massive round-tube ladder frame replicates the Shelby chassis.

usual hard paints used on exterior steelwork, and less likely to chip or flake off later.

Getting to the rolling chassis stage is one of the quickest parts of a build. Assembling suspension components is quick and simple, and it's usually pretty obvious what goes where. There are mistakes to be made, though – if you fit Jaguar wishbones the wrong way round, you can accidentally increase your wheelbase by an inch or two. Some kit build manuals are good, some are less so: the ability of a manufacturer to produce a fine kit doesn't presuppose an ability to write in sentences. Quite the opposite, in fact – these are people who do things rather than talk about them.

You will need to replace any rubber bushes you come across in the suspension, which can be a pain. 'Metalastic' bushes consist of an inner steel tube bonded to an outer steel tube, and the outer steel tube is an interference fit in for instance the wishbone to which it is fitted. An interference fit means you can theoretically press or bash it in or out, but after ten years it can be a bit of a laugh getting it out – an interference fit becomes a rusted-in-and-immovable fit. When replacing bushes, it's a good idea to change the old rubber ones for hard polystyrene bushes. These are a direct replacement, and act to tighten up the entire suspension, sharpening up the geometry and making the whole car feel more precise and rigid. There's some increase in ride harshness, but the price is worth paying for the handling improvements.

Generally, the newer the suspension set-up, the simpler it is. Ford Sierra stuff is strong and simple, and not too expensive to overhaul – new wheel bearings and so on are easily available, and relatively easy to replace. Again, the Haynes manual has all the details on how to do it. The more comprehensive donor

Above: These bars securing the Jag front wishbone are always rusted in place, so save time by buying a pair of new ones rather than trying to get the old ones out in one piece.

Old-fashioned, complicated ball-joints can be a bore, but at least they can be stripped, un-shimmed to get the slop out and then used again.

With brake and fuel lines, avoid sharp corners, and secure them with clips every few inches to ensure they don't vibrate and chafe.

The Malone Skunk's suspension tubes and wafer-thin brake discs don't look strong enough for the sort of mad speeds these things do, but are plenty strong enough in practice.

manufacturers' manuals can be used as well, not least because they usually have tables of torque settings for the mechanicals as well as the engine. It's well worthwhile using your torque wrench anywhere you can find a recommended torque setting. Not only are your bits more likely to stay on the car, but your hands will learn how hard it should feel to do up an average suspension bolt, for instance, which is useful knowledge.

Jaguar suspension is still within amateur abilities, but there's a hell of a lot more of it. The big Jaguar clubs keep specialist tools to hire out, which can be useful. Some Jag parts prices are silly, some very reasonable – but where a Ford would have a rubber bush, Jaguar would tend to fit six shims, two rubber rings, two washers, six little chrome securing rings, a bearing with dozens of little chrome needle rollers, a detachable grease nipple and a tin cover with rusted-in screws. Even if each widget is a reasonable couple of quid, that's technically known as a shedload of widgets.

Jag gear does have the advantage of being very over-engineered, so once you've got it sorted it will stay sorted – apart from the back brakes. Access to the rear brakes on an XJ6 is a very poor piece of design, and very difficult – so the average mechanic simply ignores them. They do need lubrication and servicing, particularly the 'self-adjusters' for the handbrake callipers, which don't. The self-non-adjusters are pointlessly complicated and need regular attention, so make sure that unlike Jaguar, you provide access to the diff and brakes when they're in your car.

The good points about Jag rolling gear are its strength and its brakes – big four-pot vented fronts and disc back brakes cost a bomb to buy new, but come free with every £50 scrap XJ6.

There are mistakes to be made with plumbing your car. It makes

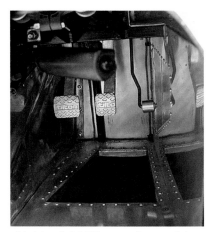

Lightweight Tilton racing pedals and cylinders are expensive, but come complete with everything you need to operate the clutch and brake hydraulics.

A very smart move, if you're on a tight budget, is to buy cheap, second-hand manufacturers' alloy wheels and have them tidied up, powder-coated, diamond-cut and lacquered – they can look fabulous for about £100 a set, all in.

Motor Wheel Services can supply either 14in wire wheels very cheaply, or gorgeous, big stainless Bentley-sized rims very expensively. Wires are stronger than alloys, and are no bother once you have them properly balanced.

superficial sense to run the fuel and brake pipes and the wiring neatly along the bottom of the chassis, except that the first road hump you go over will squash everything flat and leave you with no brakes, no fuel and lots of sparks. All the services must be routed along the inside of the chassis, well away from exhaust pipes or anything else hot. Kit builders will increasingly need to think about ground clearance and exhausts as more and more British roads are humped and made impassable, but at least you know you're not doing structural damage to a kit car chassis merely by grounding it. Underfloor exhaust silencers need skidplates welded on to ensure that a hump doesn't rip the whole system off. Sidepipes are better, being higher off the deck, but the Cobra replica pictured merrily bowling along the road on the first page of Chapter 3 lost a sidepipe to a security gate frame on the way to Le Mans. Fortunately he was in good company, and was soon sorted out.

Making suitable fuel and brake pipes is relatively easy, but having the patience to get them to look good is part of the discipline of a good build. If you're sloppy and rushed, it'll show. Pipes have to be carefully bent around things

such as jamjars and spray cans to get smooth curves, and to avoid kinking them. If a pipe folds over and kinks, it's scrap.

Brake piping in cupro-nickel is easier to deal with than steel, but the same rules apply. All pipes must be secured every few inches to avoid any possible vibration and resultant fractures. Making brake lines is a nice rhythmic thing to be doing, and brake pipe flaring tools are quite cheap. One thing you will do at some stage is to flare a pipe end without first pushing the relevant union on, so allow extra piping for when you do that.

The actual assembly of a rolling chassis is a remarkably quick process, and many people will see a chassis on its wheels after an enthusiastic weekend's work; it's the preparation and the details that take up the hundreds of hours. Bolting wishbones and axles on is a satisfying process, but that's the point at which the real work starts.

Wheels are a matter of money and taste – manufacturers usually have some choices on offer, and will know what sizes and offsets will go under the wheel arches. Offset means the position of the hub inside the rim – basically, front-wheel-drive cars have the

rim towards the inside, and rear-wheel-drive cars tend to have the rim towards the outside, which looks better. Old Ford alloys are very cheap and can be creatively refurbished to look fantastic. Just don't use Capri RS-style four-spokes on Escort hubs, as the nuts aren't compatible and the wheels will fall off. Several different manufacturers may use the same wheel PCD, or pitch circle diameter, which puts the wheel studs in the same places. This means you can use some Peugeot wheels on some Ford hubs. That's not much use as Peugeots are all front-wheel-drive, but it does give you more second-hand alloy wheel options in some cases.

Don't automatically use the biggest wheels you can jam in under the arches. They may look good, but with a light car and huge tyres the 'footprint' of the tyre can be too lightly loaded to offer much grip, and the steering also tends to get nasty with really big wheels, as every fault is amplified. Even if roads look okay, there can be poor repairs beneath the surface that cause big tyres to tramline unpleasantly.

With your chassis powered, fuelled, braked, on its wheels and almost drivable, it's time to pop the body on.

Chapter 10

Bodywork and GRP

The first car with a glassfibre (GRP) body was the Jowett Jupiter, made about sixty years ago. Jupiter bodies may have deteriorated through neglect and abuse, but not because of any other reason – so we know that GRP bodywork will last as long as you want it to.

GRP is also surprisingly easy to work with, although undeniably stinky and icky. (Let me know if my language is getting too technical for you.) As a complete novice, I was able to make huge repairs to a written-off Cobra replica body, and the end result looked perfect. I also made a back door for a Jeep kit which didn't have one originally, so even somebody inexperienced and cack-handed can get good results with GRP.

The basis of GRP bodywork is a hard, shiny outer layer called the gelcoat, which is bonded to several layers of glassfibre matting impregnated with plastic resin. A catalyst or hardener sets off the curing process in both the gelcoat resin and the resin in the matting, and after a few hours the curing of the layers has mostly taken place and you have a strong glassfibre shape with a shiny outer coat.

The word 'plastic' means flexible, and new panels remain flexible for a good few weeks until the full curing process has finished. Ideally, GRP panels would be left in their moulds for that long to support them in exactly the right shape. However, this would be expensive as a regular commercial practice, and only a few manufacturers can afford to keep moulds occupied much beyond the initial curing. Intermeccanica in Vancouver make their Speedsters this way, and their bodies are perfect.

You need to know about this because you may well buy a kit, and take a year or so over overhauling and assembling the rolling chassis and running, leaving the bodyshell in your garden. You may then be shocked and hurt to find it no longer fits the chassis, which is made of steel and has stayed the same shape. You have to be careful to support the body properly until you want to use it. This is particularly so with Cobra replicas, which have heavy front and back ends connected by thin sills that can go out of shape easily. If the body really won't fit, you may have to hack it about a bit until it does, and in doing this you'll inevitably damage the gelcoat.

Gelcoat finish from a top-quality mould can be so good that you really don't need paint. Indeed, it can be quite difficult to tell whether some kits have been painted or not – Chesil Speedsters and Pilgrim Sumos, for example.

Gelcoat does eventually fade in colour. Red gelcoat in particular used to be fade-prone and was then improved, but the EU now

Making a GRP panel: the first part of the process is to polish the mould with carnauba wax seven to ten times and then coat the inside with mould-release fluid.

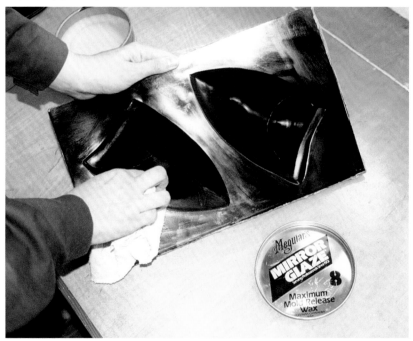

The gelcoat is (optionally) mixed with pigment paste, and a few drops of catalyst fluid are added to the mix. The gelcoat is then painted on to the mould surface with a paintbrush in an even layer.

says the required cadmium red pigment is naughty, so reds will start fading again. In the first few years of a kit's life, it may be possible to match repairs with the same coloured gelcoat, but after that you'll need to think about paint. If you can stall paying for a

The resin bucket is filled up, and the measured amount of catalyst is added and stirred in. (The bathroom scales still haven't recovered.) Also, bare feet and sandals are not recommended clothing for working with industrial chemicals.

paint job for a few years until the gelcoat gets tatty, great.

When it comes to fitting the body to a kit chassis, things are usually pretty civilised these days, and for a home kit builder to have active involvement with raw GRP is relatively rare. If you require

Beloved Wife demonstrates how to stipple the resin into the glass matting, after painting a layer on to the mould first. The overalls and surgical gloves are definitely recommended clothing.

to – or wish to – bond a body to a chassis, the materials can be bought in small amounts and in the right mixing ratios. In order to achieve a suitable curing time, it's possible to vary the amounts of catalyst a little if you have to work in very variable temperatures. If it's hot, the standard mix of resin to catalyst may 'go off' before you've finished, so reduce the amount of catalyst a little. If it's really cold the mix may not go off at all, in which case more catalyst is required. Just mix small amounts at a time, partly because it wastes less when you make a mistake, and partly because a 'hot mix' with way too much catalyst can actually heat itself up so much that it catches fire – at which point it burns pretty fiercely. Make sure you know where you're going to chuck it so that it doesn't set fire to anything.

Ideally, all body panels in a kit would be 'unstressed', which means they carry no weight and are not intended to be part of the strength of the car. The exceptions are GRP monocoques, and Beetle-based kits in which the GRP body tub adds considerable strength to a relatively weak sheet-steel structure.

Nearly all kit cars with steel chassis have the opening body panels hung from steel structures

The brush gets a lot of the glass impregnated, but big and small rollers are also used to soak the glass fibres completely. There can be tricky corners on moulds, and you have to get rid of all the bubbles or they will come back to haunt you later.

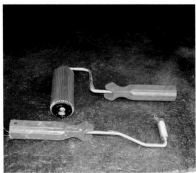

When the matting is all wetted, the panel is left to cure. It's a good move to trim the edges within a few hours while the resin is semi-soft and it's still easy to cut with a craft knife.

welded to the chassis, which is the best way of doing it. Mounting bonnets and boots on steel is less crucial, but doors are definitely best hung from steel hinges attached to the chassis. Doors can be a bitch to hang, partly because they're so visible. Think about asking the manufacturer to hang them before delivery: the price they quote will tell you how hard the job is.

If you do finish up hanging a bootlid from external hinges on the body, make sure you use big washers inside to spread the load over as much of the GRP as possible. GRP is strong, but too much stress on a very small area, such as the bolt holes for hinges, will promote cracking. Of course, this principle works with steel as well – most MGB doors eventually crack by the quarterlight where the point stresses weren't thought through well enough at the design stage.

It is possible to bond steel plates into GRP panels at weak points, but steel and GRP expand and contract at different rates with the ambient temperature, and eventually bonded-in plates can show through the outer surface.

When drilling holes in GRP, remember the gelcoat is hard and brittle, and likely to chip or crack if drilled. Put masking tape where you want to drill the hole and mark the position on the tape, and be very gentle until you're through the gelcoat. Start holes off with small drills, and work from the outside in if possible.

Buying a rough old kit car and doing the body up, or even

changing it to suit your own purposes, is an excellent idea. My old yellow Eagle Jeep only cost me £800, because it was in a fairly horrible state although it was on the road and usable. The up side of its condition was that I could do what I liked to it without losing any of its relatively minimal value. I lived in Ladbroke Grove, in fairly central London, at the time, where a soft-top is seen as an invitation to slash: so I started by bonding the hardtop on. A sunroof was also bonded into the roof, and the doors remained detachable. With an open sunroof and the huge doors taken off, that's as convertible as anybody needs. The rear window originally used to flip up, but with the rear-mounted spare tyre on its original frame, you couldn't open the window more than two inches. There wasn't a tailgate, as the Eagle had originally been designed for a VW Beetle donor. I cut a new door out of the back panel, added a frame to the window glass and then attached it to the new door. I then hinged the door sideways and made a door frame, and hung the spare wheel frame on the door so that the whole lot swung out. It took a while to sort out a few leaks, but the point is that the whole thing was thought out and executed by an amateur whose real job is writing amusing stories, not redesigning cars. If I can do it, so can you.

Repairs on existing panels are also quite easy, with just a few things to remember. First, a crack in the gelcoat goes a lot further than you can see, and can even appear as 'referred damage', where it can show up on the other side of the car from the original impact.

Steel panels get dents, and GRP panels get 'star-crazing'. This is where damage radiates outwards from the point of impact. You have to use a grinder and chase each crack outwards until you've cut it out completely. When you've finished, it looks a right mess, but

The back end of a Sebring Healey replica, in good quality coloured gelcoat. With the flashlines (where the mould pieces join) ground off, this will polish into a finish almost as good as paint.

you've now dealt permanently with all the cracks. If the damaged area is extensive, it may be a good idea to beef up the panel from behind with new resin and matting before you start. If you're repairing a panel that's in several pieces, strap them back together with strips of aluminium riveted on – the rivets can be drilled out later when the panel has been reassembled.

When your repairs are at the stage where there are no holes going right through the panel and all the cracks have been ground out into vee shapes, it's time to fill in the cracks and damage.

There are two sorts of filler – the (usually red) stuff marketed as being for bridging gaps when repairing rusty old donor cars, and the (usually grey) filler used for filling dents. The red stuff is plastic resin and chopped glassfibre, and is really the same sort of material that the GRP body is made from. The grey filler is basically resin and powder, and has no structural strength. If you use this on its own to repair a GRP panel, it will crack.

Start with the red stuff and fill in the vee-shaped cracks to just proud of the surface, and then sand it back until you get the right basic shape. You can then use a thin skim of the grey filler to finish off the repair, and after that it's down to using finer and finer grades of wet-and-dry paper until it's ready for paint. Always use a sanding block, as fingers leave little channels that show up when the gloss coats go on. Make sure you use a primer that will isolate the GRP and the previous paint from your top coats, or you can get bubbles and strange reactions going on under the paint.

The GRP industry also offers very useful two-pack expanding foam plastic, which can be used to fill body cavities in GRP cars to add rigidity and to cut down noise. Make sure there's enough room for the excess to escape as it expands, though. A friend of mine

Seriously top-class cars are always painted. This is one of Boyd Coddington's Boydsters – a sort of kit rod. The prep work starts with the perfect gelcoat, as far as he's concerned.

The author's written-off and remanufactured Cobretti shell is stretched over the body mountings as the body fitting begins. Fitting involves many bolts, rivets and bonding, so it takes a while.

The extent of the body repairs can be seen here – the nearest rear wing has been completely replaced, as has a large chunk of the front wing. The split bootlid was clamped back together and re-gelled. If I can do it, so can you.

The author, wondering if it had been entirely wise to cut off half the back of his Jeep. The chopped-out section would reappear later, having been converted into a door.

The new door has the old window sealed into a new ally frame bonded to it, and the whole lot including the spare wheel swings out on a hinge post welded to the bumper. The new door works a treat.

split the sills wide open on a TVR because he didn't leave enough escape holes.

Another thing to remember is never to wear anything woolly when working with GRP, because spiky bits get deep into the material and acupuncture you mercilessly until you throw the glassfibred sweater away.

Work in the open if possible, as the stuff really stinks, and use a mask as the dust isn't good for your lungs. Other than the above and its undoubted general ickiness, GRP is really quite approachable stuff.

When it comes to paint, the crucial thing to remember is that preparation is all. Car paint forms a very thin layer, and any runs, dips or chips will show up. Black is the worst possible colour for showing up dodgy prep work: lighter plain colours are kinder. Silicon on pre-paint bodywork is an absolute pig to get rid of, and makes unpleasant paint blemishes if there's a trace of it left on the body. Mould release wax is also a nuisance. Some primers don't work well with GRP, so make sure you buy from a paint shop whose staff know what they're talking about. If you stick to a plain colour and cellulose paint, you can get a remarkably

good finish working in your own garage. Clean the floor to get rid of the dust from rubbing-down before spraying, use a sticky 'tack rag' to get rid of particles on the surface before each coat, and then just splosh the paint on wholesale. When you have a nice thick layer on the car, cut it back with the finest wet-and-dry paper (used wet) and then T-Cut and polish it up to a good finish, being careful

Mad Frank from Belgium spends thousands of hours creating insane one-off vehicles such as this 6-litre V8 Mini. The prep for the paint job took him hundreds of hours before the car was covered in a nice metallic blue.

not to cut through the paint on sharp edges.

Metallic paints look good, but can't be easily touched in afterwards and are harder to work with. Avoid isocyanate two-pack paint, as it will kill you if you get a good dose of it. Paint with cyanide in it genuinely needs an external pressurised air feed to a helmet when you're using it.

When your car is resplendent

Hang on, it's not blue, it's gold, um, orange, er, purple? The paint on this car is actually a four-way flip-flop to Frank's own mix, and costs hundreds of pounds a litre. It is spectacular though, isn't it?

The Police Cobra's optional wheelarch extensions extend outwards by several inches to accommodate big wheels and wide axles. If the full-width cop car rear axle is used, the front track obviously needs to be wider also, to avoid the car looking like a Reliant Robin. The temporary buck, from which we'll take the moulds, is made of foam plastic and plaster.

Above: Once the mould is fully cured in a week or two, it's pulled off and is then ready to be waxed eight times and used to make future sets of wheelarch extensions. Waxing can be done indoors while watching telly and throwing toy lobsters for the dog.

Right: The plaster wheelarch that was temporarily added to the car is broken off and disposed of, and the original arch can be re-prepped ready for taking the main moulds. The wide-arch option isn't needed for Police Interceptor-based Ayrspeeds with narrowed rear axles, or for the British BMW or MX-5-based versions of the car, although it remains an option if you want the baddest-looking Cobra around.

The final shape follows the line of the original arch, and also refers to the angle of the original wheelarch bubble. It's carved, smoothed, sanded and sealed, and then waxed and polished eight times before mould release fluid is applied. It's then ready for the mould to be taken.

in its gleaming new colour, a good way of keeping it that way is to use underseal on the inner wings, anywhere a stone could be thrown up. GRP is hard and brittle, and a stone thrown up by a tyre can easily cause a star crack that runs right through the panel and shows up in the outer surface. Use clear underseal on gelcoat-finished cars, as it has been known for the black colouring in underseal to leach through the GRP and show through the gelcoat.

Just to illustrate the point that it is relatively easy to change the

The gelcoat goes on first and is left to partly cure until it's tacky. Then glassfibre matting is laid over it, and the mixed resin and hardener are stippled in. Moulds normally have several extra layers for strength.

shape of a GRP kit car to suit your own ideas, here's a fairly dramatic change I've had to make to my new Ayrspeed Police Cobra's bodywork in order to use the very wide Police Interceptor axle. I had to make a set of optional widened wheelarches which are attached to the bodywork to cover the wheels if the full-width axle is used. I'm also going to make a different bonnet with a rearward-facing air scoop, which will help cooling and aerodynamics.

Everything I've done here, you can do too.

Chapter 11

Keeping the smoke in the wires

Smoke in the wires? Has he lost it only halfway through the book? No, the smoke in the wires is only partly nonsense, and like all the best nonsense it has a thread of logic running through it.

Electricity is actually made of smoke, you see. If the smoke stays in the wires, everything works. If the smoke comes out of the wires, everything stops. So obviously electricity is smoke.

In your world, smoke is the result of electrical energy emerging in the wrong place as extreme and unwelcome heat, rather than in the right place such as turning your starter motor. The spontaneous production-car fires that leave all those roadside burnt patches are usually down to an electrical short circuit. It's wise to leave battery terminals slightly loose during electrical work, so that if smoke starts curling up through the dashboard wiring, you can pull the positive terminal off without looking for a spanner first. It's an even better idea to include a racing-style isolator switch with a red plastic key on the positive battery cable, so that switching off the power is instant. This is also an excellent anti-theft method as the key is detachable, and you can get a little bypass wire that feeds current to clocks and coded stereos when the main current is disconnected.

Keeping the electricity not only in the wires but doing whatever it's supposed to do is actually easier than you would think, particularly with a brand-new kit car wiring loom and a brand-new steel chassis. Most of us have had problems with both car and kit car electrics, but these are usually down to age and corrosion on production cars, and down to GRP bodywork and bad earthing on kit cars.

Fitting a new and properly earthed kit car loom is well within the competence of anybody capable of reading this book. If the loom is for a specific make of kit, it should already be fitted with the right colours and lengths of wires, which will terminate in the right connections to be plugged straight in. On anything Sevenish with a

With a new loom earthed to a steel chassis, making everything work is mostly a matter of logic and patience. Electricity usually obeys the laws of physics, although Sod's Law comes into it as well, and volts and amps can sometimes just sulk.

Standard old wiring looms pulled out of scrap donors used to work well enough with everything cleaned up and proper earthing, but that approach is becoming more and more tricky with a tenfold increase in electrical and electronic complications.

Above: The manufacture of kit car wiring looms is pretty low-tech. This is Alan of Premier Wiring making up a kit loom on a large pegged board. You can get a loom made with whatever colours and connections you want, although his universal kit car loom is a good deal.

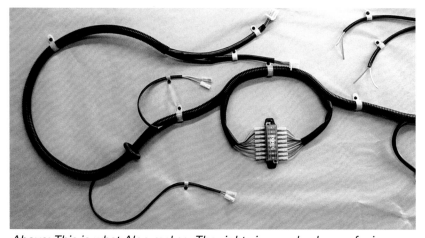

Above: This is what Alan makes. The right sizes and colours of wires are collected, wrapped up in tape and fitted with the correct connections. The central blade-style fusebox is a good idea.

Right: Don't chuck away a dodgy starter motor, as having a unit to exchange cuts the cost of a replacement. Bear in mind that 'reconditioned' may just mean stripped, cleaned, lubricated and painted, which you can do yourself.

good and simple loom, it really is pretty obvious what goes where once you've studied the loom and the car. Centralised and simplified fuseboxes make life even easier.

For example, let's look at a left-hand tail lamp cluster. A red wire goes to the parking light filament of the stop/tail bulb, and a green wire with a purple trace goes to the thicker brake light filament. A green/red wire goes to the left flasher. A black might go to earth. That's it: that corner of the car is wired.

To a great extent, the wiring loom is self-explanatory. It may come in a plastic bag looking like electric spaghetti, but as soon as you've spread it out on the floor and had a look at it, 90 per cent of its purposes are instantly obvious. All the wires are coloured, and there's a fixed set of colours for each loom. Ford colours are different, but most UK kit car wiring looms still use Lucas

ETB's digi-dash provides a wealth of information and is designed for amateur installation.

Starter motors and alternators are basically electric motors, so you can often repair them yourself. Bearings and electronic components fail, but the big bits are usually okay.

This is an ECU, apparently. Most of us wouldn't have a clue whether it came from a car or a television, or whether it was in peak health or fried. Check sensors and connections carefully before buying a replacement ECU.

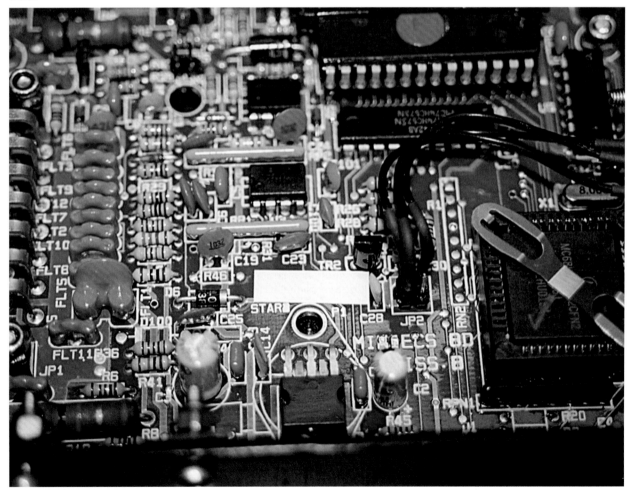

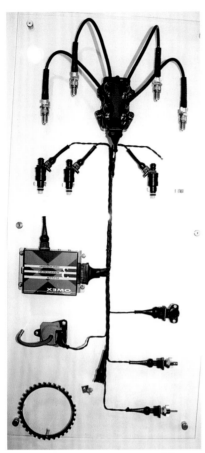

From the bottom: crank position sensor and ring, engine sensors, ECU, injectors, distributor block and spark plugs. Omex again, with their complete replacement loom assembled and ready to install.

colours. These are pretty simple, and are based on seven main colours.

Anthony Stafford, erstwhile supplier of shiny bits to the kit car world, commissioned presses to make new MG headlamps which are still on sale years later from SVC, and still at a sensible price.

The American classic car world provides an excellent supply of good repro parts. This Model A-style rear lamp is in stainless steel and is very nicely made.

BASIC LUCAS COLOURS

Black earth

Green auxiliary ignition controlled items – wipers, flashers etc

White base colour for ignition circuits

Red parking lights and numberplate lights

Blue headlights – white trace for main beam, red trace for dipped

Purple non-ignition controlled items – interior lights, horns

In any case, it doesn't matter what the colours are – British, American, Chinese – once you know what red means, you then know where red wires should go.

It is also possible to retain and recycle a donor loom, and to design and make your own loom. The problems with using donor looms are not too bad, and are mostly to do with complication and barely adequate wiring thicknesses. Most of the functions of a modern production loom are irrelevant to a kit, which only needs basic wiring. When you've stripped out what you don't need and re-packaged what's left, you still have to cut and extend various wires to match the new components, and many of the plugs and connections will need to be replaced. Donor car manufacturers also tend to use the thinnest and cheapest wire they can get away with, and for instance, may rely on a single wire remaining in open air to stay cool, which it may not when tightly wrapped up in a new loom.

Making your own loom from scratch is also a possibility, and is a nice clean therapeutic tabletop business. However, the best way to make a new loom has to

be to start with a semi-universal loom, such as the one offered by Premier Wiring and other kit car magazine advertisers. Premier will sell you a basic kit car loom with the right connections such as a Lucas alternator, bullet headlamp wires and standard instrument wiring, with a central fusebox, and with extra long wires to go beyond where the extremities of your car might be. These looms are based on updated Mini or Spitfire wiring, and contain all you need, but nothing extra. You can of course specify extras if you fancy them – my own loom has extra wiring for map lights and front spot lamps, while rear fog lamp wiring is now universal on new looms. You get a good price dealing with these small companies on this sort of thing and you have the freedom to fiddle with the loom, but you don't have to buy half a mile of different coloured wires and a couple of hundred assorted connectors. You can also rest easy in that the wires will all be plenty thick enough to keep their smoke inside them.

Getting the electrics under control is one thing, but electronics are a different matter. I am a great believer in keeping things simple, and if it's possible

Speedy Cables can help out with most instrument and sensor problems. As well as re-calibrating speedos, they can alter rev counters to provide stable readings for any number of cylinders.

to avoid an ECU I will do so every time. The ECUs themselves are relatively reliable: about 50 per cent of failed ECUs traded in for exchange are working perfectly, but you're not going to get them sent back with a refund, are you? In addition, if you try to use a Ford loom and ECU and you haven't dealt with the circuits for the missing door-shut connections on the now-missing rear doors, your engine won't start. How would you go about tracing that one? I also happen to be in on the secret that bad idling can be caused by failing to bridge the contacts for a missing air conditioner, but imagine the bill you could run up trying to find that out.

If you don't have an engine with a distributor, you do unfortunately need electronics. If you do, I'd recommend buying the whole lot from the same place, such as Omex or Weber. Their stuff is guaranteed and they know exactly what they're doing. They will sell you mappable ignition and fuelling which will liberate a lot more power from a modern injected engine, and if you're running a turbo as well you can dial in some mad power as long as your engine can hack it.

Using very second-hand engine electronics has to be a bad idea. If you left your hi-fi out in the street for 15 years in all weathers, then stripped it and put it back together, you wouldn't expect it to work, would you? Multiple, delicate corroded connectors also send current in all sorts of odd directions, so even fault-finding by dedicated computer systems can result in expensive substitution mistakes.

The whole-system approach with a complete, new matched set of components should get you the first ten years' reliability with no problems.

The system itself usually comes in a self-contained loom. This is the engine and computer loom we're talking about, rather than the simpler and mostly separate chassis loom that works the lights and charging system. Starting from the spark plugs, follow the HT leads to the distributor or distributor block, then the next four wires go to the injectors to time their pulses. The next connection is to the ECU, then the throttle position sensor, then (optionally) the MAP sensor, which measures the Manifold Absolute Pressure of a turbocharged

engine. Next is the air flow sensor, and finally the temperature sensor, which tells the ECU to keep extra fuelling going until the engine is up to temperature. With no distributor, you need a crank sensor to tell the ECU where the crank is. This is a toothed ring that spins in front of a sensor that records where the teeth and gaps are.

The engine sensors usually work on a changing current basis, so a higher temperature might result in a stronger signal to the ECU. This is why mixing and matching systems can be tricky – Omex and Ford, for example, use completely different signals.

You do need mappable ignition and fuelling for a high-powered modern turbo engine, and you can get a lot of extra power out of them. The manufacturer's standard chipping is designed to avoid warranty claims, but you can push your own luck much closer to the real limit of the engine. Ford's rev limit might be 6,000rpm, but you can take a Zetec much higher as long as you back off the ignition a few degrees right at the top end to make sure it doesn't melt a piston.

However, none of this is amateur stuff. You need to have a fully mappable ECU, and an experienced tuning bunny sitting in your car for several hours with a laptop and a rolling road. Check back through that sentence and you'll find there are no cheap words in it.

If you don't want to go all high tech and pay for somebody to squeeze the max bhp out of your engine, and if you still have a distributor, you're in luck. You can combine the simplicity of points and carbs with the reliability of just a few key electronic components to get the best of all worlds. In my XK, there will be an SU fuel pump with a Burlen electronic conversion that replaces the actual points, which wear and burn out. There will also be a magnetic Hall-effect switch inside the distributor to

When you buy an exchange alternator, remember to retain the fan off the front, because recon units don't come with fans attached.

get rid of the main ignition points, for the same reason. However, everything else will stay as simple as possible. A throttle cable will open the throttles, and as long as there is fuel coming in and a spark to the distributor the engine will run. There is almost nothing to go wrong, compared with hundreds of optional failures in an electronic set-up.

For an example, until you have a problem you may not even know that there are two temperature senders in a modern engine. One goes to the ECU, the other to the dashboard temperature gauge with all the other instruments. Getting the dashboard one working a treat doesn't fix the other one.

When it comes to your instruments, your approach will depend on money and time, and how much you have of both. I've seen very clever adaptations of bog-standard complete Ford instrument binnacles made to look like expensive sets of separate dials, just by the clever use of sheet metal, bezels, Perspex and paint. Using a complete old loom and instruments saves a lot of

hassle, although it can generate some as well. This is becoming less easy with more complex modern car electrical systems, but on a bike-based car an excellent option is to use the complete instrument assembly. Bike clocks usually look good too, unless somebody's banged their helmet on them in the process of writing the bike off for you. With older donor cars life is simpler. If all wires are cut back to clean copper core and all the connections are clean and shiny, there's no reason why it all shouldn't work for many more years. There's also the advantage that the engine temperature sensor already works, the gauge works, and the two are designed to work together. Having said that, my Jag fuel sensor and gauge, from a completely standard Jag set-up, only ever reads between 1/4 and 3/4 full. When it says 1/4 full that means it's empty. I don't care – as long as it always does the same thing, you know where you are. (If all your instruments read low, that suggests the dashboard voltage stabiliser is shot. If just one instrument reads low, replace it or live with it.) However the original instruments were earthed, you have to duplicate that, but you have to earth to your steel chassis, not to your GRP body.

Most of the usual dash instruments are fairly easy to get under control, but speedos are a real problem for SVA – they have to be absolutely accurate or read a small percentage over. You can have a speedo that reads 31mph when you're doing thirty, but it can't read 29.95mph at that speed.

Fortunately, people like Speedy Cables can recalibrate your speedo to get the reading right, and it's not even too complicated. You push the car forward for six revolutions of a road wheel, and note how many turns the speedo drive cable has made: then you send the whole lot off and get the speedo back reading correctly. The same people can interfere

with a tachometer to make it suit your purposes. I'm replacing a straight-six with a V8, so the large XJ6 tacho had to be re-jigged to register eight pulses per revolution instead of six, with new electronics to stabilise the reading. They also very usefully make one-off combination drive cables, such as the one connecting my own Rover V8 gearbox speedo drive unit to my Series 1 XJ6 speedo.

It makes life easier if you buy your whole dashboard in one go, complete with all senders and dials. Complete instrument sets usually come with an electronic speedo, which works from sensors attached to the propshaft. These are easily adjustable for calibration, and can even be adjusted sometimes during the SVA test if you ask nicely. Instructions can be poor, though – if the reading makes no sense despite flipping the correct switches, check with the maker.

Digidashes are a relatively new phenomenon, using computer technology to add a lot of extra information and data processing to the old-style dash display with separate gauges. ETB's budget digidash comes with its own harness and sensors and replaces the entire instrumentation of the car. It shows rpm, speed, trip, miles, all fluid levels, pressures and temperatures, and includes shift lights, an accelerometer and some basic datalogging. You can add lots of fancier applications such as tax bandit camera warnings and GPS functions, and the basic system costs around £400. It doesn't have the jewellery appeal of a gleaming array of chrome-bezelled clocks, but it definitely bungs you the maximum info, and a digidash looks good in a minimalist bike-Seven.

If you're still having fun reading about wiring, there's more at the end of the Fuel chapter in a new in-depth section on computer-controlled electronic fuel injection.

Chapter 12

Fuel, bits and bytes

Until recently I thought that the SVA test meant mandatory electronic injection, but it now turns out that even a pair of fat twin 45 Webers on a dirty old Pinto engine will still get through the test, as long as there's a good enough bolt-on catalytic convertor fitted – and it happens that Fisher Sportscars are currently selling just such a cat.

That being the case, you are still free to use carbs or injection if you want to.

Sticking with carburettors gives you slightly less power and smoothness overall, but is a lot simpler and often cheaper. The fuel system for carbs involves a tank, a pump and a carb or carbs. The tank nowadays needs a flush or soft-edged fuel filler cap to pass SVA, and must have a venting system that does not leak fuel – a vented cap is fine. Some kits can use tanks from donors, which saves money, but often the limited space in a kit car means it's worth using a dedicated tank. It will also be made of nice thick steel and won't have flakes of rust in it from ten years of condensation.

If you do use an old tank, be aware that even if you've washed out the old fuel very thoroughly, there can still be enough residual fumes to make it a very effective bomb.

A single fuel line runs from the tank to the pump, which can be either an electric SU-style low-pressure type or a mechanical one fitted to the engine. The old-style SU pump is still okay, but it has points which eventually burn out. There's now a conversion kit to electronic points available from Burlen, which should make the pumps even more reliable. A fuel filter is crucial, particularly with new hand-made tanks and freshly cut fuel lines, otherwise tiny pieces of debris and crud soon jam the float valves and your car stops while you strip and clean the carbs seven times on the way to Le Mans. (Yes, you do hear the voice of hard-earned experience again.)

A carb is a simple mechanical device that organises the air being sucked in by the engine and squirts a little fuel into the air stream to make it explosive. A butterfly or other throttle device operated by your foot controls how much air and fuel gets in, and there are secondary devices such as a choke to richen the mixture when the engine's cold, and sometimes extra accelerator jets to squirt more fuel in for more power. If you get the choice, use a carb with a manual choke, as autochokes are based on bimetallic strips, usually switch off too late, and always fail in the end.

Putting free-flow air filters on is a good idea, as the standard ones are restrictive. However, when you let an extra 40 per cent of air into the engine, you need to match it with more fuel, which means fitting different jets and needles. This is best done on a dyno rolling

Two fat Webers on a Zetec is what most kit people visualise when somebody says the word 'carbs'. Surprisingly, these monsters are still legal on a new kit, given the right catalytic convertor.

96

Even a Mini engine can be fitted with a respectable amount of carburation, if you can find room for a reasonable-sized airbox. This installation is in a Mini, so the speedo must have been moved somewhere else to make space for the airbox.

road, which will set the engine up correctly and will usually pay for itself quite quickly in saved fuel costs. It also gets the max power out of the engine – you can easily lose 40 per cent of your available power through bad timing and carb settings.

An injection system also gets fuel into the engine, but if working well is more accurate, more efficient and less environmentally messy. You need the same vented tank and filtering, but usually a fuel injection system will have double fuel lines. One is the main high-pressure feed, and the other is a return line to the tank – there's usually fuel in circulation all the time. A fuel injection pump is a much more ambitious high-pressure affair than a pump for carbs, and it pressurises a fuel rail running along the side of the engine. The fuel injectors are connected to this permanently pressurised rail,

Ford's early BDA slide injection system. It didn't ever work very well, but it certainly looks cool, doesn't it?

The Cosworth Sierra Turbo gives you 205bhp standard, and much more with chipping and higher boost pressure. It also comes with a good gearbox, but anything bearing a Cosworth logo is expensive.

and when an injector is sent a signal from the ECU, it opens for a few milliseconds and squirts the correct amount of fuel into the incoming air to fire the cylinder. Earlier mechanical fuel injection is unlikely to figure in new kit car builds, as most people will either be using old-fashioned carbs or modern high-techery.

ECUs nowadays control both fuel and ignition, but fuel computers often used to be separate. If you try to use fuel injection from late 1980s Rover V8s, be aware that your Lucas fuel ECU does not have a good reputation. Weber produce a replacement, and can also supply some interesting fuelling

conversions to suit older donor engines. They are currently developing retro-fit electronic fuel injection for Ford Kent (Cortina) engines, which the Lotus Seven-style racing boys will be interested in.

Fuel lines for kit cars should be made from fairly large bore copper or cupro-nickel piping, and must be secured every few inches along the inside of the chassis. Be careful not to run the lines too close to any exhaust pipes, and be prepared to use heat shielding in the engine bay, as fuel will vaporise at high engine bay temperatures, and your car will simply expire in the middle of a traffic jam until everything cools down.

The classic car industry in the UK is doing us all proud at the moment, as Weber and SU Burlen are expanding rather than contracting the number of old carbs for which they can supply parts and overhaul kits, and you can still buy twin 40s or big 2in triple SU set-ups brand new, with new manifolds, linkages, the lot.

Fuel itself was quite good when it had lead in, and lean-burn technology was progressing well. Fuel and car producers were concentrating on increasing efficiency and cutting fuel use, until the unleaded bandwagon got going. Unleaded fuel was initially pretty poisonous, with lots of proven carcinogenics such as benzene and toluene. In many laboratories the standing rules would require Super Unleaded to be in a sealed chemical cabinet rather than exposed to atmosphere. Fire departments are also less than keen on unleaded, as it's harder to put out once a fire has started.

Catalytic convertors are largely a waste of time, as they don't work on cold engines and don't last very long anyway. However, no politician will have the courage to point this out, so we're stuck with them, as we are with unleaded petrol.

To avoid detonation and

Bigger fuel injectors are needed to match higher turbo-boosted air supply with an increased fuel supply. This richens the mixture enough to stop the pistons melting at 7,000rpm.

pinking with unleaded, it's usually necessary to back off your ignition a few degrees. This takes the edge off your engine's efficiency and performance and burns more fuel, but we have to live with it.

Older engines ran fine on leaded petrol because of its cooling and lubricating lead content, and their valve seats were usually cut straight into the cast iron of their cylinder heads. As unleaded fuel burns hotter, and the friction from its lack of lubrication adds to the heat, the valves get micro-welded to the seats, and tear off tiny pieces of valve seat as they revolve. An A- or B-series BMC engine will last about 5,000 miles on its old valve seats before they burn out, although some other older engines can last quite a while longer. The Federation of British Historic Vehicle Clubs' tested and approved lead-replacement fuel additives will keep things going for a while, but the most sensible course of action is simply to back off the ignition and drive your car on unleaded until the seats recede and the compression goes. The bits you are damaging will be cut out anyway, so you lose nothing.

'Fuel catalysts' in the form of pellets that drop into the fuel tank to prevent valve seat erosion are about as effective as sacrificing a chicken at a crossroads at midnight, but much more expensive. There was a big sales push for them a few years ago, and many MG owners are now suing as their valves burn out after 5,000 miles or so, exactly as if they hadn't put a 'fuel catalyst' in the tank at all.

Something well worth putting in your tank if you run a big engine and have enough room for the tank is liquid petroleum gas (LPG). The big advantage of this at present is taxation. UK petrol prices are nearly all (80 per cent) tax, but LPG is currently taxed much less heavily. Even when the government gets greedier in a

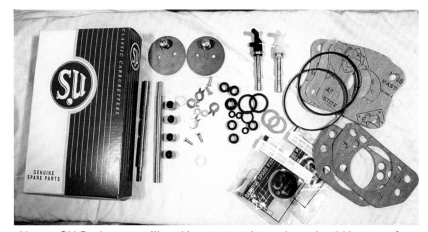

Above: SU Burlen are still making new carbs and overhaul kits even for quite early applications. These kits are comprehensive and even include replacement bushes for the butterfly spindles.

Repairing and overhauling carbs is a nice evening tabletop affair, and can be carried out indoors with music and coffee to hand. No drips down your neck, no danger and no pain.

This is a freshly overhauled set of carbs for my V8. Every wearing part other than the spindle bushes has been replaced, but the increased airflow from the K&N air filters means I'll need different needles.

The old SU petrol pump still works fine for most British-sized engines, although American V8s require rather more fuel volume than the tick-tick British pumps can provide.

couple of years, there will still be a useful saving – in some areas it's about 40 per cent on fuel costs at the time of writing.

The LPG system involves a very strong pressurised tank, piping and safety valves, and a regulator that lets gas into the manifold,

If you're planning any serious track action, a racing fuel cell is a smart move. These also come in useful shapes and sizes for general kit car use.

SU are now selling a conversion kit that replaces the old points in their pumps with a circuit board instead, which won't need a thump with the thick end of a screwdriver to wake it up.

either through carbs or injectors. There's also a changeover switch that switches off the petrol supply when the LPG system is on, and there are connections to the ECU if you have one fitted. A system will cost about £1,000 to have fitted, or you can hunt around and buy

a DIY kit, and do the donkey work of tank and pipe fitting yourself. Commissioning the system should be left to someone who knows what they're doing. You tend to lose a significant amount of power, and you lose in-car space depending on the size and shape of the tank. If you're genuinely interested in the environment, LPG is also very clean.

Lotus are currently working on a natural gas compressor and tank that will cost even less to run, as it won't be seriously taxed until after LPG has been hit. It's interesting that they managed to get a tank and system in an Elise, hiding it behind the seats. If gas power is part of your build plan, you can design in a space-saving installation before you start working on the car.

RPI are also currently developing an interesting LPG installation that automatically changes to petrol when you want power and reverts to gas when you want economy – a good compromise.

A typical well-sorted kit car fuel tank set-up. A rubber-mounted pump, filter, tank, piping and sender wiring – all neatly tidied up and secured.

Politicians making mileage out of environmentalism won't seriously attack multinational car corporations, but classics and kit cars are an easy target, and the gentlemen's agreement that laws for new cars are not backdated and applied to old cars relies on the government being gentlemen. That, nowadays, would be unreasonably optimistic.

Realistically, we will all have to use computerised fuel injection and catalytic converters before long. However, the up side is that we can usually get significantly more power and/or a useful increase in fuel economy out of our engines. A big V8 with a four-barrel carb and a spiky cam will probably get 10mpg, maybe 15mpg if you're careful. The newer Ford 4.6-litre V8 with an ECU controlling its injection and sparks offers 250–300bhp and around 25–30mpg with its autobox retained. If you resent paying £4 in tax for every five-quid gallon of petrol you buy, paying £8 in tax for a ten-quid gallon will feel even worse – so I'm going to come to terms with computers and consign the 40DCOEs to history. Mind you, Weber/Omex sidedraught ECU-controlled throttle bodies are basically injected 40s, so that's an option.

Modern engines don't have distributors, and no longer have an intake manifold suitable for a carb, so the options are narrowing unless you deliberately go retro with an older engine design. Bike engines will all soon be injected too.

Automotive computing is complicated in detail, but simple in essence. The ECU tells the coil or coils when to spark, and tells the injectors when to open to squirt fuel into the engine: it does this more accurately than a distributor and carb. You don't need to know how unless you want to, in the same way that you don't need to understand mobile phone technology to order a pizza.

Wiring up an engine to work with an aftermarket ECU is reasonably easy, and at a basic level mostly just involves identifying and plugging in the sensors. If you fancy learning to design a fuel map (which is a 3D picture of your fuel and spark instructions) on a laptop with your car on the dyno rollers, you can do so – but you can also just use something like an Omex system right out of the box with a good fuel map already programmed into it. You can also hire a tuning professional and a dyno to refine the fuel map to explore your ideas if you want to. You can have a temporary MoT-passing emissions map too, depending on the extent of your respect for the authorities, but you'll only need to do that if you're trying to use a full-race engine on the road.

What Ford want from ECU software is the opposite of what we as kit builders want. They want no warranty claims, low emissions, adequate drivability and enough power to ensure that their more expensive models using a particular engine have more power than the cheaper ones. We, on the other hand, want max power, adequate emissions, and some protection for the engine, but at a level much closer to its real limits.

WIRE DIETING, PIGGYBACKS AND STANDALONES

You can still recycle the standard ECU, injection system and wiring from the donor engine. This is apparently quite easy with Honda FireBlade bike engines and with Mazda MX5 donors, but extremely difficult with a 4.6 Ford. My 4.6 V8 Police Interceptor wiring loom would need something like 60lb of junk wire and widgets removed or dieted, and a reflash of the ECU to get rid of the PATS anti-theft programming and Ford's traction control, both of which can cause major problems if

left in the system. As it turns out, it's impractical to use the Ford ECU for Ayrspeed Cobras anyway, because Ford have been complicating the 4.6 control systems continuously from 1989 to 2007. Even using a standard ECU with the wrong year of 4.6 engine can cause problems.

If you can successfully separate the engine wiring and ECU from a donor car and get it working, you have the option of a piggyback ECU upgrade, which changes the stock ECU's programming and possibly gets you more power. It just plugs into the original ECU, so it's easy. Boy racers with Japanese cars are an easy target for bullshit, though, and some cheaper performance 'upgraders' delete some power at 2,000rpm, then let it back in with a bang at 3,000rpm. This feels like the engine has more performance.

Standalones are new high-performance computers, which completely replace the original ECU and engine wiring. They are inevitably fairly expensive, but simple and pure of purpose, and are designed to be fitted to racing and kit car engines by amateurs.

Omex offer good value with their standalone ECUs and engine management. Their processors are based on GEMS technology, which is used in WRC and for many major manufacturers' road cars: good enough. GEMS use Omex and kit cars as a useful testbed for new ideas. Omex boss Richard is hard to track down as he spends much of his time charging around racetracks in kit cars testing ideas. He says this is 'research'. I should coco.

Check out all your options before deciding anything, though. There's plenty of choice: I just happen to know Omex from way back, and trust them. Omex supply their software free - download it from the net at www. omextechnology.co.uk and check it out. You can decide whether to get involved with tuning the fuelling and ignition using the software,

The crank sensor normally uses some variation on a toothed wheel to tell the computer where the crankshaft is in its rotation, and how fast it's revolving.

Wherever the throttle shaft is to be found you'll find (or fit) a throttle position sensor.

There are lots of engine vacuum connections on this inlet manifold: one of them goes to a MAP sensor which tells the computer how much vacuum is being made.

or you can just use the default mapping that's already in the ECU.

WIRING AND SENSORS

For any application you'll need an engine wiring loom. You may be able to build one, but some sensor plugs are unavailable. I'm working with Omex right now on the loom for my 4.6 Ford V8 Cobra, using new plugs and sensors going directly into the engine sensor holes to replace the Ford ones that are unobtainable. Omex are set up for making custom looms. Sensors can have different names, but their functions are clear, and many just update old-fashioned engine controls. There are some options in how you fit sensors, but the smart move is just to plug the new loom into whatever sensors you have on your engine where possible. Replace them if they're reasonably priced. Fitting new sensors all round on a newly built car isn't a bad idea anyway, and you can keep the known-to-be-functional old ones for spares and substitution.

CRANK POSITION/ ENGINE SPEED

Typically an engine will use a crank position sensor (sometimes known as a TDC sensor) facing a trigger wheel with a series of

teeth. This pattern of tooth/gap/ tooth is sensed by the crank position sensor and is used by the ECU to calculate the speed at which the engine is spinning. The trigger wheel will also have a missing or extra tooth at some point that the ECU can use as a reference position so it can calculate where TDC is.

Ford use a pattern of 36 teeth, which means one every 10 degrees, with one missing for the reference point. The pattern used by Bosch is 60 teeth, so it has a tooth every 6 degrees, with two missing for the reference point. Although there is more data available from the Bosch type of trigger, and theoretically more accuracy, the rate of acceleration of engines is so low (in computing terms) that the extra information is not needed and the Ford 36-tooth pattern is more than adequate.

The sensors come in two forms. The most common is a magnetic sensor that generates its own voltages, and the other is a Hall Effect sensor that requires a 12V power feed.

All modern engines have some form of crank sensor, but for engines that have triggers that cannot be used by aftermarket ECUs, or for older engines with no trigger at all, Omex can supply general-purpose kits to bolt onto the crank pulley.

ENGINE LOAD

Throttle position is often used as the primary load sensor on naturally aspirated engines, assuming air density and pressure are constant, which we'll come to later. By knowing the throttle opening and the engine speed, we know exactly how much air will be coming into the engine, and so we know how much fuel to inject to match it. Accurate fuel delivery gives more power and better efficiency.

Turbocharged engines can't use just a throttle position sensor for load, as they have the variable of boost pressure to take into consideration, and so a MAP sensor (Manifold Absolute Pressure sensor) is fitted to measure this. This is fitted between the throttle plates and the engine and so senses the air pressure that the engine is working with, and the fuelling and ignition timing can be adjusted to suit the pressure. The MAP sensor does not replace the throttle position sensor – it is used in addition, as the throttle position sensor is still required to sense when the engine is idling and for acceleration fuelling (i.e. when the throttle is 'pumped').

MAP sensors can also be used to sense load on naturally aspirated engines, but they will

This is definitely a coolant temperature sensor, but it may be the one for the dashboard gauge and not the one for the computer: to find out, trace it to see where the wire goes.

The collector box on my Cobra's exhaust system came with a threaded socket ready for a Lambda sensor.

An air temperature sensor is a useful improvement to a basic kit car ECU setup: it allows the air/fuel mixture to be adjusted for air density.

just be working in the vacuum condition all the time, as there won't be any boost. They have the advantage of making idle control valves easier to work with (idle valves can be used on throttle-position-only systems, it's just more difficult), but they have the disadvantage of making the throttle response a little slower as they have to average out all of the pressure-pulsing that occurs in the intake plenum, whereas throttle position sensors can give immediate response.

Mass airflow sensors are used on nearly all current OEM road cars. This is because they can compensate well for engine wear over the lifetime of the engine, and for small differences between the engines coming off the assembly line – very important for manufacturers who need to guarantee the emissions standards of the engine in 100 thousand miles' time. For kit cars and race cars they are never used as they can be difficult to work with, give poor throttle response, and can be quite expensive.

CORRECTION FACTORS

Coolant temperature – a coolant temperature sensor is needed by the ECU mainly to add more fuel when the engine is cold (like

a carburettor's choke would), and also to control any other temperature-related functions around the engine such as radiator fans. It is also possible to retard the ignition timing if the engine becomes dangerously hot, but of course that won't happen to drivers who check their instruments …

Air temperature – as the air temperature changes, so does the density of the air. This is approximately a 3% density change for every 10 degrees of air temp change. If the ECU knows the air temperature, it is able to compensate for these changes by providing a different amount of fuel.

Atmospheric or barometric air pressure – as the atmospheric pressure changes, the density of the air changes, meaning a different amount of fuel is required to match this. Atmospheric air pressure changes are more or less zero in areas that are close to sea level and have no significant mountains. In the Rockies and the Alps, engines can run badly unless adjusted for the missing air, and high in the Andes they won't run at all without a 50% cut in fuel supply, as there's only 50% air pressure. The posher Omex ECUs have an internal barometric air pressure sensor, and the cheaper ones can have

them fitted externally if you live in Aspen. Or Machu Picchu.

AIR-FUEL MIX

Lambda or oxygen sensors (usually narrow-band) are mainly for emissions purposes, and they're fitted in the exhaust system close to the engine and before a catalytic converter if one is fitted. Two are needed for Vee engines, one for each bank. There is a perfect (stoichiometric) air-fuel mixture known as Lambda 1, which is 1 part fuel to 14.7 parts air. The Lambda sensor is basically a switch that tells the ECU that the exhaust gas composition indicates the fuel just burnt was too lean (too much air) or too rich (too much fuel), and the ECU adjusts the mixture to suit.

In the simplest modern set-up, you'll need an ECU, a load sensor, a crank position sensor, a coolant temp sensor, an air temp sensor and a Lambda sensor if you have emissions issues and need to have a catalytic convertor. Once you know what and where they all are, no worries.

Big power gains can be made by using a standalone with some engines, depending on how much the standard ECU programming has strangled them. Some engines are also strangled by small and restrictive inlet tracts, in which case changing the ECU program won't get spectacular power gains without intake mods as well. I'll find out what the Omex ECU and a better air filter and straight-through sidepipes will do when I get the Cobra on the rollers, but going up from around 250bhp to around 300bhp wouldn't be too much to hope for if the Ford ECU is restrictive.

Creative ECU options are available if you want them. All the inputs and drivers inside an ECU are interchangeable, and can be used for whatever you want – you might decide on water injection at max revs to avoid blowing a piston, so you would tell the program to instruct the driver in the ECU to fire the water injection pump at 8,000rpm.

The software that operates an ECU is available to us for customising engine behaviour, but you can't really get into the programs and rewrite them unless you have a relevant degree. However, people like Omex can and do rewrite the software, and in the case of Omex they do it because they're techies who love fast cars – so they're developing pretty much the systems we would want anyway.

Many of the functions of good software design are automatic. For example, a software-solved problem is that injectors operate more slowly if battery power drops. Injectors have a reaction time, an open time and a closing time, all of which vary slightly according to the amount of power supplied to them. A big electric cooling fan cutting in would therefore slow down the injectors and lean out the fuel supply, but good software compensates for this. The basic shape of the fuel map is already in the program, but the map is still available to be developed to suit the individual. Personally, I want my Cobra to be a fuel-miserly pussycat at 1,500rpm, but I'd also like all hell to break loose at 3,500rpm. With a mappable ECU I have full access to those options.

Control of idling and full throttle is already sorted by the software, but you can play around with torque curves and power bands by manipulating the fuel map. You might want max power in the middle of the rev range and an extra squirt of fuel right up at max rpm to keep the pistons from melting.

You can decide where the data points or instruction points go on the fuelling and ignition map, which is how you instruct the ECU to tell the injectors what to do. At idle and at full chat the computer doesn't need much information, so you don't need many mapping points there and you can concentrate them where you most need them. You need fine control at low throttle openings and when engines come on cam, so that's where you want lots of mapping points for accurate control over fuel and ignition. In general, setting mapping points at every 500rpm and every 10% of throttle opening position will be more than enough. The software, which you operate mostly by mouse-clicking on-screen multiple-choice boxes on a PC screen, also controls other aspects of the engine.

The shift light speed and the rev limiter are useful additions, as is the ability to adapt the tacho output signal to suit any electric tacho. Tachos can be slow to respond and horribly inaccurate, by up to 1,500rpm, so a shift light and/or a rev limiter based on the rpm information from the much more accurate crank position sensor could save you a huge bill.

There are usually two fan outputs. You can decide what to do with these – some say give the engine max cooling before it brews up, some say just use one fan and switch in the other if needed. Up to you. The software delays switching the fans off until the temperature has changed by several degrees, to avoid constant starting and stopping of the fan at around the right temperature.

Fuel injection remains essentially simple, but nowadays comes with complications. An injector is basically a small electrically operated valve attached to a fuel rail containing fuel under high pressure. It opens and allows a brief squirt of fuel spray into an inlet tract. Most standard modern injectors can spray enough additional fuel to cope with an extra 20% of additional incoming air and engine power, after which you need either to fit bigger injectors or additional ones. There's usually one injector per cylinder, although there are sometimes two. Single point injection (basically replacing a carb with a single fat injector) is now rare, and was only really used for small engines anyway.

Big injectors are difficult to control at idle, and tend to give dirty emissions. Using two smaller injectors and opening up the second one shortly before the first one maxes out is a good option and one that Omex use for high-boost turbo engines: lots of extra fuel is available, smoothly delivered.

Early injection systems used to fire all the injectors at the same time. This isn't as wasteful as it seems, as the fuel charge just waits in the inlet tract until it's drawn into the engine by the sinking piston. Later systems were semi-sequential, or batch fired. Later still, full sequential systems fire each injector for its individual cylinder.

There's no extra power available from sequential injection, just better NOx emissions. It's also complex to arrange, and it needs cam position sensors which seem to be generically unreliable. Semi-sequential injection is the preferred option for kit cars, as it's easy, reliable and clean enough for SVA and MoT emissions.

Ignition coils are still basically the same as ever, and you can still fire all the cylinders on an engine with a single coil, even a V8 – although coil recharge time is reaching the limit at high revs with a V8. You can also have more coils if you like – up to one per cylinder. There's no power benefit, but it gets rid of the HT leads and looks nice.

The wasted-spark system is still very common – all of the coils are fired, and the spark that reaches a cylinder full of compressed air and fuel ignites the mixture.

If you're running a turbo you need a nice fat spark, and if you're using nitrous oxide a big fat spark is really crucial, so stock coils and spark plugs may not be adequate.

Cam control is needed for variable-profile cams. Variable camshafts mean you can change the profile of the cam lobes that operate the valves from low and smooth for a silky idle to high and sharp for max power at high revs – all with the same camshaft. Changes in cam profile can be either stepped or smooth depending on the engine design. Control is electronic and is often achieved by controlling the valve that lets engine oil pressure change the cam's profile. Switched cam profile changes can be fairly violent – I've watched a Mini with a Honda B-series VTEC engine trying to jump off the dyno rollers when the cam change banged in. However, Honda have to set the cam profile change point quite high up the rev range to comply with drive-by emissions requirements, while Omex instruct their ECU to switch it at the most efficient and power-efficient point, which is at much lower revs – so the change is much less brutal and we get more power. K-series Honda engines have a smoother system in which the cam profile is constantly changing in response to a continuous data stream.

Full-throttle gear changing is software-controlled. It can be brutal on the transmission if it just cuts the ignition, but the Omex approach is to back off the timing to soften the bang. It still feels very weird not to back off the throttle while changing gear, though.

Traction control uses a similar approach – a slipping wheel will grip if power to it is briefly reduced. That's what you do when driving to get a grip on a slippy surface anyway, but the computer does it faster.

Air temperature sensors are more important on boosted engines, as turbochargers get literally red hot and much of that heat is transferred into the engine – hence the need for intercoolers, nitrous frost sprays, water injection and so on. Air temperature sensors are also useful on ordinary engines, because each 10 degree centigrade rise in air temperature decreases air density by 3%, and it all affects fuelling accuracy. The air in your engine bay is sucked into the engine many times over every minute, so using air from outside the car rather than from inside the engine bay is an excellent idea – after all, you don't need to feed air to the top of the carbs any more. Air temp sensors should be fitted somewhere in the air inlet path, and if your air intakes just use general engine-bay air, cable-tying the air temp sensor to the fuel rail will do well enough.

Mass airflow sensors are almost universal in production cars now, and they use either a flapper valve or variations in the temperature of a heated wire in the incoming airflow to get a more exact reading of incoming airflow. They can also compensate for engine wear, which throttle position sensors and MAP sensors can't do. A MAF will be found between the throttle plate and the air filter.

Knock sensors are used on later cars, but not usually in kit car applications. Detonation is fuel exploding rather than burning, and it sends an audible bang through the piston, rod and crank. Ford engines running on 94-octane Shell fuel in Hampshire don't need knock sensing, but the same engine running dirt-cheap supermarket fuel of 87 or even lower octane in Brazil needs the ignition knocked back a good

few degrees in order to survive. Choose and use a higher-octane branded fuel when giving your engine serious exercise, and there should be no problem.

Fuel pump control is an advantage offered by many ECUs – they run the fuel pump for a couple of seconds, then turn it off if the engine doesn't fire up. With the Omex ECU, if a fuel line splits or comes adrift and fuel starts gushing, it shuts off the pump, as well as shutting off ignition and power to the injectors.

Cold starting is easy on big old V8s, but can generate major rectal discombobulation issues on some new and more precisely built engines. The latest emissions-compliant engines are fussy and a pig to start from cold, but the Omex programs written for them achieve smooth and instant starts.

There are spare inputs and outputs on the ECU, and their use is only limited by your imagination – the full-throttle signal going into the ECU could signal the NOS system to fire, could raise a Porsche-style tail spoiler or could even operate an ejector seat for annoying passengers.

There is usually a data output that can be read on a PC, and Omex's bigger ECU offers half a megabyte of internal datalogging, very useful for any sort of competition. You choose how to use it, so you can collect information on revs, engine temp, whatever you fancy – either lots of short-term info which could help find a misfire at a particular rpm number, or a lower level of longer-term info such as the revs and fluid temperatures reached during a race. If you think this is all top fun and you want to read more, Dave Walker has written a book on engine management available from Haynes.

So, you can just plug and play and stick to the supplied fuel map, or you can go to town and squeeze more power out of your engine and more performance out of your car.

Chapter 13

Cooling

A serious mistake in the cooling department can ruin a brand-new engine in a matter of minutes, so let's not make any mistakes.

The basic principle of cooling engines is simple enough – air is passed through a radiator either by the movement of the car or by fan. The radiator is full of engine coolant which circulates around the block and the radiator, and this takes out the waste heat generated by all the explosions going on inside the engine.

Even air-cooled engines have radiators – they just use oil coolers instead of water radiators, as well as having cooling fins on the cylinders. People still build kits using VW and Citroën 2CV air-cooled flat-fours and twins, and unless the airflow and cooling are good, these still seize when they overheat. Taking the fan off a 2CV engine means relying purely on forward movement for cooling air, although most people with Lomaxes seem to get away with this happily enough. VW engines without good cooling seize regularly, but fortunately piston and cylinder sets for both are relatively cheap.

For nearly all other cars, we're looking at water and antifreeze circulating through the engine, radiator and heater matrix. (Tip – if an engine is brewing up a bit, turn the heater and its fan up full to add a bit more cooling.)

In engines with aluminium heads and/or blocks, the antifreeze also slows corrosion of the waterways, and the proportion of antifreeze to water must be concentrated enough or it won't do the job. Insufficient antifreeze means freezing coolant can also pop the water gallery core plugs out of the engine block, and can even split the block itself. Repairable if it's ally, generally scrap if it's not.

There are just a few important points that the kit builder needs to know about cooling systems. First, when using the car you have to be able to add coolant into the system at its highest point – so the radiator cap or header/expansion tank cap has to be above the engine and above the heater. You'll get airlocks otherwise. A bulkhead-mounted header tank can be a useful way to get the highest point raised above the engine. Zetecs in particular need care with this.

The radiator cap itself needs to be in good condition, and you'll see a marking on it that says 13lb or whatever. A pressurised system will reach a much higher temperature before it boils, which is why the cap has a spring on it. Modern systems run higher pressures, as that allows manufacturers to skimp on radiator size, which also suits us kit car builders – we like small, light rads.

The thermostat in the water system stays closed when the engine's cool, and keeps the coolant out of the radiator. The coolant in the engine just circulates around the central

The construction of any car radiator for water, oil or air is similar. Whatever is to be cooled passes through thin, flat tubes with lots of surface area, and the tubes are connected by lots of fins or thinner sheets of metal, which also draw heat out of the tubes as air passes through the rad.

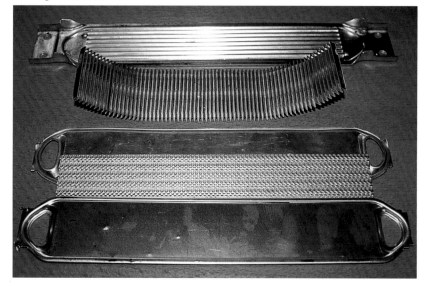

engine block until it gets above the correct operating temperature. Then the thermostat automatically opens and lets the coolant circulate through the radiator to be cooled down. Both thermostats and radiator caps are very cheaply made mass-manufactured disposables, so just because they're new, don't assume that they work.

Radiators take pumped water from a large-bore radiator hose and push it through very thin, flat brass or aluminium pipes with cooling fins attached to them. The maximum surface area is thus exposed to the passing air, and the air carries the heat away from the coolant. Aluminium radiators are more effective because aluminium disperses heat better than brass. They're also lighter, and more expensive.

An important detail is that radiators are by their nature quite delicate, and they don't like vibration and being banged about. When you fit one to a kit car, make sure it's not just directly bolted to the chassis without some sort of rubber mounting.

No radiator is very effective without lots of air passing through it, and this can be a problem for many kit cars. Cobras and their replicas have a problem because their relatively small engine bay is stuffed with a large V8. Cobras usually have two air intakes at the front and one on top of the bonnet, and there are also air outlets in the sides of the wings. At speed, this is usually enough. However, when stopped in traffic there's a very big engine in there, with two very hot four-pipe manifolds and a couple of gallons of nearly boiling water. Many owners run two cooling fans on their main rad, with one switched on by a thermostat and the other switched on manually when the temperature gauge needle starts creeping up towards the red and making them nervous.

Replica Cobras share the genuine authentic period cooling

Above: The author's Cobretti ran a 5.7-litre Chevy V8, and was cooled by the biggest radiator that would fit in the hole, aided by two Kenlowe fans. Once the initial leaks were sorted and the system settled down, it worked very well.

Right: Ayrspeed XK rads had to be made to fit a vertical rather than a horizontal hole. Top tank is from a dump truck, big fan is from Kenlowe. The system works better with the ally Rover V8 than it did with the huge cast-iron Jag six.

Below: This Ford BDA-engined Caterham sticks with a radiator size close to the original, and it's made from aluminium to increase its efficiency.

A Westfield used for racing combines the Cobretti and the BDA ideas – the biggest rad that can be jammed into the hole is also made of aluminium.

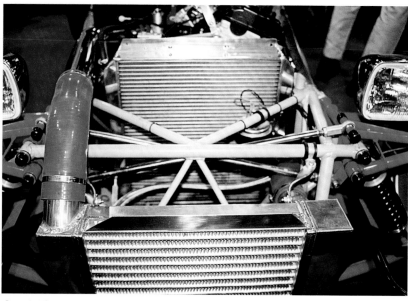

Overkill? No, this is a Dax with a bike engine and a turbocharger, and the front radiator is a charge-cooler to get the incoming air temperature down. Note the big tubes to allow free air passage.

It's possible to have a radiator made to suit, but expensive. Modern car radiators are often small and neat, and usually come with ally cores and plastic tanks. Check the scrapyards before coughing up big bucks.

This is the usual shape of an oil cooler, and it's exactly what the lower radiator hole on a 427 Cobra body is designed for.

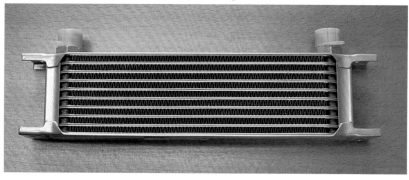

problems of the real thing, and the same can apply to other replicas. XK120s are a case in point – the same small radiator hole that helps to get seriously high speeds out of their aerodynamics also makes cooling marginal. The prototype Ayrspeed used to boil whenever it saw traffic, although everything was theoretically hunky dory. My own example, built later, has a huge radiator from a dump truck, and also has a big electric two-speed fan from Kenlowe. It normally runs on its low setting, which is enough to keep things cool most of the time. However, there's a panic-stations setting as well, so if the engine threatens to brew up big style, you can really give it some air. Kenlowe tell us that their newer generations of fans use much more effective curved blades, which do the job more quickly, more quietly and on just one speed.

My own cooling system was good enough for a skinny straight-six with one manifold, but when it comes to a short, fat V8 with two manifolds occupying most of the back of the engine bay, I expect to have to improve the hot air exits from the engine bay. The first

Mocal offer lots of different-shaped oil, air and water radiators from stock, which saves the cost of having one custom made.

Braided oil lines and radiator hose aren't of any real use, as your oil lines shouldn't be capable of chafing unless you've built some mistakes into the car. Regard them as engine-bay jewellery, and put them on the Christmas list.

phase is a fairly subtle half-inch slot along the rear edge of the bonnet, and if necessary, I'll also cut some louvres directly above the manifolds. With the standard XK bonnet, the air space above the engine has no outlet, and worse news is that the air intakes for the carbs are sitting in this hot air pocket. We definitely want cool and moving air up there, not heated and static air.

A second radiator is usually required if you use an automatic transmission, as the tranny fluid gets hot and bothered with all that thrashing and pumping. These autobox cooling rads are usually part of a composite main water radiator in the donor car, but kits will not usually have room for a big dual-purpose rad like that. Mocal can send you a complete kit including a cooling radiator, and all you have to do is cut off the steel fluid pipes coming out of the transmission and attach the rubber hoses to and from the tranny cooler with hose clips. There's minimal fluid pressure involved, so there's no problem. This also looks as though you have an oil cooler fitted, which immediately makes the car look more cool, as it were. In any case,

if you drive a 427 replica, there's a large hole in the body under the radiator gape that has to be filled with something.

Engine oil coolers are another line of defence if your main cooling system is marginal, but they are usually only of any genuine use when racing. Oil is thick when it's cold, but becomes thin and ineffective if it gets seriously too hot. Adding a cooler into the system on a regularly thrashed car can help keep the oil at the medium high temperature at which it and the engine work best. For a road car, it's okay to use an oil cooler, but best to run it with a thermostat so that it only works when the oil is genuinely getting too hot. If you run the engine too cold by over-cooling the oil, you'll pay for it in wasted petrol and in long-term wear.

Cooling the cabin can be a problem, although less so in the UK. If you insist on driving something like a GT40 or a Countach replica in Nevada, however, you have a real problem. The shape of a supercar usually involves a lot of sloping glass, which makes it an excellent greenhouse with you inside it. Unless you're a tomato, this is

not good. Closed cars of this type really do need air conditioning. Fortunately there are small, neat aftermarket systems available from the kit and classic car world, so it's not a problem to find suitable aircon equipment.

Even in an open-top car, the proximity of large engines, red-hot exhaust manifolds and your feet can be a problem. If you have no room or budget for an aircon system, it's possible to shift the heat elsewhere and gain a couple of extra bhp at the same time. If you wrap the manifold and the first part of the exhaust system with heat-reflective material, you can keep the engine bay (and footwell) temperatures reasonable. However, you have to be careful – the heat has just been shifted, not cooled, so the exhaust pipe where the wrapping stops is now almost red-hot. That's okay if it's well clear of the body and as long as it's not hanging from a rubber-ring mounting without some sort of double-skinned mount to dissipate the heat. Several GRP cars have caught fire before now due to inadequately thought-out manifold wrapping exercises.

Heaters are part of the cooling system too, and you need one

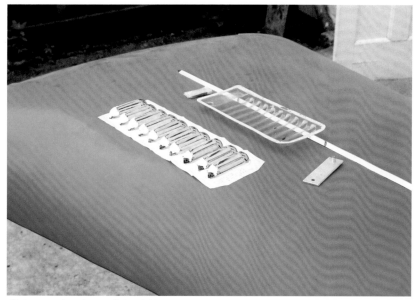

If the engine bay of the XK gets too hot with two V8 manifolds pumping out heat, a set of louvres can be cut to let the heat disperse. Chrome louvre trims will look quite good too, if a little tarty.

Using an oil cooler is always a good idea, but make sure it's on a thermostat so that it only works when the oil is seriously hot. Cold-running engines wear out faster.

to get past SVA if you have a windscreen, although an electric screen heater might get you through the test. In any case, if you propose to drive in Britain during the winter, let's face it, you're going to need a heater. The heater radiator or matrix is the same as the main engine radiator and fan, but smaller and in a box. It also corrodes and jams up with crud, just like an engine rad. Using an old Mini heater is an excellent idea as it's cheap, compact and effective. However, strip the heater

Flex-a-Lite make high-quality cooling fans in the USA, but they're having a lot of trouble with cheap Chinese fakes of their products. Be careful where you buy components.

and renew the matrix before fitting it, or it will let go halfway down to Le Mans and boil your legs, and then everyone will point at your pink knees and laugh.

Still at a rough concept stage, this will be the optional Ayrspeed cool bonnet. It's Ayrodynamic ... sorry. Major louvre action above the exhaust manifolds, and the air scoop will face the wrong way to extract air out of the engine bay rather than stuffing more in where it's not needed. It should help a little with economy and top speed too.

Chapter 14

Furniture and decor

One of the best interiors I've ever seen in a kit car was also one of the cheapest. It was in a Le Mans, which is a Ford-based Jaguar D-type replica that has sadly been out of production for some years: on its own terms, it was a nice little car.

The interior was ingenious. It had the big dials from a Series 1 XJ6, not restored but just used as found, and the seats were small buckets in black leather. The entire interior had been skinned in copiously riveted aluminium, and had then been given a light coat of matt-black spray paint from a tin, without any cleaning or preparation at all. The black had flaked off in patches, and people's feet and the safety harness buckles had scratched most of the black off the wide sills. For about £5-worth of black paint, the interior looked astonishingly convincing. If you didn't know it was a month-old fake, you would have sworn it was a genuine 50-year-old racing car. Until you heard the engine, anyway.

The point is that you don't need to spend a fortune to achieve a good interior. Most kit manufacturers offer vinyl or leather interior kits, and you can simply order one of these, fit it, and off you go. However, you can also mix and match as you feel like it, and you can choose whether to use new seats or adapt and re-trim existing donor seats.

There is one crucial mistake in trimming kit cars that I continue to make on a regular basis, and that is not trimming the car before starting to use it. Finishing it off later is the same concept as a rolling restoration on a classic car – it just never happens, and you finish up driving a rolling wreck instead. Once the car has got past the build phase and into the driving stage, there will never be time to trim it.

A glorious interior on a top-class Cobretti: red padded leather, chrome-bezelled matching gauges, a discreet sound system and a woodrim Moto-Lita wheel.

Here, at the other end of the market, a pair of standard-size production car seats have been squeezed into a tight cockpit. They don't look very convincing, but they're comfy enough to let you drive for hours without backache or bumache.

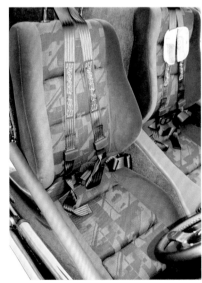

Above: The metallic blue paint on this Cobra could be teamed up with any of the trim colours shown – it's your own car so you can trim it in any colour you like.

Sound insulation for under the carpet and high-temperature, flame-retardant noise insulation for under the bonnet: the more layers, the less unwanted noise.

Manufacturers' trim kits make life easy – just drill the holes in the right place and pop them on. This is a Pilgrim door trim in leather, with a stretchy map pocket.

This Pontiac Fiero-based Ferrari replica has had the standard seats re-trimmed in black leather with red piping. The rather plasticky Fiero trim is a dead giveaway, so most Fierorarri owners go for a trim job.

Trim kits from manufacturers range from bargain plastic to fab leather, and anywhere in between. The better vinyls are very close to leather in look and feel, and Ambla in particular could just as well be suede. A cheeky but effective idea is to get some scraps of freshly tanned leather and staple them up under your seats – you get the rich smell of leather, but your (vinyl) seats won't go mouldy in an English summer. Leather actually has no smell of its own – it's the tanning chemicals that create the smell.

It's a good idea to approach trimming a kit car by starting with simpler shapes such as transmission tunnel covers and door trims. Trimming flattish panels is easy to do adequately, but hard to do well. Making a hardboard or thin plywood panel is simple enough, as is covering it with thin soft poly foam and a layer of vinyl or leather. Making it look slick and professional with deftly applied pockets and lines of stitching is another matter entirely, but worth a serious try.

Trimming is an area where traditional girly skills are of value, and even a partner who has no interest at all in any other aspects of the car can quite often be drawn into it and get involved. If you're not really committed to any particular colour or material, hand over those decisions. Be aware of the fate suffered by the late Brian Mumford of Mumford Musketeer fame, though: he asked his wife if she could possibly repair some of the holes in his overalls, and she asked him if he minded what sort of material they were repaired with. He said he couldn't care less, and as a result he finished up walking around covered in large patches of yellow flowers from a pair of discarded curtains.

For fixings and screws generally, use stainless rather than ordinary steel, as a kit car interior is not the driest place on the planet.

SEATS

Good aftermarket kit car seats
have tubular steel frames and
traditional padding, while cheaper
seats are made of trimmed solid
GRP buckets with bonded-in
wooden floors. Really cheapo
seats have thin and wobbly GRP
shells. You gets what you pays for,
but it's worth thinking about what
might happen to a very thin GRP
seat shell in a prang, or for that
matter in an SVA test.

It's possible and actually
quite cheap to make very tasty
traditional bucket seats yourself
from steel and wood: the first
Ayrspeed Six prototype's seats
had thick plywood bases, sheet-
steel backs and stiffening rims
round the backs, made of 1/4in
solid steel round tube or 'wire'
bent and welded on. Once
trimmed, these looked just like
the racing buckets on C-type Jags,
which was the idea. There

*For a vintage or post-vintage seat, use a plywood base and a steel back
with a heavy wire rim, then trim it or have it trimmed. These prototype
Ayrspeed seats were surprisingly comfy.*

*Nobody makes a replica steering wheel for a Porsche 356 kit car, but Porsche used to make them for Porsches.
This is a real one, refurbished and used very effectively to finish off a kit.*

Jaguar XK120 17in wheels are unobtainable for a sensible price, so I made a rim mould from a real wheel and got the spokes and centre laser-cut to fit a Moto-Lita boss – a coat of black Smoothrite and it looks pretty good.

wasn't enough bum padding for long trips, but one learns lessons about seat trimming literally the hard way. The backs were angled by making cardboard templates and sitting on the bases, then cutting the bottoms of the seat backs in crescent shapes so that they leant back at a comfortable angle when they were

Many kit car interiors are spoiled by plywood-coloured Moto-Lita woodrims teamed with walnut dashboards. The company will stain them down, or you can strip off the varnish and do it yourself. Just apply walnut stain until it matches, then re-varnish it.

screwed to the bases. There was hardly any padding on the seat backs, but they were surprisingly comfy nonetheless.

Trimming seats properly is a tricky business, although achievable with patience and care. The best way to approach it is to dismantle something like a Mini seat to see how it all works. There's a tubular steel bottom and back, and a stretchy rubber or sprung area across the bottom, with padding on top of it. The back is covered in more padding, but relies more on the tension of the material than on springs or stretched rubber sheeting.

In construction, the cover of a seat is like a sock – it's stretched over the frame and the padding and is then clipped, stapled and/or glued underneath – not that your socks are stapled or glued on, but you know what I mean.

Making a seat cover that fits a seat really well is a tricky biz, but not beyond the capabilities of the patient kit builder, particularly if they can get some help. A brand-new seat cover has to be designed accurately and made inside out, then reversed and fitted. Cutting a narrowed old seat cover to fit a narrowed seat frame is a good idea to start your upholstery career with. If that works, you stand a chance of making a good new one.

A disposable second-hand standard sewing machine may well survive this sort of use for long enough to finish an interior, but a second-hand heavy-duty one will still be around for the re-trim when you've saved up for some leather or been inspired by somebody who's done a whizzo job you want to copy.

I once visited a vintage Bentley restorer and saw some tarty but superb two-tone art deco sunset-themed door panels being recreated in leather, with alternating dark and light-green sunrays. They were for a rare and gorgeous car, one of the few remaining 1930s Bentley top hat saloons that hasn't

This Bennett Cobra replica from San Francisco has a bare racing interior. I'm not sure that mounting the rev counter and crucial engine-monitoring gauges so far from one's line of sight is such a smart move, though.

been retro-fitted with a replica Le Mans body, but it sank in with me that achieving a really fab interior is very possible. The principle is just the same for Beauford as for Bentley door panels. Okay, two-tone green sunbursts are a little over the top, but so's any half-decent kit car. That door panel was achievable by any of us with some leather, a sewing machine and enough patience.

Production car seats, sadly, are almost invariably too fat and too high off the floor for kit car use. One of the budget Seven-style manufacturers produced a wide-bodied car with optional donor Sierra or Vauxhall Vectra Recaros, which were the height of luxury compared with most kits, and which changed a Seven-style sports car into a genuine long-range tourer at a stroke. If you're comfy, you can drive quickly and well for ages.

This Dax has a very sexy office, finished in riveted and polished ally. The owner's dad is Dick Moss, a noted vintage Bentley restorer – so this Rush was always going to be a bit special.

A steel dash cut-out is a good idea, as instruments are easily earthed to it. You then only need one earth from the dash to the chassis. To trim it. a thin layer of soft foam plastic is first glued on to provide padding.

Next, cut around the holes and prepare a sheet of leather or vinyl with the holes cut out, but leaving enough spare to push through the holes and glue down.

Even in your usual skinny kit interior you can accomplish reasonably comfortable seats. A leather armchair with electric height, rake and reach that would cost £1,000 new is worth about £3 when you drag it out of a scrap Granada. The construction method is still the same – so you can strip it, cut the frame down, re-make the leather cover and possibly achieve some very fab seats for £9 including the glue. Skip the runners and bolt it to the floor so you can see through rather than over the screen. It has to be worth thinking about.

CARPET

Carpeting a car is one of the easier jobs, and amateurs can achieve a good finish. The suppliers at kit car shows have all the right glues and so on, and provided you make cardboard templates first and stick with the 'measure twice, cut once' rule as applied to household carpets, you should find that aspect of things amusing and satisfying.

The carpet panels will sometimes need to have cake slice shapes cut out of them to allow the carpet to curve around corners, and you'll have to use imagination when it comes to carpeting bumps. It could be regarded as cheating to cover up an unsightly junction of carpet ends with a big chrome ring and a leather gear-lever shroud, but what the hell, if it works.

Start with the tunnel, and leave about 1½in of overlap to go under the floorpan carpets. When it comes to the floor carpets, I'd recommend making them removable – so secure them with correct-coloured poppers on the floor. Interesting cars are rarely waterproof, and your floor carpets will probably spend some time drying out on washing lines – so don't glue them in place. This is definitely the case with Cobras – the more authentic the Cobra, the more persistent is the trickle

Above: Refit the instruments and clamp them all in place – you now have a nice padded dashboard for an XK. The main instruments are Series I XJ6, while the smaller ones are Series II.

The clever recycling of a Cortina instrument pod. This is actually all one pod, but the careful addition of bezels and dash cut-outs makes it look as though the instruments are all expensive separates.

of rainwater that creeps round the outside of the screen frame and dribbles down on to your knee. That's the front Cobra puddle – the rear one is caused by water trickling off the fat back arches. Some falls off the back of the

car, some collects and dribbles in under the hood.

Partly for that reason and partly for looks, it's worth trimming or binding the edge of the floor carpet in either leather or vinyl. It looks good and it stops the edge

fraying. The carpet itself should be expensive man-made material rather than wool. You don't want your pride and joy smelling like a wet sheep.

WEATHER GEAR

It is possible to make your own hood and sidescreens, but the chances of designing and making anything by hand that doesn't finish up looking like your mum's bra are not good. Even fitting a professionally made hood has its problems, mostly to do with heat.

When you're fitting a pre-made hood, be sure to do it in a hot garage with lots of fan heaters going. The material will stretch and flex better, and won't go baggy and horrible on the next warm day. Pull it tight when fitting, as it does stretch to some extent naturally. Use turn-button fasteners if you can, as the lift-the-dot ones always seem to become difficult as they get older.

With both the Midge and the XK, I've finished up using stiff sidescreens that stand on their own without the hood up. Keeping the sidescreens up and the roof down gets you out in the fresh air, but avoids the continuous battering from air coming round the windscreen sides, and makes touring more civilised.

A bezel and a pink CD transform a boring Mini instrument pod into a sci-fi fantasy. The blue and red side is temperature, and the red bit on the other side means no fuel.

Matched sets of American performance dials look the business on a modern kit, and it's always nice to know exactly what's going on under the bonnet.

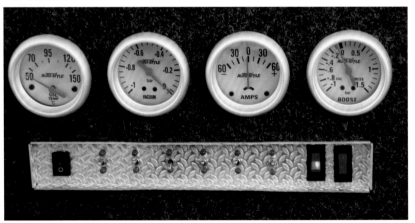

An inset central panel and a dash trimmed in two-tone green leather looks sexy as well as professional – simple ideas, but very effective and not much harder to make than a boring dash.

Some of the Sherpley Le Mans Bentley replicas are shaping up to look magnificent, with some serious work going into them. Leather buckets, fabric-clad bodywork and string-wrapped steering wheels.

Canvas or double-duck hoods are a lot more expensive than the usual black plastic, but they're probably worth it. They look better for longer, and they're also thick enough to help cut down road and wind noise.

WOODWORK

If you fancy the deep lustre of a walnut dash, you can cheat and skip all the ag of doing it the proper car trimmer's way by using the boatbuilder's method instead. Lightly rub down the fresh veneer to get rid of imperfections, then use a rag to apply grain filler against the grain. Lightly rub down again and then just keep slapping on more coats of polyurethane varnish every time the previous coat is dry. Don't bother sanding down between coats, just lather the stuff on. When it looks a few inches deep, use very fine wet-and-dry paper, wet and with a flat block, to flatten down the whole surface evenly, then use T-Cut to get the surface gloss back. Even with a walnut dash, don't be satisfied with the usual boring kit-car slab. If you design in a recess in the middle of the dash filled with maybe some machine-turned ally or another layer of veneered wood, the whole thing will look more interesting and more professional. Another tip is not to put too many instruments in.

Veneered woodwork along the door tops in the same colours looks fab too, but there's one detail that spoils so many kits, which is the inevitable light-coloured Moto-Lita woodrim wheel. The wheels themselves are lovely, but as standard they come in a light plywood finish, and look silly against a deep walnut dash. If you send the company a piece of dash in the right colour, they can stain the wheel to more or less match the dash. If you don't want to pay them to do this, you can do it yourself – just strip the varnish off, stain the plywood rim and re-varnish it afterwards, with as many layers as you have the patience to apply. Moto-Lita can also (off the menu) supply up to 16in thin-rimmed wooden wheels covered in black or coloured leather, which look the biz as well.

This budget Pilgrim Sumo interior matches beige interior vinyl with a similar-coloured hood to good effect. For light colours, plastic is more practical than leather anyway.

Chapter 15

Civilising the beast

A surprising number of kit car manufacturers worldwide get suspension details wrong, and the current SVA/IVA test makes no examination of rack height or the correct Ackermann angle (although woe betide anybody with a sharp-edged nut on a rear numberplate light). If you buy a kit that steers weirdly or handles oddly, the causes could be in the suspension design as well as in your execution of the build. Most kit car suspension works well enough, but getting one really set up properly can be a revelation.

As an example, getting the steering rack at the right height is tricky, and is more important than many people realise. If the rack height is wrong, you can get evil bump steer as the rise and fall of the wheel in its arc pulls or pushes on the trackrods. The steering will also kick like a Birmingham vindaloo, and will pose similar dangers to your trousers after a few corners. This isn't limited to small kit manufacturers – some pre-Wheeler TVRs had evil steering kick.

This chapter has been checked by the steely gaze of Gerry Hawkridge, maker of painstakingly accurate Cobra and Lancia Stratos replicas, who knows both the theory and practice of how to get suspension sorted out. He used to be a teacher, so sit up straight and pay attention.

As soon as your car is legally mobile, it should be taken to a four-wheel tracking centre to find out what's doing with your suspension settings, unless it uses pre-set suspension such as complete MG axles.

Tracking is the relationship of the front wheels to each other from the steering point of view. If the front wheels are parallel, the

Present and future generations of Hawkridges. The silver car is a 289 replica running on updated MG running gear and is powered by a Rover V8, while the yellow car is on pram running gear and is powered by feet.

119

Budget coilover shocks. The springs are detachable and easily changed, as is the ride height to some extent. Adjustable performance gas-filled dampers should be capable of being turned to both softer or harder settings than you want, to achieve the ideal shock rate.

Jaguar suspension can be adjusted for camber and castor by adding and removing shims. Match the new rack position to the original Jag geometry and you'll avoid bump-steer problems.

You can still buy replica Andre Hartford friction dampers, which combine with cart springs, cast-iron beam front axles and steering boxes to give you an authentic 1930s driving experience. It's a bundle of fun, but hard work.

degree of tracking is 0. Tracking is adjusted by loosening the securing nuts and lengthening or shortening the trackrods by turning them relative to the trackrod ends. The lengths of the two trackrods should remain equal, so if you want to add two

degrees, add one to each side. The rear end tracking can be out of line as well, and there may be adjustment or shimming available for that. On independent rear suspension, slight toe-in helps stability. If both tyres on an axle are wearing on the inside or the

Marlin have been making their own suspension components since the 1980s, so we can assume they've got it sorted out by now. Unequal length front double wishbones are almost universal for performance and kit cars.

outside, that generally suggests a tracking problem.

Camber is how much or little the wheels lean in towards each other. If the tops are closer together than the bottoms, that's negative camber. Negative can be a good thing, as it means the tyre and wheel tend to stay upright as the car leans over in a hard corner, and the tyre tread then makes good contact with the road. Too much negative camber causes excessive tyre wear.

Castor means the lean-back angle of the imaginary pin on which the front wheels swivel. No castor angle means the pin or axis point is vertical. More castor gives heavier steering and a stronger tendency for the wheels to return to the straight ahead position as you exit a corner. Insufficient castor not only stops this self-centring effect, but makes the steering feel woolly and vague. Fully adjustable suspension allows the castor angle to be changed by adding and removing shims to move the rod ends or wishbones back or forwards relative to each other.

The Ackermann angle starts getting out of the area where you can fiddle with it. As you turn a corner, the inner wheel must swivel to a different angle from the outer wheel. Don't buy a chassis from a manufacturer who doesn't know what an Ackermann angle is. You don't need to know how to calculate it, but he sure as hell does.

Rack height and positioning are critical. If the rack body is too short or too long, or the rack is positioned wrongly, the upward motion of the wishbones during a road bump comes through the steering wheel as bump-steer and/or kick. In practical terms, a very small change in rack position can make the difference between sublime and horrible steering, so be prepared to make arrangements for adjusting your rack position by shims or other positioning methods. If you think

Rose joints add precision and razor sharp responses to steering. Sadly, they also cost a bomb and wear out very quickly as dirt erodes the exposed metal.

Very low-profile Yokohama tyres stick to the road like glue and look dead sexy on big rims, but the lack of sidewall depth gives a rough ride compared with higher profile tyres, particularly on neglected roads.

you have a problem, any of the basic books on racing suspension and chassis design will bring you up to speed on the theory.

Rack ratios can also be changed to reduce the number of turns of the steering wheel required. This makes the steering sharper, heavier and quicker. Ford Escort high-ratio Quickracks are cheaply and easily available, but a

V6 Sumo owner found that one of these made the steering so heavy that he had to get rid of it and go back to a standard rack.

Spring rates and damper settings are critical to comfort and speed. Ferociously hard suspension makes you go fast for a short period, but you become so knackered after a short drive that a) you slow right down, or b) you

Engine bay insulation sheet absorbs engine and gearbox noise and cuts down the drumming from flat steel footbox and bulkhead panels.

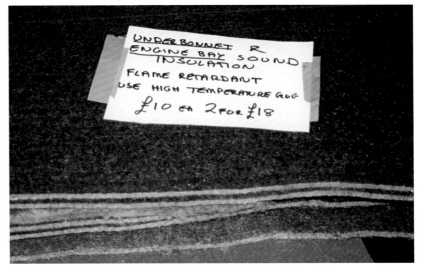

I picked up these Muff-Diver silencers and tailpipes for £20 from a Cobra owner converting to sidepipes. Keep your eyes open; there are some bargains about.

The ubiquitous Mini heater is still a good deal. Small and neat with an internal fan, and new matrices are cheap and available.

feel a strong desire to abandon the car at the roadside and get a taxi home. Colin Chapman's approach to designing the suspension for Lotuses was to go for long, soft springs and hard dampers. Ever heard anybody complaining about Lotus ride or handling?

If there is an option for softer springs with the kit you're buying, take it. When it comes to aftermarket sports dampers, their softest settings are often much harder than the dampers on a standard production car, and an average production car is twice the weight of a kit. AVO and Dampertech both advertise in *Kit-Car* magazine and sell to kit car people, so they'll have suitable dampers with the right valving to suit a lightweight application. AVO say that their 20 settings on a kit-recommended damper should go both softer and harder than you are likely to want, which is all you can ask. Don't chuck out the standard donor dampers without giving them a try first, though – if they're a bit knackered for a heavy saloon, they could well be just right to give a firmish ride on a kit car.

Tyre pressures are critical on any car, and the garage charts have no figures for kit cars. Your car is half its original weight, and its tyres may well be bigger than the originals, so your crucial contact patch where the tyre touches the road is all over the place. Too small and you'll skid, too big and you'll aquaplane. Even when experimentation gets you into the right ballpark with the pressures, you can either upset or improve various handling characteristics by adding or taking away a few pounds. Keep adjusting front and back until you've got the best out of it.

Engine tuning is not only important for getting the most power and economy out of your engine, it's also needed quite urgently on a new and modified engine installation to avoid potentially serious damage. If

CONDENSATE DRAIN HOSES

AIR CON KIT £479

£529

HEATER / AIR CONDITIONING UNIT

HOT WATER FLOW VALVE WITH CABLE

3 ROUND OR ~~ VENTS

REMOTE FAN SPEED AND TEMPERATURE CONTROL MODULE WITH WIRING

For anything with a roof that is to be used in the hotter American states, air con is essential. Modern aftermarket units can be diminutive, but still powerful enough to keep you cool even in Death Valley.

you've fitted a pair of K&N filters, you have increased the airflow by something like 40 per cent. If you don't introduce some changes in jets/needles/injectors/chips to tip in a matching increase in fuel, your engine will be running a very lean air/fuel ratio, particularly when it's high up the tacho. Any enthusiastic driving could well melt a piston.

A dyno session is relatively expensive, but it is the only way to get everything checked, adjusted and working 100 per cent. Once sorted, you are pretty well guaranteed to have the best power and the best economy you're going to get, and some surprisingly obscure problems can be identified with a well-handled scope – would you believe it can check individual cylinder compressions?

NOISE

With your suspension adjusted and tuned, your engine purring, your springs comfy and your dampers set just so, your next irritant could be exhaust noise. How much of this you want to put up with depends on how much you want to use the car. If it's just for quick summer blasts on the odd Sunday and you love the sound of a V8, go for the open sidepipes and to hell with it. You'll get huge roaring and blattering, you'll frighten babies and dogs and you'll set off car alarms just by driving past. However, you'll get a headache and one deaf ear if you try to drive any distance, and the undeniably delicious song of a badly silenced V8 will benefit everybody else rather than you: unless you're sitting in the

middle of the car you can actually only hear four of the cylinders. Quieter sidepipes are an option, but underfloor systems can offer lesser but better-quality noises. What you really don't want is booming or resonating when you're cruising. After becoming bored with the loud exhaust droning noise on my six-cylinder Triumph-based Midge, I finally added a second silencer into the system to act as a resonator box. That finished up sensibly quiet, but really a little too quiet. The same happened with my original single XK exhaust – in the end I settled on two Cherry bombs welded into the single exhaust pipe, one as a resonator and the other as a silencer. That gave a nice rich baritone thrum but didn't drone at me on the motorway. Of course, the most familiar

This Nostalgia XK interior is the biz. Nice comfy original-style leather seats, lots of thick carpet, map light, clock, chrome bezels on Jag clocks, some tasty walnut and the steering wheel stained down to match. This one has an XJ40 engine, so it probably starts without Eezistart and doesn't even rattle. Nice.

noise from the Jag exhaust was stumbling splutters and then silence as it coasted to a halt yet again, followed by the clonk of the bonnet release cable, and shortly afterwards by the piquant beeps of my mobile 'phone ringing the AA. Again.

The exhaust on the revitalised V8-powered XK consists of two four-into-one MGB V8 block-hugger headers, then two 2.5in pipes going under the gearbox, then two yard-long 3in bore Muff Diver silencers with chrome downward-facing tips. With 2,000rpm for 60mph, the engine just grumbles fairly quietly to itself when cruising, but if it needs resonator boxes or a balance pipe between the systems it will get them.

Cockpit noise can be deafening and very tiring, particularly with steel internal bulkheads and floors. It's worth putting some effort into deadening unwanted noise inside. Nice thick carpet

with underlay certainly helps, but it has to be worth sticking sound-deadening mat on some of the large flat steel panels that are such a familiar feature of kit car chassis.

MUSIC

Fitting a sound system is probably the last thing on your mind at this stage, but consider this – coming back from the Nürburgring is a long day's drive, and is immeasurably enhanced by alternating Robert Plant, Billy Talent and Vivaldi, as long as you can hear them properly. I consulted *Car Audio* magazine on the basic principles of a system for a noisy open-top car, and they had some interesting things to say. First, use a lot of good-quality power in the main amp to keep the sound pure at higher volume – watts RMS is the only figure worth listening to. Secondly, don't bother with two bass speakers, as you won't be able to hear where the

bass is coming from anyway. Just use a single central bass speaker or boom box, which can even go in the boot if you've got one. Thirdly, use some good mid-range speakers or mids with central tweeters, fitted in sealed custom boxes on the footwell sides with the cones tilted upwards and backwards towards you. (With strong grilles to stop you kicking them in on day one.) Fourthly, use four tweeters, mounted high in the cockpit, and fifthly, rubber-mount CD changers and heads, as even the subtlest kit car suspension tends to be pretty brutal compared with a production car.

It is possible to get a kit car quiet and smooth as well as fast, but if you want your action raw and nasty, build a cheap Locost with a screaming, hysterical bike engine and no trim at all – you're a kit bunny so you can make up your own rules and just do whatever you like.

Chapter 16

Bumf and emissions

UK BUMF

The British Single Vehicle Approval (apparently now to be called Individual Vehicle Approval) regulations were the usual shambles that results when the British Government attempts anything, and the rules finally lurched into effect after a number of long delays. The continuing delays were very bad for the kit car industry, as nobody wanted to buy a kit and then find it would be illegal to use by the time they'd finished it.

The regulations in the end are pretty ferocious, and go into absurd detail: it's apparently dangerous not to have a soft radius on the inner edge of a rear bumper, and the slotted screw heads on rear numberplate lights are also regarded as dangerous.

Some aspects of SVA are so idiotic they approach surreal comedy. The sharp edge of the rim on an exterior-mounted spare wheel is dangerous and requires covering in case you reverse into a pedestrian, but the other four identical wheels spinning on the car – which might actually hit a pedestrian – are regarded as safe. Filler necks must be narrow to avoid accidentally using leaded-fuel petrol pumps … which are all gone. (On the same basis, we had better close down London's theatres sharpish to avoid the spread of bubonic plague.)

However, on the positive side it's unlikely that a brand-new production car would pass an SVA test, so it must inspire confidence that the kit industry can jump successfully through a very complicated bureaucratic hoop.

Rather like annual MoT tests, the knowledge and attitude of those who operate the test centres is of variable quality, and if you join a local kit car club you should find out what sort of service the local test centre provides. If it's unsatisfactory, go somewhere else.

The test itself will take several hours, and you can expect to have to return the car one or more times to get through the whole test. Your emissions might be 0.5 per cent over the limit, or you may have left a dangerously sharp-edged nut on the suspension.

The test is currently being extended, at the usual public expense, to cover the few dozen three-wheelers registered every year, but after that we can expect further fiddling with the main test as the civil servants concerned hunt around for something to keep them looking busy.

Kit-Car magazine publishes sets of SVA regulations as they change, and the government's manual costs £37. *Totalkitcar* also offers SVA advice, and a very useful guide to the complex official bumf and forms required to achieve registration once the SVA test is passed. If you would rather eat your own arms than spend hours scribbling potentially wrong answers in lots of little printed

The edges of these replica Cobra rear overriders are too sharp to be safe, so they have been edged with adhesive chromed plastic trim. They're now SVA legal.

This fork may at some stage form part of a kit car's picnic basket cutlery, so I've made it SVA safe as well; you can't be too careful.

boxes, Paul Jepson on 0118 984 2303 or 0778 702907 runs a useful and inexpensive service that will do all that business for you. *Kit-Car* magazine also regularly publishes an SVA guide. Rather than go into detail which will probably be out of date by the time you read this, I'll go through the basics of what you'll need to comply with.

1. Anti-theft
You need an anti-theft device. It seems that an original steering lock from a manufacturer's original steering column is OK, and some people have passed with just a battery kill switch.

2. Demist/defrost
If you have a screen, you effectively need a heater and blower to defrost it. If available, a windscreen with heated electrical elements will also pass.

3. Wipers
A windscreen also requires wipers that self-park and work within the correct range of speeds. There is now apparently a pressure test carried out on the screen washer pump.

A sensible SVA requirement. The seat belt upper mount on this Royale is at the correct height to spread a crash load across the ribs rather than breaking the collar-bone.

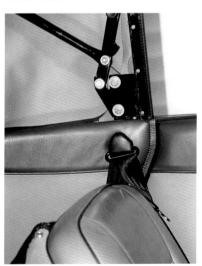

4. Seats
Seat frames must be well secured, and adjusters must work correctly.

5. Seat belts
Belts and anchorages must be secure and at the correct angles and heights. (This can be tricky with Cobra replicas, but can usually be solved by using central upper seat belt mountings and by keeping the seats low.)

6. Interior fitting
No sharp edges or switches are allowed inside the car, unless close to the steering wheel, which can't have sharp edges or dangerous holes in the spokes. Dangerously sharp gauge bezels are also out.

7. Suppression
HT ignition leads must be marked as being suppressed.

8. Glass
Windscreens must be British Standard marked or E-marked.

9. Lights
This can be a pain. Headlights must be the correct height, which

is tricky with some Cobras. Indicators on Seven-style cars may have to be out on long stalks. Measurements are taken from the very outside of the mudguard rather than the body, and are not necessarily sensible. Everything has to be correctly E-marked. You need a fog light, which must also be in the correct position.

10. Mirrors
These must also be correctly marked, and are checked for field of view. Many Cobra replica builders fit mirrors to the top of the screen to comply. They must flip back if hit; and watch for 'dangerous' sharp securing screws even on E-marked mirrors approved for use on production cars.

11. Tyres
Tyres must be correctly marked with speed ratings that match the vehicle's top speed.

12. Latches
Doors must have double latches. Suicide (rear-hinged) doors must have safety bolts and an audible warning device. There doesn't seem to be a requirement to have

It's still possible to build your own car from scratch and get it through an SVA test, but it requires careful study of the rules at the design stage.

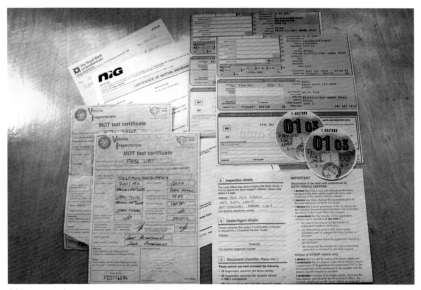

You can change a new registration number or a retained period one for a numberplate with no year letter, or for an Irish plate which has no identifiable year letter – there's bumf and tax involved, but not too much.

a double catch on the bonnet, though – which is mad.

13. Exterior projections
Dangerously sharp petrol caps on rear wings or tonneau panels are out. Eared wheel spinners are out. The sharp edges of wheel rims are not dangerous when on the axles, but become dangerous when mounted on (the back of) the body: you need to cover up a spare not just with a cover but with a wooden or hardboard circle under the cover.

14. Steering
Not a check for dangerous steering geometry as you might have hoped, but a check for soft steering wheels with no holes through which you can put your fingers, and a collapsible steering column. Self-centring steering is now part of the test. If your geometry is challenged by this, pumping your tyres up harder might help.

15. Design and construction
The examiner looks at the chassis and suspension, and checks that rotating components don't foul anything. Fuel filler tubes are checked for the correct diameter, and the system is inspected for

leaks. The electrical system is examined visually for suitability and secure fastenings.

16. Brakes
A visual check of the system, including servos. Low fluid warning/system failure warning, side-to-side and front-to-rear balance are checked, and main brake and handbrake efficiency are checked on rollers. Front-to-back balance is important – front brakes must always lock up before rear brakes. Brake hoses and even servo hoses need to have BS markings.

17. Noise
Silencers and exhaust system are checked visually, then tested with a decibel meter. The noise limit is 101 decibels.

18. Emissions
This test relates to the year of manufacture of the engine – later engines face fiercer requirements. However, Fisher Sportscars' aftermarket catalytic convertors can clean up most engines enough to get through.

19. Emissions, diesel
Diesel? What?

20. Speedometer
Speedometers can be inaccurate in that they give a fast reading, but must not read even 1 per cent slower than the true speed. Crucial in any case because of tax bandit cameras.

21. Design weights
The design weight of the vehicle and the front axle should be provided by the manufacturer, but can be calculated if not.

Kit-Car's Nigel Dean has some useful advice for approaching an SVA test. Take documented proof of your engine's age – the fact that everybody knows it's been unavailable new since 1975 doesn't count for officials.

Choose a low but realistic max-power rpm to declare for your engine, as the noise test is carried out at 66% of that rpm number.

Always ask for a morning slot, as test centres don't like starting tests in the afternoon.

Make sure your car is clean and shiny and looks as though it ought to pass.

Take tools, bits of rubber, cable ties and so on in case you get the chance to cover forgotten sharp edges or secure loose pipes or wires.

Keep any thoughts you might have about the test or the civil service to yourself, and be cheerful and helpful.

Fill the car up with petrol to get the design weight right.

Hire a trailer, rather than risking making the drive to the test centre your car's maiden voyage.

Check that the chassis number is the same on the car and the bumf.

Finally, relax – the worst that can happen is a retest, which will probably happen anyway.

Much of the SVA test is rather silly. If you run over a pedestrian with a Cobra replica, the last thing they are going to worry about is being cut by the not even very sharp edge of the rear over-rider as they emerge from beneath the back of the car. The silly aspects of the test bring it into contempt, and many kits are temporarily disfigured with correct test-passing bits and pieces and then restored the day after the test. At the time of writing, stuck-on temporary protective SVA measures such as bits of rubber hose taped over Cobra bonnet latches are illegal, but any temporary SVA bodge that is screwed on and requires a tool to remove it is regarded as SVA legal. An interesting point is that it's completely legal to buy a new Vauxhall Vectra and fit it with wire wheels and lethal winged spinners, so how would it be illegal to do the same to a newly tested and registered kit car the day after the test?

Overall, however, the concept of individual kit car testing has been a good thing, as any car that gets through it is well sorted out.

Once the test has been passed, registration beckons. At the moment the situation seems to be as follows:

You can have a new-car registration number if everything on the car but one major component, usually the engine, is new. The rebuilt component must be remanufactured to as-new specifications with receipts to prove it. Also needed are a Declaration of Newness (form

Filler caps these days are usually flush. They're SVA compliant this way, so that if you reverse into any pedestrians, you won't scratch them as they roll over the fuel cap.

V267), an insurance certificate (you can insure the car on the chassis number), the SVA certificate, and enough money for a registration fee and six months' tax. Some civil servants believe you also need an MoT for a new registration: you can argue with them, or you can just go and get one. In any case, it's not a bad way of checking brake balance, headlight aim and so on.

Donor-based cars based on a single donor can get an age-related registration plate with an SVA certificate, a V55/5 form, proof of insurance and an MoT.

Make sure you have receipts for absolutely everything.

If you are unable to establish with paperwork the source and age of the components of your car, it may be registered with a non-changeable Q-prefixed number plate. This means it's officially a vehicle of indeterminate age. It's not a big deal if you're keeping the car, but people in general don't like Q-plates, so it could hurt the value if you come to sell.

If you use an unmodified original production manufacturer's chassis with an existing identity, you don't have to bother with any of this, as the car retains its old identity. It's legally treated in the same way as a hearse or a motorhome: all it needs is a

Dax's new Camber Compensation suspension design still needs its exposed nuts covered with plastic condoms for safety and SVA paperwork.

current MoT. This works with JC Midges built on Triumph chassis, specials built on old Bentley chassis and so on, and some beach buggies. Some Speedster replicas with slightly modified VW floorpans retain Beetle identities: I won't tell if you don't.

Get some numberplates made at your local accessory shop (to the correct Euro size and with the correct Euro numerals and letter fonts, of course, and nowadays also remembering to provide the correct documentation to be allowed to buy them), bung the tax disc inside a sealed motorbike tax disc holder to make it more difficult to steal, and off you go.

In order to get a tax disc you need insurance. Fortunately the kit car mags are full of insurance ads, as kits are profitable business. People don't spend two years building a car then get drunk and stuff it into a wall, and personal injury claims from passengers are also low. There's lots of competition for your insurance budget, so shop around. Basically, the bigger the engine and the lower your age, the more your insurance is going to cost.

NORTH AMERICAN BUMF

An overview of bumf in the States is more complicated, as each state has its own bureaucracy. However, California is pretty ferocious on emissions in particular, which is perhaps not surprising in view of the state of the air in Los Angeles. The California Bureau of Automotive Repairs, the Environmental Protection Agency and the South Coast Air Quality Management District all have an avid interest in smog emissions, so life for kit cars is likely to get more difficult rather than easier.

LA-based title and registration specialist Larry Marsh (916 501 9549) makes a living by helping people through the paper trail to get their kits on to the road.

In California, the recent Senate

Bill 100 showed a little sympathy and encouragement to those who recycle old Mustangs back into new Cobra replicas. Each year, 500 replica kit cars can be allowed through on the basis that they are tested according to what they look like – so a replica of a 1966 Cobra would be regarded as a 1966 car for emissions and other purposes, i.e. no problem at all. Big block, big carbs, big exhausts, no cats. In 2002, it took until September for these 500 opportunities to run out, so it's not too long to wait in the queue for the following year. However, if No. 501 wanted to get on the road in the same year, he would need to register his car as a specially constructed new vehicle and fit it with electronic fuel injection and catalytic convertors to comply with that year's emissions regs.

There are some legal relaxations for companies making less than 500 cars a year, and those apply to individual car-makers as well. The major manufacturers have very serious rules to obey involving crash testing. A nice thought is that the only car ever to have been driven away after a 30mph concrete-wall crash test was a kit car.

The typical paper trail for a kit builder in California starts at the Bureau of Automotive Repairs, who send you to the California Highway Patrol, who carry out a safety inspection and issue a VIN number. You take the VIN number to the Department of Motor Vehicle Inspection, together with all receipts collected in its construction, and they levy taxes on the value of the car as registered, and any other tax they can think of. You also pay sales tax, which is presumably an additional tax on selling the car to yourself, as you already paid sales taxes on the car's components when you bought them. The usual damage is about 10 per cent on average, and then you have the title and registration, and off you go.

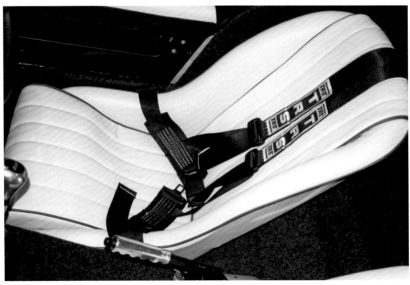

Cheap seats (not this one) can be too floppy for an SVA pass, and must be located on steel rather than GRP. Harnesses must be mounted high enough for collarbone protection.

At least you know that a kit with an SVA test pass has been far more rigorously inspected than a brand-new production car.

In open-top cars, tax discs are vulnerable to thieving, so it's a good idea to mount them in a motorbike-style holder and bolt it on to the car.

Many people choose to use an expert like Larry, who doesn't actually bend the law but knows how to help people to avoid giving the wrong answers to questions, and who can find easier ways of achieving the desired results than somebody new to the game. For instance, getting Alabama paperwork can make life easier and cheaper, but Alabama title isn't accepted everywhere, and in any case the right words have to be painstakingly prepared in the right order, or the whole pile of bumf can be thrown out.

Body conversions such as Ferrari replicas on existing car structures such as Fieros keep life nice and simple, as they are simply tested as the same vehicle with a body conversion. If your 365GTB lookalike is a skin job on an '86 Fiero, then '86 testing and emissions regs apply.

When it comes to Canadian bumf, selling completed kit cars in British Columbia is such a nightmare that Intermeccanica in Vancouver don't even bother trying – they just export their Speedsters and Kubelwagens straight down to the States. Rather a shame for the Canadians, as these are excellent cars. By contrast, the paperwork on a home-built kit in Calgary, Alberta was no bother at all for Darcy Hrychw, who built an impressive

Hummer from a Chevy Suburban. The local DMV and police checked the car for basic safety and mechanical condition, gave him a tin plate with his VIN number on it and wished him happy motoring.

EMISSIONS

The amount of air pollution produced by motor cars is tiny compared with what is produced by millions of farting cows and the dirtier industries, and the amount of crud produced by weekend fun cars is tiny compared with that of commuters. If you feel guilty about running a big-block 427 with open headers and a double-pumper for a few miles a week, balance it up by becoming a vegetarian. In any case, the energy used in building a new car is vast compared with its lifetime emissions, so anybody recycling a car built for a ten-year life into a kit car with a 50-year life is doing the world a huge favour anyway.

The propaganda put out by both the car industry and the green industry is unreliable, and political decisions are made by people who don't listen, advised by people who don't know what they're talking about, based on two sets of opposing half-truths.

Nobody mentions that causing massive industrial pollution damage by ordering a brand-new production car while your old one still works has to be the most serious environmental crime an individual can commit, but there you go. Turn a Jag into a Cobra replica and save the planet.

As mentioned earlier, recent bad news for German car enthusiasts became good news for UK kit people, in that aftermarket cats are now compulsory on all cars driven in Germany – even vintage and classic cars. Retrospective legislation like this has not happened so far in Britain, but the German rules are likely to be enforced in the UK before too long. The up side

of this is that you can now get a cat and Lambda sensor to fit any car exhaust, and even a dirty old Pinto with two spitting 45DCOEs on the side can be got through UK emissions testing.

Using older engine blocks can also get you around some of the emissions rules, as the emissions requirements are usually based on the date of the engine's original manufacture. You will require proof, but that can be achieved with reference to the manufacturers and to books on the subject. If you want serious race-style power, a forest of carb trumpets and wild cams with buckets of overlap you would be best to start with a pre-1972 engine block, for which the UK annual emissions test is whether it emits visible smoke. Sadly, my XK failed even that, before the V8 replaced the Jag sixes.

If you're starting a build soon that you would spread over a few years of evening and weekend pottering, you would be wise to look ahead at emissions and the EU. The most powerful nation in the EU is Germany, and the French tend to tag along after them. The Germans have decreed that all cars driven in Germany must have a catalytic converter: even an 1899 Benz, comically, would require a cat on its tailpipe. If the Germans decide that all cars in the EU must have a cat, that's what will happen. No big deal, as long as you've left space for a cat in your car.

Oddly enough, I was in on an early discussion of SVA policy, in which the Brits were getting advice from German TUV engineers. The Brits were civil servants, proposing the sort of nitpicking over sharp-edged number plate light nuts that eventually became the SVA test, while the Germans were qualified engineers trying to get them to forget about the trivia and concentrate on achieving basic safety. That was one of the weirder days of my life.

Chapter 17

Pride and joy

There are as many reasons for building your own car as there are kit car enthusiasts, so there's no such thing as a representative story. Here are six very different cars and builders, who have all got what they wanted out of building their cars, in their own individual way. They're not the absolute best or the most expensive or the fastest – they're just typical cars picked at random from a summer's shows in Britain and America.

AUBURN SPEEDSTER

John Boyd's Auburn Speedster replica was built 22 years ago, and has still only covered 6,000 miles. That sort of tippy-toe mileage wasn't planned, but John and his wife Sylvia finished up living in all sorts of different places such as India and Australia, and the Auburn just sat in a garage in Pacific Palisades waiting for them to retire and start having some fun with it. They've now done just that, and I caught them at the American Handcrafted Auto Association's annual Spring show at Knott's Berry Farm in LA, where they won two large and well-deserved trophies.

The Speedster kit was by California Custom Coach, in Pasadena, California. John says the kit components were of excellent quality, apart from the build manual, which was a dozen or so typed sheets with hand-drawn scribbles as illustrations. He threw it away and got on with the job himself. Fortunately, the concept of the car was simple – take a full-size 1974 Ford LTD, throw the bodywork away and then fit the replica Auburn bodywork to the chassis and running gear. It's never as simple as that, of course, but it does save a lot of hassle if all the mechanicals have worked together before.

The car is simply gorgeous. There's no way anybody on a normal income could afford a genuine Auburn Speedster without selling their house, but the kit got John a lot of the way there without breaking the bank. A single donor also allows you to spread some of the cost over a few years by picking a donor car in good mechanical shape and just using stock second-hand running gear while you work on a serious motor at your leisure. Mind you, this car doesn't really need an uprated motor. Rather than running a more sensible 351 Windsor in the car, John opted for the big-block 429 Ford. When he was 22 years younger and starting the kit, massive power was the natural choice to make, but nowadays better gas mileage would be nice, and a small-block would be plenty as far as power goes. The original LTD weighed 4,200lb, but the Auburn weighs 'only' 3,000lb – so there would be no shortage of grunt even with a few litres missing.

Mind you, the real purpose of such a car is to cruise around enjoying the California sunshine, not to go charging around burning

John Boyd pops his hood to show us the big-block nestling in his vast engine bay. A 351 would have been plenty, but as Carroll says, too much is just right.

The Auburn replica's chest-high radiator grille is as imposing as the real one was 70 years ago – but this time round you could possibly own one.

The chromework on this replica is gorgeous, but building any car to this standard is not going to be cheap, even if the donor car is an old Ford wagon.

Most of this vast car is wasted space – the interior is snug and the luggage space is laughable – but the golf club compartment in the side has been faithfully reproduced.

rubber. There's more than enough power for effortless progress, and the big displacement means the exhaust note is deliciously deep and burbly.

From the outside, the replica looks spot-on to anyone but an Auburn devotee. The chromed Auburn bits, rather like XK Jaguar brightwork, are still available as exact replica parts, which are beautifully made and expensive. The inside of the car is not faithfully accurate – it was just designed and trimmed the way John fancied it. The wheel is a small but stylish Nardi, the gear lever is actually a disguised auto shifter, and the instruments look relatively modern. There's a stereo, too. It was just the shape of the body that really got John going all those years ago, so the authenticity of the cabin was less important. Still, if he starts spotting the odd period instrument and perhaps a nice banjo steering wheel at autojumbles, I wouldn't be entirely surprised to see the car back at Knott's Berry Farm in a couple of years with a Clark Gable look to the interior as well as the exterior.

RICKMAN RANCHER

Des Haslam's Rickman Rancher is the industry's kit camper, and offers incredible value compared with any commercial camper or motorhome. The prices of any newish commercially made camper are based on freshly retired and relatively wealthy people buying them, so although they're basically just a van with windows, a cooker and comfy seats, they cost an astonishing amount of money – £40,000 for a small one isn't unusual.

Any competent kit bunny can fit out an interior no bother, so the Rickman Rancher was a sad loss to the kit world when the company stopped production. The Rickman Owners' Club now has the rights to the design, though, and this is the first of the new generation Ranchers.

Des is delighted with it, and says the simplicity of the whole thing is one of its joys. The donor vehicle is rear-wheel-drive Ford Escort, which keeps things very cheap and cheerful. Rickmans (Rickmen?) aren't very fast, but that's not the point – they get around okay if the

Des Haslam gets a lot of fun out of his Rickman camper, or mini-RV. Having enjoyed building it, he can now get away every weekend in it.

gearing's reasonable, although in use, the Escort rear axle has proved to be not quite up to the job. Des has had two bearing failures on Escort rear axles, and in one case the wheel and halfshaft went wandering halfway across the road before he realised there

The Rickman Rancher is a development of their neat, Escort-based Jeep, and as well as a mobile home it provides a very useful, cheap and practical everyday vehicle.

The fitting-out of a camper is completely open to your own ideas. Using office carpet on the ceiling is a cheap and attractive solution, and cuts down noise and condensation.

Tony Icke has spent 2,000 hours pottering quietly away over five years to achieve this delightful Gentry MG replica. His secret is to commit to doing something every day, even if it's something tiny.

was anything wrong. However, kit people are not fazed by details such as wheels falling off, and the Rickman Owners' Club has discovered that the Bedford Midi van axle fits a treat and doesn't break at all, as it has much bigger bearings.

Building one of these kits is a doddle, according to Des – he got this one rolling in a weekend, and it passed its MoT test in 40 hours. Because it's a motor caravan, it's 'coach-built' – so it doesn't need an SVA test, just a straightforward MoT. He's been fitting it out since, and it's now perfectly usable for weekends away, although there is some detailing still to be done.

The quality and design of the GRP from Rickman was always excellent, which of course makes life easier. From the financial point of view, there aren't many things cheaper than a tatty old touring caravan, and nearly all cheap old ones will contain a perfectly good cooker, sink and all the pipes, brackets and hinges you could want to fit out a kit camper.

If you want to mess about with it more fundamentally, the Rickman chassis allows plenty of

room for different ideas, and Des is thinking about changing the entire concept. There's no reason why there shouldn't be a whole front-wheel-drive subframe in the front end. This would allow much bigger, modern and more efficient engines with a choice of petrol or diesel, and a dead axle and flat floor at the back, giving more room inside. It's a kit camper, so by definition, Des and his ilk can do whatever the hell they like with it. There's even room for a V8 . . .

GENTRY TF

Tony Icke's Gentry represents an investment of relatively little money but a vast number of hours. Like the similar Midge, you don't just assemble a Gentry kit, you have to make the parts first. Tony has put 2,000 hours into this car, and it shows. The project was started in 1994 and took five years to complete. Getting one of these time-heavy kits finished can be a big psychological challenge, as so much effort goes in but no results are quickly visible.

A friend of mine started building one of these 25 years

ago, and it's only now being dragged back out of his garage to be completed after a 15-year pause. It was a kit when he started it – now it's a barn-find classic as well.

The way Tony kept his project on track was to do a little bit every day. Even if it was just half-an-hour or so spent on cleaning or tidying things up, making the commitment to give it a little daily effort kept the build from stalling. The mechanical basis of the car is the rear drive Ford Escort with a standard 1,300cc engine and four-speed box. This isn't the sort of car you rush around in: Tony and his wife use it for ambling around country lanes, so power and handling are irrelevant.

The pre-electronic and pre-fuel injection Ford mechanicals are a breeze – just get a spark to the distributor and some fuel into the carb and away you go. Clean the points every few months and life is rosy.

The engine's obviously not the correct tall and skinny MG XPAG engine, but it looks nice and old compared to any modern engines, and the detailing in the engine bay is to a high standard – polished ally rocker cover, chrome air filter, and not a self-tapping screw in sight. Every fastener is the proper thing, either captive bolts or nuts and bolts.

The exhaust note from Tony's little TF replica is nice and fruity. The exhaust was taken off the donor car, left in the garage rafters for five years and then pulled down again, and the baffles all fell out of the end in a shower of rust. The acid left in the exhaust had eaten them, but rather generously spared the outside of the silencer boxes.

There is serious detailing in this car – just check out the walnut dash. The glove-locker is on a chromed piano hinge, and its interior is as neatly trimmed as the rest of the car. There's a lot of chrome about, all of which is kept beautifully polished. You wouldn't

believe it to look at it, but the grille is actually plastic.

Once you've got used to the idea of spending a lot of hours fiddling with your car as you gradually build it, chrome wire wheels are an excellent way of keeping you busy afterwards, as it takes a week to clean and polish each of them.

DAYTONA COBRA

Roger Hanson's Daytona is his second. The first was an early Factory Five kit, but the company bought the finished car back and gave him another kit as part of the deal. Fortunately, Roger likes building cars, and took advantage of the chance to apply all the lessons he'd learned first time around and make the car even better.

The Factory Five kit is more of a lookalike than a replica, really. It's a good bit bigger and longer, and the floors have been dropped by 6in compared with the original. This is useful if you're as tall as Roger. After spending a lot of time building

The chromed wires are authentic, as are the bumpers – but the grille is forward of its position in the genuine car, and is actually made of plastic. A gentle wipe rather than bashing at it with chrome polish, then.

The two-level dashboard looks good, and is augmented by Triumph Herald glovebox fittings. Tony still needs to get that steering wheel stripped, walnut-stained and re-varnished, though.

The frontal gape of the 427 Cobra was what stopped it going over 200mph – the aerodynamics slowed it down. Daytona's slopy front end sorted that, though.

Roger Hanson is a glutton for punishment – this is the second Factory Five Daytona he's built.

Recognisable chassis design, with fully adjustable wishbones. Roger now has to tune the forest of Webers above the inlet manifold.

The flip-up tail spoiler and stumpy back may not be too elegant, but they keep the back end down on the track at insane speeds.

two of the things, he's finally going to get to drive this one, so he's spent some time and money on the engine and drive train to make sure it's well worth driving.

The engine is expected to produce about 450bhp when it's finally settled and tuned. Its base is a 392CI (slightly over six litres) Ford Racing long block, built up for strength and revs, and topped with $6,000 worth of Weberology – eight huge 48-sized chokes.

The Tremec five-speed should be big enough to handle this, and the back end is based on the Thunderbird independent rear end. With the whole car weighing in at 2,200lb, power-to-weight is going to be amusing.

Roger knows his technical limitations, and although he's made an excellent job of building and presenting the car, he's found it difficult to locate anybody around his home town of San Diego who can work on tuning the engine. Faced with the prospect of jetting and balancing eight Weber chokes, most of us would have chickened out and bunged on a couple of Carter four-barrels.

FIREBLADE F27

Chris Andrews owns this Formula 27, finished in 2007. The car represents a lot of development from the original low-budget F27 project, and this one is a good example of a potent bike-engined Sevenesque that uses

light weight and new tech to good effect.

He tells us the car's very low weight is down to the minimal bodywork, with carbon fibre used here and there, and to the light chassis, but mainly to the engine and gearbox that you can more or less pick up and dance around with, although you'd look pretty silly.

Chris doesn't really use the car much: this is partly because it's rather extreme for general road use, although it would be sublime on the track. Its performance, he says, is definitely too fierce for wet roads: 0–60 comes up in 3.9 seconds which is definitely getting up there.

The engine has upgraded carbs and obviously a custom exhaust, and its output is around 150bhp. The revs are 1,000rpm per 10mph, which means 70mph is 7,000rpm. That becomes a pretty tiresome exhaust drone before too long. There's also no cush drive as there is in the donor bike's rear wheel, so if you're on and off the power at low throttle during road use you get some clattering and banging through the drivetrain. The paddle-shift sequential gearchanging is also a bit brutal, but it works fine for flat-

The F27's unfeasibly long bonnet seems to go on for ever, but the longer the wheelbase the more stable it is in corners. Long bonnets look nice too.

The office is very businesslike, with decent comfy seats and a carbon fibre dashboard. That won't save more than few ounces in weight, but does it look cool? Oh yes.

Above: Honda's 900cc FireBlade four was the first superbike engine commonly used in bike-powered kit cars. Small, light and potent, it's still a good choice.

out charging on the track – scream clack, scream clack, scream clack, scream clack, scream clack, screeeeeeeeeam, brakebrakebrake, click click click down the box, end of corner, scream clack, scream clack etc. Again, top fun on the circuit but tiresome on the street after a while.

The total lack of torque in the 900cc FireBlade engine also takes some getting used to – at 12,000rpm there's plenty of punch,

Below: Does Chris look like a bloke who's having fun? 'Course he does.

but at 1,000rpm you could stop the engine by poking a pencil down a spark plug hole. Getting going without stalling takes some practice, as you have to more or less dump the clutch at 5,000 – and traffic queues and car parks are no fun at all. Chris prefers to use the gear lever rather than the paddles as it has a direct mechanical connection to the gearbox, so he can apply a little mechanical empathy and learn how firmly to twitch the lever, but the electric paddle change just bangs it in.

It sounds as though Chris doesn't like the car much, but he does thoroughly enjoy taking it out for a thrash now and again when the weather's right. He lives in Cornwall, where the tax camera plague is less virulent than in more crowded parts of the UK, so there are places he can play. He just needs to organise some track days to get the full benefit of the car's as yet unexplored capabilities. It's very much a four-wheeled superbike rather than a car, although thankfully, unlike a superbike you don't have to cling to the top of it like a monkey on its mum.

GTM LIBRA

Paul Curtis bought his GTM five years ago, but only spent three

months building it: for the other 4¾ years he's been charging around in it and getting it the way he wants it. GTM have been quietly updating and developing their cars for years, and the result is now slick and professional. He says that as a first-time builder, the entire process was not just painless but intriguing, and describes the resulting car as very entertaining. There's also a large and active owners' club, with all the assistance and social benefits that brings: when I picked Paul's car from the row of GTMs at the Exeter kit car show his club comrades all crowded round to take the piss like proper British mates.

If the kit can be built in three months by a first-time builder, there can't be much DIY hassle left for the buyer to deal with. In any case, you just have to look at the detailing – bonded-in windows and a gleaming gelcoat finish right out of the box. Paul just got the car built and on the road and began to play with it and make it his own. The interior has been reworked a little so that it's tailored just for him, which is a major reason for choosing to build a kit car. The spoilers and front air splitters are his own additions, and he says they keep the car nice and stable at high speed. The 1,800cc MGF/Rover 200/Lotus Elise engine with variable valve geometry is good for 157mph, at least on the dyno rollers, so it's probably best to add a few air dams in case he ever finds himself on an autobahn. 0-60mph time is 5.3 seconds, respectable for a car with a solid shell, a standard car engine and plenty of daily-driver mod cons inside. There are also plenty of smaller K-series engines available for increased economy and decreased insurance premiums. The MGF has a problem with overheating and warped head gaskets, but of course you would expect a kit car company to do a proper job with the cooling system design: GTM will have got the issue sorted out at the design stage.

Handling, of course, has been continuously developed along the way and is what you would expect from a stiff rear engine/rear drive kit car with a GRP monocoque. This approach began with the chassisless Mini-Marcos, which is the GTM's grandpa: the concept progressed through the Midas to the GTM, which was developed from the convertible version of the

The GTM Libra has evolved way beyond its Mini-Marcos roots, but still uses the design principle of a very strong GRP tub and no chassis.

Midas. The immense strength of a composite body tub is exploited by the newest GTM just as it was in 1965 by the Mini-Marcos – the mechanicals and the suspension are bolted straight to the tub with no need for sub-structures. Racing cars caught up with this idea a decade or two after Marcos, and doubtless production cars will catch up with GTM in another decade or two.

Pride and joy – six completely

different people and six completely different dreams. One with an attainable replica of an unattainable art deco classic, one with a quick and practical DIY camper, one with a five-year hand-made jigsaw puzzle, one with a storming Cobra coupé, one with a purist bike-powered Sevenesque and one with the comfort of a GRP monocoque. All six are happy bunnies who got exactly what they wanted and hoped for out of their kit cars.

The Kamm tail worked in 1966 and still works just as well in 2008. Respeck to the Marsh man, innit.

Neat interior has been reworked to suit Paul's own detailed preferences. Nice red piping works well against the black.

Chapter 18

What next?

Some people just love building cars, some enjoy thrashing them and some get off on polishing them. For most people there will come a point where the car is finished, and some will just sell it and then buy the next one. Most of us, with a couple of years of blood, sweat, tears and quite often a near-divorce having gone into our dream car, would rather have our fingernails pulled out than get rid of our freshly finished pride and joy.

So what to do with it now it's finished? Apart from the obvious point that you've just finished building a very fast, sexy and useful way of getting around the place, there are three main things to do with a kit car – you can race it, you can show it or you can just drive it to nice places.

Some kit racing is pretty hardcore, and if you're up for serious competition you will already have designed and built your car with that in mind. Caterham Sevens and other Sevenish kits are very quick indeed, and on the track they occupy a place between the weekend racers' modified saloons and the smaller single-seaters.

A race grid of Caterhams or Westfields will generally be full, and some serious speeds and lap times have been recorded.

As always with racing, it takes pretty frightening money to get to the front, but a lot of people have a lot of fun in the middle of the pack, and at the back. If you're on a budget, you can join in with general kit racing rather than becoming involved with the generally more expensive one-make series, and a home-made Locost with a FireBlade engine will get you in among some pretty frantic action.

Shall we let her drive? Why not, she's faster than most of the men on the circuit. Heather Mills races a V8 Gardner Douglas Cobra replica at Mallory Park.

Westfield's sprint day allows all Westfield owners to explore the limits of their cars' handling. It's not a competition, but there's no shortage of stopwatches at the finish line. This one is steering on the throttle, with the wheels turning into the skid to balance it up. Neat and tidy.

A Caterham Seven at Harewood hill-climb. This corner is safe with lots of kitty-litter run-off, but a hundred yards back there's a narrow and very solid wooden gate you have to go through, which is scary.

A bike-engined car is actually more at home on the track than the road anyway. You have to slip the clutch to get it going quickly, and after that you don't use the clutch at all. The engine spends its time screaming its nuts off, and the six gears allow it to be kept above 10,000rpm where the power is.

Track days, where you drive your car to a circuit and thrash it round without actually racing, are becoming more popular all the time: there were over 500 track day events in the UK in 2007.

Tips: if you get the red mist and start racing for real you'll get black-flagged off the circuit; tighten up your wheel nuts every hour or so; and bring a spare set of front brake pads and your own helmet, or risk sharing a manky communal one with dandruff in it. A quick check of *Totalkitcar*'s track day calendar will sort you out a local event.

Racing needn't involve just going round in circles. Hill-climbing and sprints are also good fun, and many kit cars do very well at both. Rather than playing rugby with thirty other Sevens

This Tiger has two Kawasaki bike engines fitted. At the Santa Pod dragstrip it did 0–60mph in 3.15 seconds, which disappointed the owner: the sticky surface apparently slowed it down.

The Brighton Speed Trials day has been going for a century or so. It's mad, with cast-iron poles and lamp-posts to hit on either side and some evil dips in the road. Kits do quite well here, with their good handling and power-to-weight ratios.

around Castle Combe, you're competing against yourself and on your own, so you can push your limits at your own speed.

For hill-climbing, Prescott offers tuition as well as a long and distinguished history. It's the home of the Bugatti Owners' Club, and is a twisty and demanding 1,127 yards. You can book a training day for £148 which includes demo runs, convoy runs, walking the course and lots of timed runs in your own car. There's a break to have some lunch and to watch videos of your performance, and another break later for afternoon tea and more video appraisal. All very civilised, apart from the actual driving.

Sprinting is one of the cheapest forms of motorsport, and usually involves a kit car club renting a small local circuit such as Curborough for a day's play. Competition is not allowed, so nobody gets to win anything. However, those in attendance are all keeping an eye on who's fastest, so there's enough of an edge to the whole thing to add some excitement. Sprint circuits are usually short, narrow and tight, and that evens things out between fast and slow cars. A well set up and well driven crossflow-engined car will not necessarily lose out to a bike-powered car or even a V8, although a light alloy Rover V8 in a good chassis takes a bit of beating – you just use the torque and don't have to waste time coasting for an eighth of a second while changing gear.

There's also rallying of various sorts. The Liège-Rome-Liège sort of endurance rallying takes place on public roads, and can involve charging through France and Spain to North Africa, dodging stones thrown by Moroccan children, and pushing yourself and your machine pretty hard up mountains and goat tracks. *Kit-Car*'s editor Ian Hyne loves all that, and prefers to do it in open Westfields and Ginettas so that he gets snow in his teeth across

The Dutton Owners' Club rent a cheap circuit in Wales for a weekend every year, and enjoy 48 hours of total full-on driving and partying fun: they spend the rest of the year recovering, and repairing their cars.

Continental rallies and club outings are mostly for classics, and can range from serious events to gourmet touring weekends; kit owners seem to be very welcome.

The lunch-stop on the kit car Le Mans trip is at a little town called Gace, where the main square becomes an unofficial kit car show. The Bar du Centre offers a good cheap lunch.

food to the equation. The car preparation required is minimal, and the only expensive item is an electronic time and distance log that costs £100 or so. If you think you might get serious about classic rallying, you could consider using (or building) something like an NG, based on and bearing the registration of a donor MG, which could get you into the 1960s.

Classic rallying is carefully organised to keep within the law, with speeds averaged at 26mph. If you don't make a mistake reading the tulip-diagram directions, completing the stages at 26mph is possible. However . . . if you make a mistake, the temptation is to retrace your steps and catch up with yourself, which means going at 26mph x 3. There are some seriously prepared cars and some pretty hairy driving goes on. Having said that, you can also just bowl along with the roof off and take a classic rally as a nice little weekend away with some navigating games to play. There are no winners, either – that would make it competition on public roads, and thus illegal. Everybody who joins in gets the same plaque. However, those whose times are spot-on get the respect, and those whose times are worst get a proportionate amount of piss-taking at the post-rally dinner. This was once focused almost entirely on the driver/navigator team of your narrator and the rally organiser, who came last on a Belgian weekend rally. Somewhat embarrassing, but at least it gave everybody else a laugh.

Much more relaxed, if a little less adventurous, is driving to amusing places and races with good people just for fun. From direct experience, I can enthusiastically recommend this – in fact I organise several low-budget Continental trips for the readers of *Kit-Car* magazine. A favourite is the five-day camping trip to Le Mans. The group mostly collects at Calais after catching the ferry from Dover, and forms a

the Alps, and sand and flies in his teeth across the desert. Some of us would rather just save time and stand in a cold shower tearing up fivers. Still . . . with kit cars, as ever, you can do whatever blows your frock up.

There's also a limited amount of semi-serious classic rallying you can do in a kit car. Technically your car should have been built before 1968, which was a rule brought in to avoid plebs in low-

rent Escorts getting involved. However, there's an increasing awareness among classic rally enthusiasts that being too snotty about dates and about cars will mean a grid of two period-correct Healeys and a TR4, and no more classic rallying at all. Quite a few of Continental's rallies are open to offers from later cars and kits. They're also largely held in Belgium and France, which adds a great deal of fun and decent loose convoy cruising on the two-lane Route Nationale to Abbeville for dinner and an overnight hotel, then on to Gace in the morning, where the market square becomes an unofficial lunchtime kit car show. The trip gets into Le Mans early to allow time to catch night practice, and then a day is spent just wandering around the pits, drinking beer and coffee at the Arnage cafes and talking about fast cars. The 24-hour race is the climax, and with the likes of Bentley and Morgan getting involved again, the whole thing is more fun each year. Background knowledge helps – we don't join the huge post-race Sunday traffic jam, we go back to the campsite and take it easy, driving back the next day instead. We avoid the circuit campsites as well now, because they're dirty, noisy and crowded with shouting drunks. The bogs are nasty and the queues are worse. The trick is to use the campsite passes as car park tickets, and to retire to a decent campsite to get some sleep.

There's a new historic race at Le Mans, which is shaping up to resemble the Goodwood events but with no rain, and the Circuit Historique de Laon has been very well recommended by a couple of kit clubs, so that looks like a possibility too.

All these trips are designed to offer some great driving on good, uncrowded roads, without being too demanding on drivers or cars, and none of them are exclusively male – they're very much social events as well, so wives and girlfriends are very welcome.

North American readers would also be welcome on these European trips. Hiring kit cars probably isn't practical, but it is possible to hire classic cars in the UK and tie that in with flights and hotels. In the same way, if there are any good outings in the USA that American readers think British kit car enthusiasts would enjoy, do get in touch with details at www.ayrspeed.com

Tagging along at the end of a kit car convoy to Le Mans. It's best to stay off the motorways and just bimble along at fiftyish with the roof off while somebody at the front navigates.

Even if you don't feel sociable and just want to take your car out on fast, empty A-roads, rural France offers lots of space, good road surfaces, good food and no speed tax cameras.

A trip to the Nürburgring for a historic race meeting allows you to drive on the old Chimay road circuit for a few laps, until the local cops come and chase you off.

All for one and one for all – a kit with a dodgy alternator gets help (and some baling wire) from others in the party, and is kept in the convoy.

The kit car clubs, particularly those within reach of Dover, also organise some excellent trips of their own, and quite often go charging around the Continent having a fine time. The clubs without exception have regular meetings in pubs for general socialising, and there are many opportunities to go off to visit castles or parks or races, or whatever ideas anybody comes up with, as well as attending kit car shows en masse.

You're not just stuck with the one-make club for your own particular brand of kit car – you can also join a local area-based club. This applies even more in the States, where getting to a meeting of a one-make club could involve a thousand-mile trip. In the UK, the Kent Kit Car Club is a good example. Nobody's bothered what sort of car you drive, as long as you bring some enthusiasm and £10 a year for your membership.

With most one-make kit car clubs, you don't have to own an example of the club's make of car – you just have to want one. Even the Bugatti club doesn't exclude non-owners, because of course it wouldn't be a very big club if it did – there are many more Bugatti enthusiasts than there are Bugattis to go around. Joining a relevant one-make club is often an excellent way to acquire a car, though: once you're a member, the others will enthusiastically help you to find something you can afford, and if anybody knows where the bargains are, it's the club members.

For a lot of people on both sides of the Atlantic, the pleasure of kit cars is in building them as close to perfection as possible, and then showing them. The kit show scene in the UK has been expanding, with more and more events. None of the manufacturers can afford to go to all of them, so some of the shows have become rather thin. The major UK kit car show is still Stoneleigh, and the big show for the clubs is Newark. Both of those are in Spring. The other kit car shows are all worth a visit and the dates are advertised in *Kit-Car* magazine. Malvern is one of my favourites, as it is largely a classic car gathering, and there's a little extra variety. The season closer in Exeter in November is also getting more and more popular.

In the USA, the industry's big annual show is at Carlisle, Pennsylvania. However, if you live in the West, the American Handcrafted Automobile Club's spring show at Knott's Berry Farm

The London–Brighton classic car run now has a kit car event running in parallel. It's a navigation run that features a stately home and a steam railway en route, and ends with a show of kits and classics all along the seafront.

There's a concours at most kit shows, with an increasingly high standard of entries. You get points for your own creativity in design and execution.

If you just like a bit of sociable fun, there are events like the Running Board Rally in Henley-on-Thames, which is organised by a few kit clubs and welcomes individuals as well.

At the Running Board Rally, you can win pots for the concours, but you can also win them for driving there from Orkney and for putting yellow plastic ducks in a bucket during their fiendishly difficult driving games.

in LA is a smallish but friendly affair, with a couple of hundred cars showing up. A number of manufacturers attend, but the whole thing is very low-stress and just makes for a nice weekend. If you have to drag an unenthusiastic family along, they can be sent off to amuse themselves in the theme park while you spend a few guilt-free hours discussing glassfibre and carbs.

Whether you become obsessive about winning concours pots or just think you've made a good job of your car and want to show it off a little, there's room for both. The kit clubs have a presence at nearly all the shows, and it's a chance to get together, exchange gripes about useless build manuals and burn bits of dead things on barbecues.

The side stands and autojumbles at shows can be extremely useful, too. The stand owners won't thank me for this, but the best time to buy is just before they start packing up to go home. The psychological pressure to let something go cheaply rather than heave it all into the back of a van and take it home again can be further encouraged by waving wads of pounds or dollars about with a cheery smile.

Whether you buy a completed kit car of build your own, there's definitely no shortage of amusing things to do with it – the tricky part is trying to make up your mind which will be the most fun.

Many kit builders have no interest in doing anything at all with a freshly finished kit car, and see it as a jigsaw – once it's done, it's of no further interest. In that case, next up is a new kit, and if you picked the right car and built it well, you should be able to sell it for enough to upgrade to a more exotic kit.

In my case, I'm downgrading, not because I need to but because I want to. The Ayrspeed Cobra replicas currently being developed involve big money and complex problems. They'll be cheap to buy but they're not cheap to develop, and there's no room for mistakes. I can't supercharge my own one because I might need that money to ship over the UK demonstrator. It's serious business, with limited fun involved at this stage.

However, I made the mistake of visiting Marcos Heritage and trying out a Mini-Marcos: after a mile I realised they were so much fun that I needed one badly and as soon as possible.

In complete contrast to frightening development budgets, year-ahead chassis development plans, months of precision bodywork and specialist custom computer software, a comprehensive Mini-Marcos kit is still available for around five grand and a dead Mini. Strip the Mini, reassemble it into the gelcoat-finish Mini-Marcos monocoque and you don't even have to paint it. The car handles better than a Mini, is quieter than a Mini and at only 1,000lb, goes like a squirrel on crack: it can get 140mph and 50mpg out of a 1275 Mini engine, although perhaps not both at the same time. It's also an instant classic with a Le Mans pedigree, and there isn't a computer in sight, just an SU carb or two. And possibly a turbo from an MG Metro if one shows up at the right price, for a further cheap 30bhp.

When thinking about what comes next, it's perhaps worth deliberately bearing in mind that there is as much fun to be had at the bottom of the kit car budget range as at the top. Keep an eye open for the Ayrspeed Marcos project at www.ayrspeed.com.

Not the prettiest car ever, but it does have charm. The high bonnet line is because the Mini engine is on top of its integral gearbox. A high rear roof line offers luggage space and Kamm tail aerodynamics.

The hatchback is one of the very few changes made to the monocoque Mini-Marcos shell that was the only British entry to finish at Le Mans in 1966. The original moulds are still in use.

Above: Plenty of room for a Mini engine/box/diff/subframe/ suspension/steering package to bolt straight in. There should be room for a 225bhp Honda B1800 Type R engine and box instead, for 450bhp/ton. Oo-er Missus!

Right: A thick glassfibre one-piece shell means a quiet and civilised interior: the driving position is also far better than the donor Mini.

Appendix

Useful contacts

This list of contacts is based on Totalkitcar.com's constantly updated web-based contacts list, courtesy of editor Steve Hole. If the information here changes, up-to-date information will be found on www.totalkitcar.com.

If anybody wants to tell me personally about anything, I can be contacted via www.ayrspeed.com

WEBSITES

www.totalkitcar.com
Part of CAR PR;
Warlingham, Surrey
01883 372 085 (Mon-Fri 9.30-5.30)
Fax: 01883 624 964
E-mail: steve_h@sportscar.
fsbusiness.co.uk
An alternative to the UK magazines: knowledgeable, amusing, outspoken, energetic.

www.kitcar.com
Crusading Curt Scott's comprehensive US site. He doesn't like cheats.

www.kit-cars.com
Kit-Car UK's site. A more mobile version of the magazine.

www.cobracountry.com
Curt Scott's US Cobra site. A useful overview of the US Cobra rep scene.

www.kitcarclub.com
The site of the National Kit Car Club (USA) led by ex-KCI editor Jim Youngs.

www.ayrspeed.com
Iain Ayre's site. Mostly nonsense. Good trips, kit import/export.

KIT-CAR
The major UK publication, written by hands-on kit-car builders.
33 Golden Farm Road, Cirencester, GL7 1BP, UK
Editor Ian Hyne Tel. 01285 642298
Website: www.kit-cars.com

COMPLETE KIT CAR
Replaces the defunct Which Kit, with new and much improved ownership.
Editor Ian Stent
Tel. 01823 335443
Website: www.completekitcar.co.uk

TOTALKITCAR MAGAZINE
See website www.totalkitcar.com

KIT CAR BUILDER (USA)
The major US publication, independent and growing. Expert writing.
Editor
Jim Youngs. jim@kitcarclub.com
PO Box 434 Castle Rock, Colorado 80104-0434 USA
Website:www.kitcarclub.com

KIT CAR (USA)
Commercial US mag: was owned by Primedia corporation, now swallowed by Source Interlink corporation.
Editor D. Brian Smith. Corporate HQ Tel. 714 939 2400
Website: www.kitcarmag.com

UK MANUFACTURERS

Courtesy of www.totalkitcar.com

A1 AUTOCRAFT
www.a1autocraft.co.uk

ACTION AUTOMOTIVE
www.stormwarrior.co.uk

ADRENALINE MOTORSPORT
www.adrenalinemotorsport.co.uk

ADR ENGINEERING
www.adr-engineering.co.uk

AEON SPORTSCARS
www.aeonsportscars.com

AK SPORTSCARS
www.aksportscars.co.uk

ALTERNATIVE CARS
www.midascars.co.uk

ALEXANDER'S 2CVS
01359 252 113

AM SPORTSCARS
www.amsportscars.co.uk

AMPHIJEEP
www.amphijeep.biz

AQUILA SPORTS CARS
www.aquilasportscars.com

ARCHER'S GARAGE
www.sebringsprite.com/replica.htm

ARIES MOTORSPORT
www.ariesmotorsport.co.uk

ASQUITH MOTORS LTD
www.asquithmotors.com

ATLAS (KLY)
www.taydec.impendo.org

AUTO SPECIALI
www.thecar2own.com

AUTOTUNE RISHTON
www.autotuneuk.com

BAY AREA RODS
www.bayarearods.co.uk

BDN SPORTSCARS
www.bdnsportscars.com

BEAUFORD CARS
www.beaufordcars.co.uk

BELFIELD ENGINEERING
01597 823 992

BGH GEARTECH (FISHER)
www.bghgeartech.co.uk

BLAZE MOTORSPORT LTD
www.blazemotorsport.com

BLITZWORLD
www.blitzworld.co.uk

BOOM TRIKES
www.boom-trikes.co.uk

BRAMWITH MOTOR COMPANY
www.bramwith.com

BUGLE BEACH BUGGIES
www.buglebeachbuggies.co.uk

BURLINGTON MOTOR CO
www.turn-the-crank.com

BURTON CAR COMPANY UK
www.burton.bevs.org

CABURN ENGINEERING
www.caburn.demon.co.uk

CATERHAM CARS
www.caterham.co.uk

CLASSIC CHASSIS SERVICES
www.ctype.biz

CLASSIC ROADSTERS
www.classicroadsters.co.uk

CRENDON REPLICAS
01296 651 985

The Exeter show in November in the UK is the last before the winter. It's been going for 12 years and is a good show.

CYANA SPORTS CARS
www.cyanacars.com

DAKAR 4X4 DESIGN & CONVERSIONS
www.dakar4x4.me.uk

DARRIAN CARS (TDE)
www.darrian.co.uk

DC SUPERCARS
www.dcsupercars.com

DEAUVILLE CARS
www.deauvillecars.com

DJ SPORTSCARS (DAX)
www.daxcars.co.uk

DNA AUTOMOTIVE
www.dnaautomotive.com

DOONBUGGIES
www.doon.co.uk

DOOSTER
www.dooster.co.uk

DYNAMIC PERFORMANCE
See MR2 Bodykit

EAST COAST MANX
www.eastcoastbuggies.co.uk

EDGE SPORTSCARS
www.edgesportscars.com

ERA
www.tigerracing.co.uk

EUROPA ENGINEERING
www.banks-europa.co.uk

EXACT 355
www.exactreplicas.co.uk

EXTREME CAR CO
www.extreme-sportscars.com

FACTORY FIVE RACING UK
www.factoryfive.com

FIERO FACTORY
www.fierofactory.com

FINDHORN CARS (NG)
www.ngcars.co.uk

FIORANO
www.corsaspyder.com

FISHER SPORTSCARS
See BGH Geartech

FLATLANDS ENGINEERING
www.flatlandsengineering.co.uk

FURORE CARS
www.furorecars.co.uk

GARDNER DOUGLAS SPORTSCARS
www.gdcars.com

GENTRY MOTORS
www.gentrycars.co.uk

GKD SPORTSCARS
www.gkdsportscars.com

GRAHAM HATHAWAY ENG
www.globalgtlights.co.uk

GREAT BRITISH SPORTSCARS
www.greatbritishsportscars.com

GRINNALL SPECIALIST CARS
www.grinnallcars.com

GT SUPERCARS
www.gtsupercars.co.uk

The 0–60mph Challenge attracted most of the British kit car industry, Lotus and AC, but no sign of Ferrari, Lamborghini, Aston et al. They knew they'd get creamed by the kits, of course.

GTM CARS
www.gtmcars.com

HAYNES ROADSTER
www.haynes.co.uk/forums/index.php

HR ENGINEERING
www.hrengineering.net

HRB AUTOMOTIVE
www.hrb-automotive.co.uk

HAWK CARS UK
www.hawkcars.co.uk

HOPPA STREET BUGGY
www.hoppastreetbuggy.com

IJF DEVELOPMENTS
www.grp.co.uk

IMAGE SPORTS CARS
www.imagesportscars.co.uk

JAS SPEEDKITS
www.beachbuggies.co.uk

JAVELIN SPORTS CARS LTD
www.javelinsportscars.co.uk

JBA ENGINEERING
www.jbacars.co.uk

JIMINI AUTOMOBILE CO
www.jimini-cars.co.uk

JZR VEHICLE RESTORATIONS
01254 760 620

KELLFORMS WOODMASTERS
www.kellforms.com

KINGFISHER KUSTOMS
www.kkvw.co.uk

KMR BUGGIES
www.beach-buggy.net

KOUGAR CARS
http://hugop.users.btopenworld.com/
kougars/newmain.htm

LANGLEY MOTOR CO
01260 253 460

LEIGHTON MOTOR CO
www.leighton-cars.com

LIEGE MOTOR CO
http://groups.msn.com/liegecars

LUEGO SPORTS CARS
www.luegosportscars.com

LYNX AE
www.lynxae.co.uk

MAC#1 MOTORSPORTS
www.mac1motorsports.co.uk

MADGWICK CARS
www.madgwickcars.co.uk

MAGNUM ENGINEERING
www.magnum-engineering.com

MALONE DESIGN
www.malonecar.com

MAMBA MOTORSPORT
www.mambamotorsport.co.uk

MARCOS HERITAGE SPARES
www.minimarcos.com

MARKHAM STREET RODS
www.markhamstreetrods.com

MARLIN CARS LTD
www.marlinsportscars.co.uk

MARTIN & WALKER (TECHNIC)
www.904gts.co.uk

MDA GT40 UK
www.mdagt40.com

METISSE SPORTSCARS
01656 862 437

**MILESTONE MOTORSPORT
ENGINEERING**
www.ultimini.co.uk

MILL AUTO CONVERSIONS
07970 974 970

MILLS EXTREME VEHICLES
www.mevltd.co.uk

MINARI
See Peninsula

MINI SPORT LTD
www.minisport.com

MINIEXVO
www.miniexvo.com

MINOTAUR SPORTSCARS
See Pilgrim Cars

MK SPORTSCARS
www.mk-sportscars.fsnet.co.uk

MNR LTD
www.mnrltd.co.uk

MOTION CAR DEVELOPMENTS
www.avelle-cars.com

MR2 BODYKIT
www.mr2bodykit.co.uk

MR2 KITS
www.mr2kits.co.uk

NAPIERSPORT
www.superstratos.com/
napiersport.html

NCF MOTORS LTD
www.ncfblitz.co.uk

NF AUTOS
www.nfauto.co.uk

NOSTALGIA CARS UK
www.nostalgiacars.co.uk

OM SPORTSCARS
www.omsportscars.com

ONYX SPORTS CARS
www.onyxsportscars.f9.co.uk

PA MOTORSPORT
www.pamotorsport.com

PARALLEL DESIGNS
www.paralleldesigns.co.uk

PEMBLETON MOTOR CO
www.pembleton.co.uk

If you need a new cam, put in a mild performance one. Piper know what they're doing, their advice is free and their cams are well priced.

**PENINSULA SPORTS CARS
(MINARI)**
07807 424 819

PILGRIM CARS UK LTD
www.pilgrimcars.com

PRO-COMP MOTORSPORT
www.procomp.co.uk

PRO-MOTIVE FABRICATIONS
www.pro-motive.com

PULSAR SPORTSCARS
www.pulsarsportscars.co.uk

QUANTUM SPORTS CARS
www.quantumcars.co.uk

RAINBIRD RACING
www.rainbirdracing.com

RANGE OVER KITS
www.rangeover.co.uk

RAW UK LTD
http://web.mac.com/rawuk/iWeb/Raw/
Home.html

REALM ENGINEERING LTD
www.realmengineering.com

REGENT MOTOR COMPANY
01744 818 516

**RESTORATION & AUTOMOTIVE
CREATION**
07796 130 482

RHINO TRIKES
http://rhino-trikes.co.uk/

ROAD RUNNER RACING
www.roadrunnerracing.co.uk

RODBODYS
www.rodbodys.co.uk

RONART CARS
www.ronart.co.uk

RV DYNAMICS
www.pythoncobra.com

SDR COMPONENT CARS
www.sdrsportscars.co.uk

SEAROADER CARS
www.searoader.com

SEBRING INTERNATIONAL
www.sebringcars.co.uk

SHELSLEY CARS
www.shelsley-cars.com

SIMOD DESIGN
01249 461 306

SOUTHERN GT
www.southerngt.co.uk

SPECIALIST AUTOMOTIVE
www.chronozone.co.uk

SPEEDWELL REPLICA CARS
www.speedwell-replicacars.com

SPIRE SPORTSCARS
www.spiresportscars.co.uk

SPM
01527 591 590

SPYDER ENGINEERING
www.spydercars.co.uk

SPYDER SPORTSCARS
www.spydersportscars.com

STIMSON DESIGN
www.stimsondesigns.com

STORM BUGGIES
www.stormbuggies.com

STUART TAYLOR MOTORSPORT
www.stuart-taylor.co.uk

SUFFOLK SPORTSCARS
www.ss100.com

SYLVA AUTOKITS
www.sylva.co.uk

TALON SPORTSCARS
www.talonsportscars.com

TAYDEC
www.taydec.impendo.org

TDK RACING
www.tdkracing.co.uk

TEAC SPORTSCARS
www.teacsportscars.co.uk

TEMPEST CARS
www.tempestcars.com

TIFOSI SPORTSCARS
www.tifosi-devon.co.uk

TIGER RACING
www.tigerracing.co.uk

TOMCAT MOTORSPORT
www.tomcatmotorsport.co.uk

TONIQ R LTD
www.toniqr.co.uk

TORNADO SPORTSCARS
www.tornadosportscars.com

TRIKESHOP
www.trikeshop.co.uk

TYGAN MOTOR COMPANY
www.tygan.co.uk

ULTIMA SPORTS
www.ultimasports.co.uk

VANWALL CARS
www.vanwallcars.com

VERANTI MOTOR CO
01257 252 700

VINDICATOR CARS
www.vindicator.co.uk

VOODOO SPORTSCARS
www.voodoosportscars.com

**WATSON'S SPECIALIST CAR
CENTRE**
www.watsonsrally.co.uk

WEST MAINS AUTOMOTIVE
www.west-mains-automotive.co.uk

WESTFIELD SPORTS CARS
www.westfield-sportscars.co.uk

WILDMOOR MTC
www.wildmoormtc.co.uk

WILKI ENGINEERING
www.jbaroadsters.co.uk

XK180.COM
www.xk180.com

XK EVOCATION
www.xkevocation.com

Z CARS
www.zcars.org.uk

Very cheap, very light, very hard, very fast indeed. No pansy nonsense about an interior, either.

USA & CANADA
MANUFACTURERS

Courtesy of *Kit Car* USA, www. kitcarclub.com and www.kitcar.com

ACE
427 Cobra replicas
818 885 5097

AFFILIATED MOTORS
Ferrari 288 GTO replica
712 239 1206

AFFORDABLE COMPANY
Ferrari 308, T-Bucket, 500SL, TR512
978 373 7389

ALDINO
K/O512 Boxer
www.sit.wisc.edu/~ahbucha

AMERICAN CUSTOM ENG
Fiero Conversions
970 259 4156

AMERICAN FIBERBODIES
427, Diablo, Testarossa, 5000s and R390
937 372 4900

AMERICAN STREET ROD
32 Roadster and 32 coupé
www.americanstreetrod.com

ANTIQUE AND COLLECTIBLE
427, SS100, 34 Ford, 35 Chevy and XK120
800 245 1310
www.acautos.com

ANTIQUE REPLICAR
Dio Tipo 61
www.kitcar.com/dio

ASPP INCORPORATED
GT40 lookalike
520 689 0100

AUTOMOBILE ATLANTA
Porsche 914 (9014)
770 427 2844

AUTO SPEED MOTOR CARS
Speedster, 427, HalfVee and 32 Highboy
714 289 9964

AUTO HAUS BUGGIES
Warrior, Sandfox, Venture and Stalker
www.autohausbuggies.com

BALASHI AUTOWORKS
Countach
561 585 9334

BALLISTIC AUTO DESIGNS
B.A.D. Jeep
800 806 5313

B&B MANUFACTURING
427 and 34 Ford
417 472 3547
www.cobracountry.com/bbmfg/home

B&C FIBERGLASS
32 Ford and 34 Ford
417 472 3547

BECK DEVELOPMENT
760 949 0227
Lister 'Knobbly' and 550 Spyder
www.beckdev.com

BENNETT FIBERGLASS
427
510 782 0705

BERRIEN BUGGY
Classic 295, Venture, Stalker, Sandfox 4X, Stalker 2+2 and Nostalgia
www.berrienbuggy.com

BERLINETTA MOTORCARS
308
516 423 1010

BGW SPECTRE
VW Rod Kits
www.bgwspectre.com

BIG BOYS' AFFORDABLE TOYS
427
905 790 7686

BIRKIN AMERICA
Birkin S3
www.birkinamerica.com

BLACKLAW
Cobra 427
www.geocities.com/motorcity

The huge and imposing Beauford, styled loosely around a 1930s Packard. A top wedding and touring car, usually built on cheap Ford bits with a Nissan straight-six.

BRADEN RIVER ENG
E-Type
941 761 8498

BRITT MOTOR CORP
Stallion GT-1
www.bmc-usa.com

BROOKLANDS CAR CO
Renaissance and 350S
http://noisette-software.com/
brooklands

CAN-AM MOTORCARS
427
www.canammotorcars.com

CAROLINA GROWLER
Growler and
Wolverine
www.carolinagrowler.com

CAROSELLI DESIGN
Sedan Delivery, Rodster and Rodster
Super Deluxe
310 322 2767

CARTER'S CONVERSIONS
Fiero-rarri
810 724 2333

CATERHAM AMERICA
303 765 0247
www.uscaterham.com

CAV
Monocoque GT40
858 342 3246
www.gt40cars.com

C-F ENTERPRISES
California Ace
562 404 0522
www.calace.com

CHAMPION MOTOR CARS
Locost 7 and 11
www.championmotorcars.com

CLASSIC ANTIQUE REPLICAR
Dio Tipo 61 and Van
405 755 5522
www.kitcar.com/dio

CLASSIC FACTORY
Auburn
909 629 5868

CLASSIC ROADSTERS
427, Sebring MX and
Badlands RT
www.classicroadsters.com

CK3 DESIGN
KR, 512, Rossa and Stingray
www.ck3.com

COBRA SHOP
427
www.cobrashop.com

COMPOSITE RACING
Countach
www.crpdesign.com

COACH AND CHASSIS WORKS
34 Plymouth and Dodge
412 812 1900

COAST TO COAST FORD
39 Roadster
www.ford39.com

CORVETTE CENTRAL
Concept 57
800 345 4122

CRD
Cavaliere Healey 3000 rep
941 635 6363

CREATIVE COACH
DVL 30th and DVL VT
http://home.inreach.com/ccoach

CREATIVE SAFETY
S-Vee Hummer replica
www.creative-safety.com

CUSTOM TOYS
SL, 512TR, F40 and Diablo
714 680 9744

CY
1966 George Barris Batmobile rep
www.cyproductions.com

DAVIS MOTORSPORTS
Cheetah
http://goracin.com

D&B ENTERPRISES
Maserati Barchetta
360 887 1673

D&D STREETRODS
32 coupé
www.ddstreetrods.com

D&R REPLICARS
Deceptor, Diablo and
Python 2000
610 434 2225
www.kitcar.com/d%26r/home

WWW.DECORIDES.COM
Discrete Illusions
Blaze, Elite and 427
www.discreteillusions.com

JB DONALDSON
1935-36 three-window coupé
rod
602 278 4505

DOWNS MANUFACTURING
Ford 37 Coupé and 37 Pick-up
www.downsmfg.com

DRAGON
Original Italianate sports
603 863 5272
www.dragonmotorcars.com

DULOUX MOTORS
37 Cord 812 Sportsman
www.kitcar.com/cord

DYNAMIC MOTORSPORTS
S1
www.superformance.com

EAGLE COACHWORKS
XK120 and SS100
716 897 4292
info@eaglecoachwork.com

EASTON ARMSTRONG
GT
713 461 3834

EASY ROD SHOEBOX
Body conversion for T-Bird, Mercury
609 693 1631
www.easyrod.com

EMERSON MOTORSPORTS
427
530 275 0435
billscobra@aol.com

ENCORE MOTORS
53 Corvette
734 241 8106

ERA REPLICA AUTOS
289, 427, Grand Sport and GT40
860 224 0253
www.erareplicas.com

EURO-WORKS
Mirage K and Mirage S
937 293 6834
www.euroworksltd.com

EVERETT MORRISON
427
www.everett-morrison.com

EXCELLENCE MOTORS
Excellence Roadstar
www.classicreplicas.com

EXOTIC ENTERPRISES
Countach, Fierossa, Machiavelli,
Mongoose,
Beamer 3, 500SL and 5000 MR2
973 956 7570

EXOTIC ILLUSIONS
Eurosex 1000 and Eurosex 2500
717 383 1206
exotic@usnetway.com

EXOTIC REBODIES
25X/S, Diabolic Coupé, Diabolic 6,
Diabolic
Roadster and Rattlesnake
702 565 6201
www.exoticrebodies.com

FACTORY FIVE RACING
427, Daytona and 250 Cal
Spyder
508 291 3443
www.factoryfive.com

FANCY CARS
512 and 355
www.coolcustomcars.com

FIBERJET INDUSTRIES
427, Bravossa, 959, Enos and Buggy
916 783 3198
www.kitcar.com/fiberjet/home

FIBERTECH INDUSTRIES
Hum 7
800 541 9402

FIERO CONVERSIONS
Fiero kits
519 972 4989
www.fieroconversions.com

FINAL CONCEPT
Final Vision Countach
941 764 1966

FUNCO MOTORSPORTS
Big Five and Hustler
www.funco-motorsports.com

This is a standard Saturday afternoon for many Westfield owners. Lined up and waiting to get out on the track for a thrash, then drive it home.

GARY'S CUSTOM EXOTICS
Diablo
www.gscustom.com

G&K CLASSICS
427
864 224 7770

G&S MOTORSPORTS
427
805 688 0600

GLASS HOUSE STREET RODS
909 592 1078

GLASS STATION
Pro V and Pro V8
www.prostreetbug.com

GROUP FIVE
Vette to Cobra conversion
480 610 1202
www.vipercarparts.com

GSR INC
Grand Sport coupé and Roadster
www.grandsportreplica.com

GULF COAST MOTORS
Vitesse
www.vitessesportscar.com

HAINES COACHWORKS
Synchro 917
http://web.wt.net/~jal/lasermain.html

HARWOOD INDUSTRIES
1932 and '33 Ford rods
800 822 3392

HELD MOTORSPORTS
Fiero-based kits
www.heldmotorsports.com

HIGHLAND DAYTONA RACING
427, 427FIA and Daytona replicas
406 947 2300
www.hdrcoupe.com

HI-TECH
427
561 743 0616

HOLDEN MOTORSPORTS
427
www.holdenmotorsports.com

HUNTERS KIT CARS
427 (ex-Integrity)
www.missionlabs.com/hunters

IFG/WARLOCK
Interceptor and Phantom
www.ifgonline.com

INDYCYCLE
Three-wheeled single-seater with bike
back end
810 724 7080
www.indycycleonline.com

INDY EXOTICS
Auburn Speedster, 427, Cheetah and
34 Ford
www.indyexotics.com

INNOVATIVE STREET MACHINES
427, 1933 Vicky rod, '35/6 roadster rod
888 888 6645

INTERMECCANICA
Kubelwagen and 356
604 872 4747
www.intermeccanica.com

JAXSPORTS
Streetster
www.jaxsports.com

JBL
Semi-Monocoque 427
760 723 2293
www.enjoya.com/jblmotor

JM DESIGN
Paladimo (original design)
819 688 2631

JOHNEX MOTORSPORTS
289, 427 and Daytona replicas
www.johnex.com

JOVI LTD
AutoBahn and Diablo VT
http://members.aol.com/joviltd/jovi

JPR CARS LTD
Griffin, Gatsby and JPR Wildcat
804 758 2551

JPS MOTORSPORTS
Halfvee, 57 Speedster and Highboy
818 985 8891
www.unionmall.com/ps

JR'S KITCAR
Jisod 8F402 and Daytona
www.kitcarman.com

JURASSIC TRUCK CORP
T-Rex 1-B
www.jurassictruck.com

KAMOTO INDUSTRIES
KD-1 Dragon and SR-71
www.telusplanet.net/public/kamoto

KANOFF
RS, SS and SL
www.buggykits.freeservers.com

KIRKHAM MOTORSPORTS
289 and 427
801 377 8224
www.kirkhammotorsports.com

KITS THAT FIT
Vyper and GTS
305 956 3352

KOOBLEKAR
Kooble T-82R
www.kooblekar.com

KURTIS CO
Kurtis
661 393 7706

LA CONCEPT CARS
Countach
941 505 1166

RV's Nemesis, with mid-rear-mounted Jag V12 power. While using this car for a week, two separate Ferrari owners tried to buy it from me.

LA EXOTIC CARS
Z3, F50, 328, 355, 500SL and 940
818 315 2068

LAMBOSHOP
LS Countach replica
www.lamboshop.com

LAMINAR CONCEPTS
Evo, Viking BE, Sport and TT
www.laminarauto.com

LEAR 2000
Diablo
www.lear2000.com

LEVY RACING
GT40
480 446 8442
www.roaringforties.com.au

LIGHTNING MOTORCYCLE
V8 Trike
888 999 1958
www.lightningmotorcycles.com

LONE STAR CLASSICS
LS427, LS32, Growler, LS53, LS300,
LS40 and
LSSV
877 572 2277
www.cobrazone.com

MAC'S AUTOBODY
Countach
http://members.tripod.com/
~macsautobody/index.html

MARK'S CUSTOM KITS
Firebird kits
941 327 0312

MADD STUFF
Madd
www.maddstuff.com

MARAUDER
McLaren, Lola, MKX and BRX
www.kitcar.com/marauder

MARK'S CUSTOM KITS
Knight Rider KITT rep on Firebird
321 697 5445
www.markscustomkits.com

MASTER STREET RODS
Street Rod
www.masterstreetrods.com

MATT ADAMS
VS, EV, SE
831 659 7660

MAXIMUM TORQUE
Corvair V-8
414 740 1118

MIDSTATES CLASSIC CARS
427
402 654 2772
www.midstatesclassics.com

MITCHAM STREET RODS
Street Rod
814 967 2309

MULLEN MOTOR COMPANY
Mullen M-11
www.mullenmotorco.com

NERIA YACHTS AND CARS
Neria
http://members.aol.com/carphreak

NORTH AMERICAN EXOTIC REP
Countach
www.kitcar.com/exotix
info@exoticreplicacars.com

NW EXOTICS
427
503 667 0427

OKESTERS CUSTOM RODS
1932 coupé, '34 coupé and
'41 Willys
http://users.aol.com/okesters1.htm

OLD CHICAGO STREET RODS
1934 Chevys
503 655 1941

OUTLAW PERFORMANCE
1940 Willys
412 697 4876

PERFORMANCE FACTORY
Dodge Viper replica
416 893 3140

PERRY DESIGNS
550 Spyder
909 279 6498

The London–Brighton kit car run visits several interesting places along the route. This Cobra rep is cruising through the Sussex countryside to Madeira Drive to join the open-air kit show at the end of the run.

Sylvas are very pretty, and use a race-bred chassis similar to a Seven. This one is quick and bike-powered, but they're more usable when they have car engines fitted.

PIGEON PERFORMANCE
427
450 831 2791

PIRANHA MOTOR CO
Piranha Roadster
714 642 7701

PISA CORP
602 273 1616
Artero, Finale, Scorpion, XTC/GT, ZR-2
and Pisa-Fiero
www.cybercars.com

POWER PERFORMANCE
427
www.pwrperformance.com

PRECISION DESIGN
250GT California rep
760 740 0230
www.calspyder.com

PREDATOR PERFORMANCE
Jaguar D-type
813 539 0218

PRO SCA
Porsche 940S
805 251 5910

PROTOTYPE RESEARCH
500k, Auburn, MGTD and '57 Belair conv
705 653 4525

QCE
Blaze
949 253 6549

RAVON STREET RODS INC
1932 Ford
800 735 9189

RAYCO INC
986 Boxster
314 621 1321

REBEL YELL INC
Rebel Roadster
www.rebelyellinc.com

RED DAWG RACING
Porsche 940
805 823 6747

REGAL ROADSTERS
T-Bird and Thunder
608 273 4141

R&D DESIGN CONCEPTS
427 and Daytona replicas
402 572 0176
www.rnddesignconcepts.com

'R' MOTORSPORT
Diva Roadster and
Speedster
716 924 4194
www.divaroadster.com

RIOT
VW powered original
619 444 1006
www.thunderranch.com

RISING HOUSE MOTORS
Maserati Birdcage
316 467 2265

ROARING FORTIES
GT40
480 446 8442
www.roaringforties.com.au

ROBERT Q RILEY ENT
Tri-Magnum, Doran, Urbacar and Phoenix
www.rqriley.com

RODSTER
Rodster, Blazer body conv
310 322 2767
www.rodster.com

ROWLEY CORVETTE
Rowley GTC
www.rowleycorvette.com

ROYAL ROADSTERS
427
919 598 3639

RTS BUGGIES
619 938 0839
Info@fundooners

Raffos are designed by a Lancastrian Italian, at the bottom of his garden. The ideas are extreme, but somehow the whole thing hangs together in the end. Very rapid, too.

RYAN MOTORS
718 Spyder
310 598 3054

RU CAR CRAFTERS
427
918 245 1512

SHELBY AMERICAN
CSX 4000 and CSX7000 Shelby
Cobras
702 643 3000
www.shelbyamerican.com

SHELBY CUSTOM EXOTICS
SCE Countach
www.shelbycustom.com

SHELL VALLEY
427
402 246 2355
www.shellvalley.com

SIMPSON DESIGN
Miata Miami and Miami Roadster
www.simpsondesign.net

SO-CAL SPEEDSHOP
So-Cal Special and Brookville 32
www.so-calspeedshop.com

SOLID STERLING
VW-based Sterling
503 366 0553
www.kitcar.com/sterling

SPECIALTY MOTOR CARS
427
501 443 7072

SPEEDSTER MOTORCARS
Auburn Boat Tail
www.speedstermotorcar.com

SPEEDWAY MOTORS INC
Track T, 32 Lo-Boy and 34 Ford
402 474 4414

SPIRIT CARS
23 T-Bucket
www.spiritcars.com

STABLE AUTOWORKS
Isabella
www.zcarkits.com

STANLEY INTERNATIONAL
F-355
www.stanleyinternational.com

STEVE'S AUTOS
1934 Ford
503 665 2222

STRAND COMPONENTS
1932 Ford
219 987 6062

SUN RAY PRODUCTS
Bradley GT
800 333 3494

SUN VALLEY
Veepster
602 991 8975

SUPERFORMANCE
S1, 427 and Daytona
www.superformance.com

**SUPERIOR GLASS
WORKS**
Rods
503 829 9634

T-3
GT40
www.t-3cobra.com

TATONKA PRODUCTS
Bummer
www.bummer-kit.com

TEAM-C RACING
427
860 228 3936
www.team-c-racing.com

THUNDER RANCH
550, 250GTO, 32 Ford,
FunVee, 34 Roadster and
Riot
www.thunderranch.com

TOP GUN CO
Callista
818 606 0623

This is 66 per cent of the entire output of Ayrspeed Sixes ... not the world's biggest commercial success. I should stick to writing stories.

TOTAL PERFORMANCE
1923 Model T and
'32 Highboy
203 265 5667
www.tperformance.com

TRIANGLE G
Exotics and hardtops
818 769 1624

UNIQUE MOTORCARS
289 and 427
256 546 3708
www.uniquecobrareplicas.com

ULTIMATE PORSCHE 914
Porsche 914
www.ultimateporsche914.
bizland.com

URBAN MANUFACTURING
Urban Gorilla 106
and 130
www.urbgorilla.com

UPSTATE SUPER REPLICAS
Daytona coupé
www.daytona-coupe.com

V-8 ARCHIE
Finale, Fino and SL500
www.v8archie.com

VETTE-ROD
59 Corvette
504 845 9893

VIPER CAR PARTS
Cobrette, Corvette-based 427
www.vipercarparts.com

VINTAGE SPEEDSTERS
356 and 550
714 538 6550
www.vintagespeedsters.com

VR ENGINEERING
Velo Rossa Spyder and 940z
www.kitcarz.com/automotive.html

VSE
427
831 659 7660

WARLOCK DESIGNS
Diablo rep
909 597 4110
www.ifgonline.com

WARP FIVE INC
Manta, Montage, Starship,
Phantom VT and Phantom VR
816 228 2960

WEST COAST COBRA
427
www.cobrakit.com

WHITEHORSE MOTORS
Scorpion SS Countach
www.kitcar.com/whitehorse

WESTFIELD CARS
Seight
541 895 3000

WILLYS REPLACEMENT
42 Willys
909 980 3022

WILLY WORKS
1941 Willys
www.willyworks.com

WINSLOW MOTORSPORTS INC
Winslow Cheetah
www.cheetahracecars.org

WORLD CAR COMPANY
Wombat (ex-Hummbug)
www.wombatcar.com

WORLD CLASS MOTORSPORTS
WCM Ultralite, Ultrabusa and
Ultralite S2K
www.worldclassmotorsports.com

WORLD PERFORMANCE +
427, 289 and 289FIA
www.worldperformanceplus.com

WRIGHT ENTERPRISES
Porsche 914
www.kitcar.com/fzero

XANTHOS USA
Xanthos 23
www.xanthos.com

ZACH ATTACK
1939 Studebaker rod
www.zachattack.com

UK USEFUL SUPPLIERS

ABBEY SPORTSCARS
Rover, Ford, Chevy supplies
01953 607274

AC COMPOSITES
Carbon fibre
01623 407868

ADRIAN FLUX
Insurance
0845 1303400

AIRPORT RADIATORS
0208 897707
www.airrads.co.uk

AJ'S TRIMMING
01628 530257
www.ajtrimming.co.uk

ALDRIDGE
Trimming
01902 710805

ALLEN'S R&D
Bike engine adaptations
01949 836733
www.allensperformance.co.uk

AUTOGEAR
Rebuild/manufacture of gearbox, o/d,
diffs: sourcing of hard-to-find parts/
lights/trim/all sorts
01268 681608
www.autogear.com

AUTOPROP
Propshaft chop and balance
01342 322623

AUTOSPARKS
Wiring
0115 949 7211
www.autosparks.co.uk

AVO
Dampers and springs
01604 708101
www.avouk.com

AW MARLOW
Insurance
01283 740440

BACKFORD BLOOR
Insurance
0151 356 8776
www.insuranceforkitcars.co.uk

BARRY BRACE
Second-hand kit cars
01702 231319

BGH GEARTECH
Ford Type 9 gearboxes
01580 714 114
www.bghgeartech.co.uk

BLACKBURN
Bike engines and catalytic convertors
01622 664444

BOYRIVEN
Trimming supplies
0208 902 9581

CADINI
Kit car builders
01202 894009
www.kitcarbuilders.co.uk

CAMCOAT
Ceramic exhaust coatings
01925 445003
www.camcoat.u-net.com

CAR BUILDER SOLUTIONS
General kit bits
01580 891309
www.nfauto.co.uk

CHESHIRE MOTORCYCLE SALVAGE
Bike engines
01625 502372
www.cheshiremotorcyclesalvage.com

CIC INSURANCE
01206 792927

CLASSIC AND PERFORMANCE
Second-hand Locost and Escort parts
07855 562464

CLASSIC POWDER COATING
From parts to full chassis
01895 270616

CLASSIC SPARES
Jaguar breakers and spares
01992 716236
www.jagweb.com/classicspares

CLUTCH SPECIALIST
07899 801391

COUNTRY ENGINEERING
Locost chassis
01782 313109

COVENTRY AUTO
Jag repro parts
01203 471217

COVERDALE
Carpets, covers
01942 244001
www.coverdalecarpets.com

CURBOROUGH SPRINT SCHOOL
Race training
01509 852235

CUSTOM CHROME
Exhausts and kits
01203 387808

CUSTOM ENTERPRISES
Superchargers
01902 494955

DAVID KELLY
Donor breakers, Jaguar in
particular
01978 843253

DEMON TWEEKS
General performance gear
0845 330 6236
www.demontweeks.co.uk

DUNNING & FAIRBANK
Propshaft chop and balance
0113 248 8788

ELECTRICAL CAR SERVICES
Auto electricians
01992 718439

Thunder Ranch are looking to the future with this Porsche replica – it's electric. Excellent kit car power-to-weight ratio helps extend its range.

ELLIOTT PERCIVAL
Shot and bead blasting
01895 824030

ESCORT RS SPARES
01570 434773

ETB
Instruments
01702 711127

EURO ENGINES
Ford head and engine upgrades and rebuilds
01708 862806

EUROPA
Comprehensive kit bits emporium
01283 815609
www.europaspares.com

FIBREGLASS SHOP
0208 568 1645

FIESTA CENTRE
01603 722333

FIESTAS UNLIMITED
01482 580305

FISHER SPORTSCARS
Bike engines, aftermarket cats
01622 832977

FOOTMAN JAMES
Insurance
0121 561 6250

FRONTLINE
Spridget gearbox conversions
01225 852777

GLASPLIES
GRP supplies
01704 540626

GLEDWOOD
Triumph spares, repairs
01895 850450

GOTT AND WYNNE
Insurance
01492 870991

GRAHAM SYKES
Insurance
0870 444 6320
www.graham-sykes.co.uk

GURSTON DOWN HILLCLIMB
Race training
07971 989517

GAZ SHOCKS
Shocks, springs
0-1709 703992
www.dampertech.co.uk

HALLMARK
Second-hand kit cars
0208 529 7474
www.hallmark-cars.com

HARWOOD
Escort RS spares
0151 339 2801

HIC
Insurance
0845 121 2212

HI-GEAR
Five-speed conversions to Ford Type 9 gearbox
01332 514503

HILL HOUSE HAMMOND
Insurance
01733 310899

IMAGE WHEELS
Alloys including three-piece race rims
0121 522 2442

INSTANTBOOKSTORE
SVA guide
www.instantbookstore.com

INTATRIM
Seats
01952 641712

JAG SHOP
New and second-hand Jaguar bits
0208 748 7824

JANSPEED
Exhausts, performance gear
01722 321833

JP EXHAUSTS
01625 619916

KENLOWE FANS
01628 823303

KENT CAMS
01303 248666

KINGFISHER CAR COVERS
0115 966 5236

KITFIT
Second-hand Ford parts for kits
01636 893453

K&N
Air filters
0121 523 3635

LEAPING CATS
XK spares
02476 313139

LINK
Insurance
0845 330 6001

LUEGO
Locost chassis, parts, electricals
01487 815643
www.luegoracing.com

M&MD
Trim
01775 640423
mandmd@supanet.com

MA SERVICES
General kit bits
01622 717720

MAGNUM ENGINEERING
Engines, chassis, suspension fabrication
www.magnum-engineering.com

MERLIN MOTORSPORT
Race gear, kit plumbing, fittings, harnesses
01249 782101
www.merlinmotorsport.co.uk

MIDAS METALCRAFT
Fabrication, chassis makers
01234 378995

The Malone Skunk is a wickedly fast trike with bike power and rear drive, relying on squashing its bike tyres out for traction on hard corners.

MILLERS OILS
Robin Longdon, 01606 836637

MOCAL
Rads, coolers, plumbing
0208 568 1172

MOTO-LITA
Handmade steering wheels, flying
jackets
01264 772811
www.moto-lita.co.uk

MSM
Insurance
01279 870535

MWS
Wire wheels, hubs, bolt-ons
01753 549360

NAMRICK
Nuts and bolts
01273 779864

NEWTON COMMERCIAL
Classic British car trim, seats,
hoods
01728 832880

NORFOLK CAPRI SPARES
01553 810487

NORTHWOOD KITCARS
Second-hand kit cars
01923 823681

NR ENGINEERING
Locost parts, kit builds
01642 863716

The view from the Skunk's passenger seat. You simply would not believe how fast this thing is.

PD SPORTSCARS
Cobra kit builders
01283 515058
www.cobraclassics.com

OMEX
Engine management, electronics
01242 681044
www.omextechnology.co.uk

PERFORMANCE TURBO SYSTEMS
01582 731733

PERFORMANCE WHEELS
Superlite, repro and original design
alloy wheels
01544 231214

PERMA-GRIT
Abrasives
01529 240668
www.permagrit.com

PIPER CAMS
Performance and custom cams
01233 500200

PLANEX
Engine hoist plans
www.planex.org.uk

PREMIER WIRING
Kit looms, supplies
0800 0742789

PROPSHAFT SERVICES
0208 844 2265

POLYFACTO
Soft tops, particularly Dutton
01323 841399

QUAIFE
Race gears, diffs
01732 741144
www.quaife.co.uk

RACELOGIC
Performance engine management,
traction control, 0–60mph timing
01280 823803

RACERS' HARDWARE
Ford tuning parts
0031 0485 441354

RALLY DESIGN
Ford performance and braking gear
01795 531871

RAW ENGINEERING
Engine tuning
01981 251875
www.rawengineering.co.uk

REAL STEEL
American and Rover V8 shop
01895 440505

RECOPROP
Chop and balance propshafts
01582 412110

RV's Bugrat is based on the humble Skoda, which depreciates faster than it drives. Good tough mechanicals, though, and a cheap and very cheerful package.

RED LINE
Rolling road tuning
01753 655522

RENOVO
Soft-top refinishing
01444 443277
www.convertiblecar.com

REPOWER
US V8 performance
parts
01903 522900
www.roadcraftuk.co.uk

RICHFIELD
Seats
01159 673020
www.richfieldseating.co.uk

RIMMER
Triumph, Rover V8 engine parts and
accessories
01522 568000
www.rimmerbros.co.uk

ROADSURE
Insurance
0208 989 3339
www.roadsure.ltd.uk

RPI
Rover V8
specialist
01603 891209

RV DYNAMICS
V8/V12 to Renault 25 and other
gearbox conversions etc
07802 813649

SATURN INDUSTRIES
Instruments, rod parts
01594 834321

SB DEVELOPMENTS
Vauxhall engine tuning
0208 391 0121
www.sbdev.co.uk

SFC
Fasteners and fixings
01803 840777
www.fastfix-direct.co.uk

SPEEDFLOW
Hoses, fittings
0208 530 6664
www.speedflow.co.uk

SPEEDY CABLES
Cables, Smiths instruments
01639 732213

SSC
Kit builders
www.specialistsportscars.com

STAFFORD
Electric, lights
01827 67714

SUFFOLK TRIMMERS
01359 250513

SU BURLEN
SU carbs, pumps,
spares
01722 412500
www.burlen.co.uk

SUPERFLEX
Poly suspension bushes
07000 787373
www.superflex.co.uk

SUSSEX KIT CARS
Kit car builders
01435 812706

SURETERM
Insurance
0700 202023

SWIFTUNE
Mini engine tuning
01233 850843

T&J
Lucas electrical spares
0121 777 3386

TERRY NIGHTINGALE
Second-hand Westfield
dealer
01638 743569
www.terrynightingale.co.uk

THUNDERBIRD RACING
Kit builds, engine work
01623 722288

TIFOSI
Fixings, fasteners
01769 581454
www.tifosi-devon.co.uk

TIGER RACING
Type 9 Ford gearbox
conversions
01733 894328

TRIPLE S
Powder coating
Enquiries@triple-s.co.uk

TRITON
Locost chassis,
components
01327 341577

TRUST ELECTRICAL
Wiring looms
01904 608899

TTS
Bike engine tuning
01327 858212
www.tts-performance.co.uk

TWO TO FOUR
Bike engines
01386 881283
twotwofour1@aol.com

UNIQUE PLAQUE
Plaques, photos
01273 891591

UXBRIDGE KITCARS
Second-hand kit cars
01895 624554

VEHICLE WIRING PRODUCTS
0115 9305454

VIKING
Rover breakers
0121 459 6866

VISION MOTORSPORT
Track time
www.visionmotorsport.co.uk

VULCAN
Heads and performance tuning
0208 579 3202

WARD ENGINEERING
Jaguar axle, brake supplies
01375 846986
www.ward-engineering.co.uk

WEBER
Carbs, injection, management
01932 787100
www.smpeurope.com

WHEEL HOSPITAL
Alloy wheel overhaul, repair,
sales
01702 545689

WIZARDS OF NOS
Nitrous injection systems
01302 834343

WOOLIES
Trim and upholstery
supplies
01778 347347
www.woolies-trim.co.uk

WUNOFF
Exhausts
01274 619070
www.wunoff.co.uk

WYE VALLEY SERVICES
Nuts, bolts, fasteners
01597 860464

ZORSTEC
Exhausts
www.zorstec.net

The Dutton Mariner was the first kit amphibian. It was surprisingly good both on the water and on the street, and you can drive it straight down a slipway into the sea, which is top fun.

USA USEFUL SUPPLIERS

ADVANCED CLUTCH TECHNOLOGY
661 940 7555
www.advancedclutch.com

APEX
Suspension, turbos
714 685 5700
www.apexi.com

AUTOLOC
Door/window solenoids, rams, electrics
www.autoloc.com

AUTOMETER
Instruments
815 895 8141
www.autometer.com

B&M
Race transmission fluid
818 882 6422
www.bmracing.com

BREATHLESS
Exhaust systems
954 925 7725
www.breathlessperformance.com

CHASSIS ENGINEERING
Cages, drag equipment
www.chassisengineering.com

CLASSIC AUTO AIR
Aftermarket A/C kits
813 251 2356

CLASSIC REPLICARS
Builds
301 722 0740

CLASSIC TUBE
Braided brake lines
www.classictube.com

DAKOTA DIGITAL INSTRUMENTS
www.dakotadigital.com

DISCOUNT TIRE DIRECT
480 443 5621

DRIVE SHAFT SHOP
To 600 bhp +
631 348 1818

EAGLE
Rod and crank assemblies
662 796 7373

ECKLER'S
Corvette parts
www.ecklers.com

EDELBROCK
Engine performance, crate engines
www.edelbrock.com

ESCORT
Speed radar detectors
www.escortradar.com

FINISH LINE INC
Cobra parts, accessories
888 436 9113
www.cobraaccessories.com

GTECH
Performance meter
www.gtechpro.com

HOLLEY
Carbs, fuelling
www.holley.com

HOOKER
Headers
www.holley.com

JE PISTONS
714 898 9763

K&N FILTERS
www.knfilters.com

KONIG
Wheels
www.konigwheels.com

A very sensible Ford-based Sevenesque kit. Manufactured to a budget and requiring some input from the builder, it uses mass production to provide value for money.

LEVY RACING
Factory 5 builds +
480 446 8442
www.levyracing.com

LG
Vette/Chevrolet
power
www.lgmotorsport.com

LM INTERCOOLERS
714 777 9766
www.blitz-na.com

LOKAR PERFORMANCE PRODUCTS
865 966 2269
Brake parts
www.lokar.com

MSD
Ignition
915 857 5200

MR GASKET
216 398 8300
www.mrgasket.com

MORE POWER RACING
Performance mail
house
www.morepowerracing.com

NOS
Nitrous oxide systems
www.nosnitrous.com

PRO-TORQUE
Custom torque convertors
631 218 8700
www.protorque.com

PRODRIVE
Shafts, gears, hubs
888 340 4753
www.prodriveusa.com

RACE ENGINEERING
Engine parts
561 553 5500
www.raceeng.com

RANDOM TECHNOLOGY
High flow cats
770 554 4242
www.randomtechnology.com

RC – Custom injectors
310 320 2277
www.rceng.com

RH – Wheels
626 962 0033
www.rhevolution.com

ROSS PISTONS
310 536 0100
www.rosspistons.com

RTEC
Air filters
972 633 8369
www.rtec-usa.com

S&B FILTERS
909 947 4483

SPEEDPEOPLE
General performance
www.speedpeople.com

SPEEDWAY MOTORS
Mustang wishbones
new
www.speedwaymotors.com

STAINLESS STEEL BRAKES
Rust-free rotors
www.ssbrakes.com

SWAIN
High temp coatings
585 889 2796
www.swaintech.com

TILTON ENGINEERING
Custom hydraulics, pedals
805 688 2353

TURBONETICS
Turbos
805 581
www.turboneticsinc.com

UNORTHODOX RACING
Light pulleys, flywheels,
clutches
631 586 9525
www.unorthodoxracing.com

Another variation on the Seven theme, but this time with 5.3-litre V12 Jag power. Not very sensible at all, but quite nippy at 500bhp/ton and actually quite drivable too.

Sadly, the designer of this Le Mans Bentley-inspired kit died recently – but he left behind a magnificent epitaph.

KIT-CAR MAGAZINE'S CLUB LIST

Updated regularly from the palatial offices of the Unfinished Kit Car Club in the throbbing Yorkshire metropolis of Ackworth Moor Top. Club secretaries, put *Kit-Car* on your mag mailing list to keep your entry up to date, and if you have any corrections to entries, please send them to Iain Ayre at i.hyne@btinternet.com

2CVGB
memsec@2cvgb.com

2CVGB MODCON REGISTER
01609 772203

289 REGISTER
www.289register.de
DWPilbeam@aol.com

750 MOTOR CLUB
01825 750760
01379 384268
www.750mc.com

AF SPORTS OWNERS' CLUB
01789 740575

ARISTOCAT REGISTER
01279 816536

ASHLEY REGISTER AND HISTORIC SPECIALS REGISTER
01258 454879

AVANTE OWNERS' CLUB (AND NOVA)
01827 705506

BEAUFORD OWNERS' CLUB
01788 547033

BERKELEY ENTHUSIASTS' CLUB
01483 475330
BEC-Membership@bigfoot.com

BOND OWNERS' CLUB
0121 784 4626

BUCKLER CAR REGISTER
01788 575519

BRISTOL CLASSIC, SPORTS AND KITCAR CLUB
12 Hortham Lane, Almondsbury, BS12 4JH

BATTERY VEHICLE SOCIETY
01258 455470

BURLINGTON OWNERS' CLUB
01203 597111

CARLTON OWNERS' CLUB
0121 243 9482
mervyn01@globalnet.co.uk

CALVY MITCHEL OWNERS' CLUB
01375 366823

CARISMA OWNERS' CLUB
01767 640892

CHALLENGER OWNERS' CLUB
01328 855281

CLAN OWNERS' CLUB
01656 744741
www.clanownersclub.com

CLEVELAND KIT CAR AND SPECIALS OWNERS' CLUB
01287 209885
ian.churms@dth.nl.com

CLUB DRK
01942 211673

CLUB DUTTON
36 Wheatcroft, Wick, Littlehampton, BN17 7NY

CLUB LOTUS
01362 694459
www.uk-classic-cars.com/clublotus.html

CLUB MARCOS INTERNATIONAL
01225 707815
www.clubmarcos.freeserve.co.uk
info@clubmarcos.freeserve.co.uk

CITROËN SPECIALS CLUB
csc.memsec@virgin.net

CLUB EVANTE
www.pharo.force9.co.uk/evante.htm

CLUB ROTRAX
01249 720946
jj.harding@znet.co.uk

COBRA REPLICA CLUB
01329 312011
www.cobraclub.com

CONTEMPORARY COBRA/ DAYTONA COUPÉ OWNERS' CLUB
0207 723 9768

COUNTACH REPLICA OWNERS' CLUB
01253 867027

COVIN OWNERS' CLUB
01452 559951

DAVRIAN REGISTER
01263 860525
101341.2312@compuserve.co.uk

(NEW) DAVRIAN REGISTER
01825 763638

DASH SPORTSCAR CLUB
01706 624504

DAKAR OWNERS' AND DRIVERS' ASSOCIATION
01780 721529
www.dakar4x4.yahoo.com

DAX TOJEIRO COBRA OWNERS' CLUB
0207 912 1135

DAX RUSH OWNERS' CLUB
www.rushowners.co.uk
RichardPope50@Yahoo.co.uk

DELLOW REGISTER
01202 304641

DOMINO CAR CLUB
01494 432074

DUNSMORE OWNERS' CLUB
Welcome Bank, Stratford upon Avon CV37 0QE

DIVA REGISTER
01705 251485

DUTTON OWNERS' CLUB
01386 423899
www.duttonownersclub.co.uk
freespace.virgin.net/amber.upton/index.html

EAGLE OWNERS' CLUB
02392 690379

ENTHUSIASTS' KIT CAR CLUB
26 Boulsey Rise, Ottershaw, Chertsey, KT16 0JX

ELVA OWNERS' CLUB
01903 823710
roger-dunbar@elva.com
www.elva.com

FALCON DRIVERS' REGISTER
01203 382130
falconshells@1950sspecials.freeserve.uk

FAIRTHORPE SPORTS CAR CLUB
01895 256799

FORMULA 27 OWNERS' CLUB
01527 457808
www.formula27.freeserve.co.uk

FEDERATION OF KIT CAR CLUBS
31 Patrick Road, West Bridgford, NG2 7QE

FUGITIVE OWNERS' CLUB
357 Classmont Road, Morriston, Swansea SA6 6BU

GARDNER DOUGLAS REGISTER
01455 2026599

GEMINI OWNERS' CLUB
01254 886819
www.kitsnclassics.com

GENTRY REGISTER
01773 719874
www.gentry-owners.co.uk
gentry.reg@connectfree.co.uk

GINETTA OWNERS' CLUB
1 Furze Avenue, St Albans, Herts AL4 9NQ

GILBERN OWNERS' CLUB
Crooksbury, Castlebrook, Compton Dundon, Somerset TA11 6PR
01458 442025
pvdaye@netscapeonline.co.uk

GRIFFON REGISTER
berry9@supanet.com

GRIMSBY KIT CAR CLUB
89 Springfield Road, Grimsby, Lincs DN33 3LG

GT40 ENTHUSIASTS' CLUB
02380 696015
musmce@hants.gov.uk

GTD40 OWNERS' CLUB
01622 831416

GTM OWNERS' CLUB
01773 875516

You don't have to build your car from a kit. This one was constructed from a dead Citroën 2CV and some alloy sheet. The builder's mad-looking eyes are bloodshot from driving the car on an African endurance run. So he says, anyway.

HANTS AND BERKS KIT CAR CLUB
3 Hillside Cottages, Frogmore,
Camberley, Surrey

HAWKE OWNERS' CLUB
01778 380131
charles.stowe@talk.21.com

HENSEN OWNERS' CLUB
01283 511201

**HERTS AND BEDS ALTERNATIVE
CAR CLUB**
01462 675092

**HERTS AND ESSEX REPLICA
CLUB**
01206 210920

HISTORIC LOTUS REGISTER
Badgers Farm, Short Green,
Winfarthing, Norfolk NR19 1TF

ITALIAN EXOTIC REPLICA CAR CLUB
01501 763288

ITALIAN REPLICA CLUB
01924 273619
www.italianreplicacarclub.co.uk

JAGO OWNERS' CLUB
01782 343691
techsec@jagoowners.freeserve.co.uk

JBA OWNERS' CLUB
01995 672230
les.fragle@virgin.net

JIMINI DRIVERS' CLUB
0121 351 5374
www.jiminidriver.co.uk_
jiminidriver@aol.com

JZR PILOTS' ASSOCIATION
01932 873200
www.geocities.com/jzrpa
michael.l.smith@btinternet.com

KARMA OWNERS' CLUB
01634 864809

KINGFISHER REGISTER
01373 461851

KENT KIT CAR CLUB
clubsec@kentkitcarclub.org.uk

KOUGAR OWNERS' CLUB
01737 246720

LISTAIR OWNERS' CLUB
01827 712720

LOMAX REGISTER
01252 620128

LOCOST CAR CLUB
01322 385102

LOCUST ENTHUSIASTS' CLUB
01634 581823
www.locustenthusiastclub.fsnet.co.uk
d.hancock2@ntlworld.com

LOTUS SEVEN CLUB
01283 791034

MAGIC OWNERS' CLUB
01252 546230

MAGENTA KIT CAR CLUB
01642 815060

**MALVERN KITCARS AND
SPECIALS CLUB**
01684 592294

MARCHES KIT CAR CLUB
01568 616627

MARLIN OWNERS' CLUB
01785 841439
marlinoc.freeserve.co.uk

MARCOS OWNERS' CLUB
0208 460 3511
ABS.labs@dial.pipex.com

MCCOY OWNERS' CLUB
0161 962 8576
dawald@aol.com

MERLIN OWNERS' CLUB
01785 840284

MICRO MANIACS
3 Pine Tree Lane, Hillam,
Leeds LS25 5HY

MIDAS OWNERS' CLUB
www.kitcarclubs.org.uk/midas/
index.htm

**MIDGE OWNERS' AND
BUILDERS' CLUB**
01782 546036
david.everall@virgin.net

MIDLANDS KITCAR CLUB
www.midlands-kitcar-club.co.uk
kim_langridge@hotmail.com

MIDTEC OWNERS' CLUB
22 Grenville Court, Silverdale Road,
Southampton SO15 2TD
01703 323256

MINARI OWNERS' REGISTER
www.minari-register.org.uk_
da-smith@ntlworld.com_

MINI-JEM REGISTER
01732 843280

**MINI-MARCOS OWNERS'
CLUB**
01905 458533

MIRAGE OWNERS' CLUB
0208 683 4980

This gorgeous hand-made one-off single-seater special must have taken years of work. The styling and finish are flawless.

MODCON REGISTER (2VCGB)
01609 772203

MONGRELS KIT CAR CLUB
01673 860438

MOSQUITO OWNERS' CLUB
01366 500872

MOSS OWNERS' CLUB
01737 645165

M6GTR OWNERS' CLUB
01252 878316

NCF DIAMOND REGISTER
01763 261109

NG OWNERS' CLUB
0208 393 4661

NOMAD OWNERS' CLUB
01977 616970

NATIONAL BUGGY REGISTER
01132 684310

NORTH EAST KIT CAR CLUB
0191 519 2671
nekcc@ijohnson.demon.co.uk

NORTH WALES KIT CAR CLUB
14 Caegals, Old Clowyn, North Wales
LL29 9DL

NOVA OWNERS' CLUB
See Avante

**NUTCRACKERS CAR GROUP
(SOUTH LANCS)**
Heys Villa, The Heys, Coppull,
Chorley PR7 4NX

**NUTCRACKERS CAR GROUP
(HOME COUNTIES)**
01702 526622

OGLE REGISTER
01444 248439

ONYX OWNERS' CLUB
01472 316597

**PIPER SPORTS AND RACING
CLUB**
azcak@zen.co.uk

POTTERIES KIT CAR CLUB
103 Chell Green Avenue,
Chell ST67LA

PILGRIM CAR CLUB
r.thorn@ntlworld.com

QUANTUM OWNERS' CLUB
01277 623523
MichaelHughes7@compuserve.com
www.quantum-owners.co.uk

RICKMAN CARS OWNERS' CLUB
0121 681 5313

ROCHDALE OWNERS' CLUB
01752 791409

ROCHDALE REGISTER
01444 241125

RONART DRIVERS' CLUB
01962 735377

ROYALE OWNERS' CLUB
366 Washway Road, Sale, Cheshire
M33 4HF

SCAMP OWNERS' CLUB
chris@cyates.freeserve.co.uk
cyates@freeserve.co.uk

SCORPION OWNERS CLUB
01923 779966

SCOTTISH KIT CAR CLUB
01506 430248
01383 623270

SEBRING OWNERS' CLUB
Hill House, Water Lane, Chelverton,
Northants NN9 6AP

**SOUTH WALES KIT CAR
CLUB**
01437 890015

**SOUTHERN DUNE BUGGY
CLUB**
020 8657 9320
www.sarsen.dial.pipex.com
SDBC2@hotmail.com

SPARTAN OWNERS' CLUB
01782 266451

**SPEEDSTERS OWNERS'
CLUB**
01934 843007

SPIRIT OWNERS' CLUB
142 New Road, Hethersett, Norfork
NR9 3HG

**SPYDER SECTION
(SEE SPEEDSTER CLUB)**

**SUFFOLK COASTAL KIT
CAR CLUB**
01473 780777

SUSSEX KIT CAR CLUB
01435 812706

STRATOS REPLICA CLUB
01285 643899
s.holloway@stratos1.demon.co.uk

SYLVA REGISTER
01622 851593

TEAL OWNERS' CLUB
01763 281412

TRIDENT CAR CLUB
0208 644 9029

TRIKING OWNERS' CLUB
07730 880180

TEMPEST REGISTER
01524 781841

TIGER DRIVERS' CLUB
57 London Road, Teynham, Kent ME9
9QW

TVR CAR CLUB
01952 770635
www.tvrcc.com
carol@tvroffice.demon.co.uk

TRIAD OWNERS' CLUB
01543 416107

TRIUMPH SPORTS SIX CLUB
01858 434424
tssc@tssc-hq.demon.co.uk_

TORNADO REGISTER
01582 737641

TURNER REGISTER
01895 256799
01494 445634

ULSTER KIT CAR CLUB
02838 329656
darrylwebb@hotmail.com
ulsterkitcarclub@btinternet.com

UNFINISHED KIT CAR CLUB
01977 612289
iain@ayrspeed.com

ULTIMA OWNERS' CLUB
5 Lovelace Crescent, Elmsthorpe,
Leics LE9 7SL

UVA FUGITIVE OWNERS' CLUB
357 Clasemount Road,
Morriston,
Swansea SA6 6BU

VINCENT REGISTER
01793 750529

**VINDICATOR OWNERS'
CLUB**
0121 459 3639

WESTFIELD SPORTS CAR CLUB
www.wscc.co.uk

WESSEX KIT CAR CLUB
01202 892328
JPHAMMOND@tinyonline.co.uk

**WEST CUMBRIA KIT CAR
CLUB**
01946 728462

WILDCAT OWNERS' CLUB
01276 23078

**YORKSHIRE ALTERNATIVE
CAR CLUB**
01977 515360

Most people would say this Jensen CV8 isn't a ... however, the body is GRP, the chassis is ... and simple, the engine and box are standard Chrysler big-block V8 and much of the vehicle comes ... production car parts bins. Even the bumpers are ... Ford Anglia. A restoration would b ... semi-kit project.

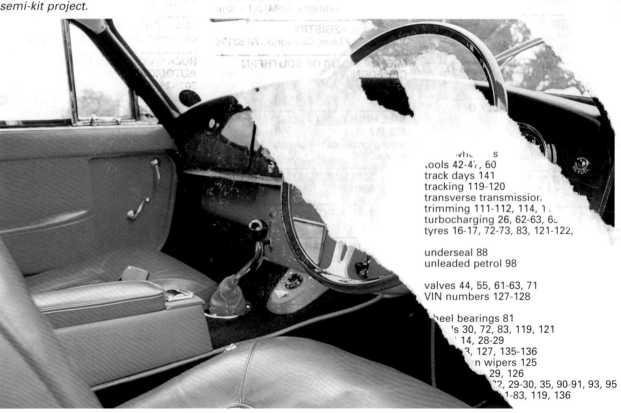

NORTH AMERICAN CLUBS

289 FIA REGISTER
5 Beaufain Drive, Sumter, SC 29150

ASSOCIATION OF HANDCRAFTED AUTOMOBILES
909 796 9946

ALABAMA'S UNIQUE AUTO ASSOC.
205 967 5310

ARIZONA KIT CAR CLUB
480 539 0489

ARIZONA COBRAS
Mike Canning
623 486 2299

AUTOTUNE US CLUB
304 743 9466
www.citynet.net/blenko/racing
Avenger/Valkyrie Registry 914 267 3748

BROTHERS OF THE THIRD WHEEL
309 797 846?

**CHIC.. ..PLICAR
AS'**
84
h'
r   car.tripod.com

..a.com

.. KANSAS KIT KAR K
. 0911

.PIRE STATE SPECIA'T
.SSOCIATION
.18 765 4771
http://members.t?
427cobra@co?

FIERO OW'
714 917 ?

GA?
P

GREATER ST LOUIS KITCAR CLUB
618 344 5698
http://members.tripod.com/GSLKCC/
GSLKCC/shankt55@aol.com
Kit Car 1 Site: www.crosswinds.
net/~kitcar1

HANDCRAFTED AUTOMOBILES OF MINNESOTA
612 4?6 2212

HERITAGE CLUB INTERNATIONAL
218 334 3500

HOUSTON KIT CAR CLUB
17718 Windy Point Drive
Spring, TX 77379

JACKSONVILLE REPLICAR CLUB
904 781 2210

JERSEY SNAKE PIT, NJ
732 545 3043

KANSAS KIT KAR KLUB
620 922 7325

KANSAS KITCAR CLUB
785 286 0911

THE KELLISON REGISTRY
608 831 2265

KENTUCKIANA HOT WHF
502 245 6346

MANTA OWNERS' ..TION
816 228 2960

MANTA OWNE   DENVER
www.sebar.com   .ANTA.html

THE MERA RF
10227 Caddy   nia, WI 53108

?NIGI CAR   ??? ?RN
.ALIFOR?
.337 Mor
Pacific P

CAR CLUB

.AR ASSOCIATION

.. KIT CAR CLUB
.itcarclub.com

.EVADA REPLICAR ASSOCIATION
702 362 2744

NEW JERSEY REPLICAR CLUB
201 391 3721
www.njreplicar.org
cyscott@aol.com

NORTH CAROLINA SPECIALTY CAR CLUB
919 247 4400

NORTHEAST OHIO KIT CAR CLUB
216 633 6554

NORTHERN CALIFORNIA KIT CAR CLUB
925 449 1149 / 510 353 9914
www.kitcar.com/club-nckcc/home.html

NORTHERN ILLINOIS FIERO ENTHUSIASTS
630 690 0324

NORTHWESTERN COBRA AND REPLICAR CLUB
206 566 0259

OKLAHOMA KIT CAR CLUB
Oklahoma City Chapter
405 794 4817
Tulsa Chapter
918 852 7493
www.okkitcar.org

OHIO VALLEY KIT CAR CLUB
513 683 3790

OREGON HANDCRAFTED AUTOMOBILE ASSOCIATION
503 362 8370

PARAGON FANTASIES
732 478 2943

PENNSYLVANIA KIT CAR CLUB
c/o NJ Replicar Club

PORSCHE 917K CLUB
609 223 9438

PUMA CAN AM CLUB
835 Arnett Blvd. Rochester, NY 14619

ROCKY MOUNTAIN HANDCRAFTED AUTOMOBILES
303 425 6807

SEBRING/CIMBRIA KIT CAR CLUB
6 Dixie Drive
Bel Air, MD 21014

SQUIRE SS-100 CLUB
602 893 9451

SOUTH FLORIDA COBRA REGISTRY
954 436 9101

SPECIALTY CAR ASSOCIATION OF TEXAS
817 540 1515

UNIQUE COBRA OWNERS' ASSOCIATION
770 445 8484

VIRGINIA KIT CAR CLUB
http://vakitcarclub.freeyellow.com
vakitcarclub@gatsbycars.com

WESTERN PENNSYLVANIA SPECIALTY CAR CLUB
412 226 3831

Index